Birdwatchers Guide to Wildlife Sanctuaries

Photo by William Claiborne

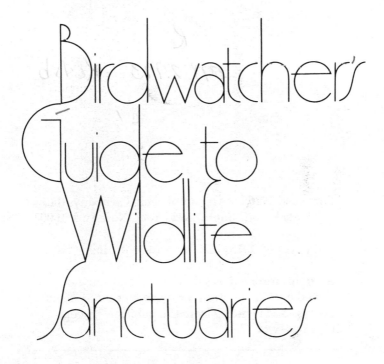

Birdwatcher's Guide to Wildlife Sanctuaries

Jessie Kitching

ARCO PUBLISHING COMPANY INC.

219 Park Avenue South, New York, N.Y. 10003

Published 1976 by Arco Publishing Company, Inc.
219 Park Avenue South, New York, New York 10003

Copyright © 1975, 1976 by Jessie Kitching

Library of Congress Cataloging in Publication Data

Kitching, Jesse.
  Birdwatcher's guide to wildlife sanctuaries.

  1. Bird watching—United States. 2. Bird watching—
Canada. 3. Wildlife refuges—United States. 4. Wild-
life refuges—Canada.
I. Title.

QL682.K57   917.3′04′92   76-5388

Printed in the United States of America

CONTENTS

INTRODUCTION   1

ALABAMA   7
  University of Alabama Arboretum   7
  Wheeler National Wildlife Refuge   7

ALASKA   8
  Aleutian Islands National Wildlife Refuge   8
  Glacier Bay National Monument   8
  Izembek National Wildlife Range   9
  Katmai National Monument   9
  Kenai National Moose Range   10
  Kodiak National Wildlife Refuge   11
  Mount McKinley National Park   11

ARIZONA   13
  Arizona-Sonora Desert Museum   13
  Cabeza Prieta Game Range   13
  Chiricahua National Monument   15
  Desert Botanical Garden   17
  Glen Canyon National Recreation Area   17
  Grand Canyon National Park   18
  Imperial National Wildlife Refuge   19
  Montezuma Castle National Monument   19
  Organ Pipe Cactus National Monument   20
  Petrified Forest National Park   21
  Prescott National Forest   21
  Sabino Canyon Visitor Center   21
  Saguaro National Monument   23

ARKANSAS   25
  Big Lake National Wildlife Refuge   25
  Holla Bend National Wildlife Refuge   25

Hot Springs National Park 26
Wapanocca National Wildlife Refuge 26
White River National Wildlife Refuge 27

CALIFORNIA 29
Audubon Canyon Ranch 29
Big Basin Redwoods State Park 29
Channel Islands National Monument 30
Death Valley National Monument 30
Descanso Gardens 31
El Dorado Nature Center 31
Griffith Park 32
Havasu National Wildlife Refuge 32
Inyo National Forest, Mammoth Ranger District 33
Joan Hamann Dole Memorial Sanctuary 34
Joshua Tree National Monument 34
Kern-Pixley National Wildlife Refuges 35
Klamath Basin National Wildlife Refuges 35
Lassen Volcanic National Park 36
Living Desert Reserve 36
Los Angeles State and County Arboretum 38
Modoc National Wildlife Refuge 38
Mount Tamalpais State Park 39
Muir Woods National Monument 39
Pinnacles National Monument 41
Point Reyes Bird Observatory 41
Rancho Santa Ana Botanic Gardens 42
Sacramento National Wildlife Refuge 42
Salton Sea National Wildlife Refuge 42
Sequoia and Kings Canyon National Parks 43
Silverwood Wildlife Sanctuary 44
Strybing Arboretum and Botanical Garden 45
Tucker Wildlife Sanctuary 45
University of California Botanical Garden 46
Whittier Narrows Nature Center 46
Yosemite National Park 46

COLORADO 48
Colorado National Monument 48
Dinosaur National Monument 48

Grand Mesa-Uncompahgre-Gunnison National Forest   49
Great Sand Dunes National Monument   50
Mesa Verde National Park   50
Monte Vista National Wildlife Refuge   51
Pawnee National Grassland   51
Rio Grande National Forest   52
Rocky Mountain National Park   52

CONNECTICUT   54
Audubon Center in Greenwich   54
Connecticut Arboretum   54
Flanders Nature Center   55

DELAWARE   56
Bombay Hook National Wildlife Refuge   56
Brandywine Creek State Park   56

DISTRICT OF COLUMBIA   57
Rock Creek Nature Center   57

FLORIDA   59
Boyd Hill Nature Park   59
Chassahowitzka National Wildlife Refuge   59
Corkscrew Swamp Sanctuary   60
J. N. "Ding" Darling National Wildlife Refuge   60
Everglades National Park   61
Florida Keys National Wildlife Refuges   62
Lake Woodruff National Wildlife Refuge   63
Loxahatchee National Wildlife Refuge   63
Merritt Island National Wildlife Refuge   64
St. Marks National Wildlife Refuge   64

GEORGIA   66
Ocmulgee National Monument   66
Okefenokee National Wildlife Refuge   66
Piedmont National Wildlife Refuge   67

HAWAII   68
Hawaii Volcanoes National Park   68
Hawaiian Islands National Wildlife Refuge   68

IDAHO   70
Camas National Wildlife Refuge   70

Craters of the Moon National Monument ... 70
Minidoka National Wildlife Refuge ... 71

ILLINOIS ... 72
Chautauqua National Wildlife Refuge ... 72
Crab Orchard National Wildlife Refuge ... 72
Forest Glen Preserve ... 73
Mark Twain National Wildlife Refuge ... 73
Mississippi Palisades State Park ... 74
Morton Arboretum ... 74

INDIANA ... 75
Hayes Regional Arboretum ... 75
McCormick's Creek State Park ... 75
Pokagon State Park ... 76

IOWA ... 77
De Soto National Wildlife Refuge ... 77
Effigy Mounds National Monument ... 77
Union Slough National Wildlife Refuge ... 78

KANSAS ... 79
Kingman County Game Management Area ... 79
Kirwin National Wildlife Refuge ... 79
Quivira National Wildlife Refuge ... 80

KENTUCKY ... 81
Clyde E. Buckley Wildlife Sanctuary ... 81
Daniel Boone National Forest ... 81
Land Between the Lakes ... 82
Mammoth Cave National Park ... 82

LOUISIANA ... 84
Delta-Breton National Wildlife Refuges ... 84
Lacassine National Wildlife Refuge ... 84
Sabine National Wildlife Refuge ... 85

MAINE ... 86
Acadia National Park ... 86
Moosehorn National Wildlife Refuge ... 87

MARYLAND ... 88
Blackwater National Wildlife Refuge ... 88
Catoctin Mountain Park ... 88

MASSACHUSETTS   89
  Arnold Arboretum   89
  Bartholomew's Cobble   89
  Cape Cod National Seashore   91
  Great Meadows National Wildlife Refuge   91
  Ipswich River Wildlife Sanctuary   92
  Laughing Brook Nature Center   93
  Monomoy National Wildlife Refuge   93
  Parker River National Wildlife Refuge   94
  Wellfleet Bay Wildlife Sanctuary   94

MICHIGAN   96
  For-Mar Nature Preserve and Arboretum   96
  Isle Royale National Park   96
  Kalamazoo Nature Center   97
  Ottawa National Forest   97
  Seney National Wildlife Refuge   98
  Shiawassee National Wildlife Refuge   98

MINNESOTA   100
  Agassiz National Wildlife Refuge   100
  Itasca State Park   100
  Pipestone National Monument   100
  Rice Lake National Wildlife Refuge   101
  Superior National Forest   102
  Tamarac National Wildlife Refuge   103
  Upper Mississippi River National Wildlife Refuge   103

MISSISSIPPI   105
  Natchez Trace Parkway, Tupelo Environmental Study
    Area   105
  Noxubee National Wildlife Refuge   105
  Yazoo National Wildlife Refuge   106

MISSOURI   107
  Bennett Springs State Park   107
  Mingo National Wildlife Refuge   107
  Missouri Botanical Garden, Arboretum and Nature
    Reserve   107
  Ozark National Scenic Riverways   109

Squaw Creek National Wildlife Refuge 110
Swan Lake National Wildlife Refuge 110

MONTANA 111
Benton Lake National Wildlife Refuge 111
Charles M. Russell National Wildlife Range 111
Glacier National Park 112
Medicine Lake National Wildlife Refuge 112

NEBRASKA 114
Chet Ager Nature Center 114

NEVADA 115
Desert National Wildlife Range 115
Lake Mead National Recreation Area 115
Pahranagat National Wildlife Refuge 116
Ruby Lake National Wildlife Refuge 116
Stillwater Wildlife Management Area 117

NEW HAMPSHIRE 118
Wapack National Wildlife Refuge 118

NEW JERSEY 119
Batsto Nature Center 119
Brigantine National Wildlife Refuge 119
Great Swamp National Wildlife Refuge 121
Sandy Hook Unit, Gateway National Recreation Area 123
Scherman Wildlife Sanctuary 124

NEW MEXICO 125
Bandelier National Monument 125
Bitter Lake National Wildlife Refuge 126
Bosque Del Apache National Wildlife Refuge 126
San Andres Refuge 127

NEW YORK 128
Arthur W. Butler Memorial Sanctuary 128
Constitution Island Audubon Sanctuary 128
Cornell Laboratory of Ornithology 129
High Rock Park 129
Iroquois National Wildlife Refuge 130
Jamaica Bay Wildlife Refuge 130

Montezuma National Wildlife Refuge 131
Morton National Wildlife Refuge 133
Teatown Lake Reservation 134
Ward Pound Ridge Reservation 134

NORTH CAROLINA 135
Cape Hatteras National Seashore 135
Mattamuskeet National Wildlife Refuge 135

NORTH DAKOTA 137
Arrowwood National Wildlife Refuge 137
Audubon National Wildlife Refuge 137
Long Lake National Wildlife Refuge 138
Slade National Wildlife Refuge 139
Souris Loop National Wildlife Refuges 139
Sullys Hill National Game Preserve 140
Tewaukon National Wildlife Refuge 141
Theodore Roosevelt National Memorial Park 141

OHIO 143
California Woods Outdoor Education Center 143
Hueston Woods State Park 143
Mill Creek Park 143
Ottawa National Wildlife Refuge 144

OKLAHOMA 145
Platt National Park 145
Salt Plains National Wildlife Refuge 145
Tishomingo National Wildlife Refuge 146
Wichita Mountains Wildlife Refuge 146

OREGON 147
Crater Lake National Park 147
Oregon Caves National Monument 147
Sheldon, Hart Mountain Antelope Refuges 148

PENNSYLVANIA 149
Bowman's Hill State Wildflower Preserve 149
Erie National Wildlife Refuge 149
Hawk Mountain Sanctuary 150
Hershey Rose Gardens and Arboretum 151
Longwood Gardens 151

Raccoon Creek State Park   151
Reading Nature Center   152

RHODE ISLAND   153
Ninigret National Wildlife Refuge   153

SOUTH CAROLINA   155
Cape Romain National Wildlife Refuge   155
Carolina Sandhills National Wildlife Refuge   155
Santee National Wildlife Refuge   156
Savannah National Wildlife Refuge   156

SOUTH DAKOTA   158
Badlands National Monument   158
Lacreek National Wildlife Refuge   158
Sand Lake National Wildlife Refuge   159
Waubay National Wildlife Refuge   159
Wind Cave National Park   160

TENNESSEE   161
Cherokee National Forest   161
Great Smoky Mountains National Park   161
Reelfoot National Wildlife Refuge   162
Roan Mountain State Resort Park   162
Tennessee National Wildlife Refuge   163

TEXAS   165
Aransas National Wildlife Refuge   165
Bentsen-Rio Grande Valley State Park   165
Big Bend National Park   166
Buffalo Lake National Wildlife Refuge   167
Hagerman National Wildlife Refuge   168
Heard Natural Science Museum and Wildlife
    Sanctuary   168
Lake Meredith Recreation Area   169
McAshan Arboretum and Botanical Garden   169
Monahans Sandhills State Park   170
Muleshoe and Grulla National Wildlife Refuges   170
Padre Island National Seashore   171
Palo Duro Canyon State Park   171
San Jacinto State Park   172
Santa Ana National Wildlife Refuge   172

UTAH 175
Bear River Migratory Bird Refuge 175
Bryce Canyon National Park 175
Capitol Reef National Park 176
Fish Springs National Wildlife Refuge 176
Flaming Gorge National Recreation Area 177
Ouray National Wildlife Refuge 178
Zion National Park 178

VERMONT 179
Missisquoi National Wildlife Refuge 179

VIRGINIA 180
Back Bay National Wildlife Refuge 180
Blue Ridge Parkway 180
Chincoteague National Wildlife Refuge 181
Mackay Island National Wildlife Refuge 181
Presquile National Wildlife Refuge 182
Shenandoah National Park 182

WASHINGTON 184
Columbia National Wildlife Refuge 184
McNary National Wildlife Refuge 184
Mount Rainier National Park 185
Olympic National Park 185
Turnbull National Wildlife Refuge 186
Willapa National Wildlife Refuge 186

WEST VIRGINIA 188
Harpers Ferry National Historic Park 188
Monongahela National Forest 188

WISCONSIN 191
Green Bay Wildlife Sanctuary 191
Horicon National Wildlife Refuge 191
Mackenzie Environmental Center 192
Necedah National Wildlife Refuge 192

WYOMING 193
Grand Teton National Park 193
National Elk Refuge 193
Yellowstone National Park 195

VIRGIN ISLANDS 197
  Virgin Islands National Park 197

CANADA—EAST 198
  NEW BRUNSWICK 198
    Fundy National Park 198
    Kouchibouguac National Park 198
  NEWFOUNDLAND 199
    Terra-Nova National Park 199
  NOVA SCOTIA 200
    Cape Breton Highlands National Park 200
    Kejimkujik National Park 200
  ONTARIO 201
    Georgian Bay Islands National Park 201
    Point Pelee National Park 202
    Quetico Provincial Park 203
    Royal Botanical Gardens 203
    St. Lawrence Islands National Park 204
    Wasaga Beach Provincial Park 204
    Wye Marsh Wildlife Centre 205
  PRINCE EDWARD ISLAND 205
    Prince Edward Island National Park 205
  QUÉBEC 206
    Forillon National Park 206
    La Mauricie National Park 207
    Parc des Laurentides 207

CANADA—CENTRAL AND WEST 209
  ALBERTA 209
    Banff National Park 209
    Jasper National Park 209
    Waterton Lakes National Park 210
  BRITISH COLUMBIA 211
    Kootenay National Park 211
    Manning Provincial Park 212
    Mount Revelstoke and Glacier National Parks 212
    Pacific Rim National Park 213
    Wells Gray Provincial Park 213
    Yoho National Park 215

MANITOBA   216
  Riding Mountain National Park   216
  Turtle Mountain Provincial Park   216
NORTHWEST TERRITORIES   217
  Wood Buffalo National Park   217
SASKATCHEWAN   218
  Cypress Hills Provincial Park   218
  Nipawin Provincial Park   219
  Prince Albert National Park   219

INDEX   221

Birdwatchers Guide to Wildlife Sanctuaries

INTRODUCTION

This is the way to see America: to look for the corners of this big land which are undeveloped and carefully set aside for wildlife, especially birds.

Most birdwatchers wend their way through the greenest landscapes and in the purest air still present on earth. The charm of the surroundings is one reason why birdwatching is growing more popular. The other major reason is the beauty and interest found in the birds themselves. It is fun and absorbing not only to recognize a bird but also to learn about it and notice where it is, what it is doing, and, if possible, why.

Notes on bird life have long been kept by National Parks and by National Wildlife Refuges (chains of wildlife preserves that provide nesting and resting places for birds on their flyways and shelters for other wildlife). In recent years, an increasing number of arboretums, public gardens, environmental education centers, and other places with moderately large tracts of land and water to preserve are discovering, cherishing, and listing the birds that fly in. Happily for bird sanctuaries, you never have to truck in the birds that use them, or worry about publicity. Word gets around.

This guide is aimed at describing most of the major and many of the smaller sanctuaries that will admit the public in the United States and Canada, and one in the Virgin Islands.

As a few of the sanctuary managers have pointed out in their letters to me, the words "refuge" or "sanctuary" do not necessarily hold true for all refuges because, in some, game birds may be shot in hunting season.

Bird sanctuaries may be rugged wilderness areas, or good picnic grounds, or parks set aside within cities; all are represented here. If you don't see your favorite birding refuge listed, please let me know.

This book began as a critical survey of bird checklists in my newsletter *Books about Birds* (P.O. Box 106, Kew Gardens, Jamaica, New York 11415). Response was so good that more lists were obtained, and this book finally came into being.

Bird checklists are ever-changing indexes to the contents of bird refuges. Checklists are, at their best, almost an art form. Illustrations and graphics are striking and clearly printed, to be read outdoors in fog, frost, or bright sunlight. Very good lists are at once practical and attractive, printed on narrow widths in pocket-sized flip-page style with pages of graduated length, with each page labeled at the base so that all labels show. Helpful information and small drawings of birds may be included.

Any bird checklist reflects devoted field work and research, usually by several people. Most conform to the names and order prescribed by the American Ornithological Union in its 1957 Checklist, with later corrections.

However, differences in bird lists leap to the eye, and not merely in size—from the enormous lists of over 200 species to the local-garden lists of 50 or so. Some listers count birds flying overhead, even if the birds don't land. Some listers don't count such passing birds. Some listers are "lumpers" and list no subspecies. Some listers are "splitters" and proudly list all the local subspecies. Some listers will specify what parts of their refuge are most productive of birds. This is helpful and most appreciated. Most listers will characterize the number of a particular species as "abundant," "common," "uncommon," or "rare." People have widely different definitions of these terms. Then there is "hypothetical," which can mean anything from the fact that only one person saw the bird to the fact that the bird was reported from just outside the refuge, or the supposition it should be there because the refuge is in its migration path. Also, there are the "accidentals" or the "casuals," birds one is surprised to find in the area and only finds once or twice.

Given sufficient income, unlimited time, and a sturdy car, any confirmed birder would leap at the chance to follow in the steps of Roger Tory Peterson and James Fisher in their *Wild*

America (Houghton Mifflin, 1955), or to trace the routes which Mr. and Mrs. Edwin Way Teale followed in *North with the Spring* (Dodd, Mead, 1951) and the other books in Teale's *American Seasons* series.

To plan an ideal year in bird refuges is a fanciful but pleasing exercise. My ideal year would start with a November visit to Aransas National Wildlife Refuge, Texas (with luck, a distant view of the whooping crane). Then, to Big Bend National Park, also in Texas (expecting almost anything, barring Arctic birds). Then on to Bandelier National Monument, New Mexico (semi-desert, with a forest and interesting Indian archaeology). A stop at Tucson, Arizona, where the Arizona-Sonora Desert Museum is a drop-in point for birds as well as people. To California for a float trip through Havasu National Wildlife Refuge.

Then back across country to catch the exciting, colorful warbler flights in the third week in April at Great Smoky Mountains National Park, Tennessee. On to Cape Romain National Wildlife Refuge, South Carolina, for a good view of the black skimmer's spectacular way of getting his food. Heading north, a stop at New York City's Jamaica Bay Wildlife Refuge (glossy ibis and bobwhite especially), then up through Massachusetts' Bartholomew's Cobble (ferns, wildflowers, and chickadees that feed from the hand). Lastly, to Moosehorn National Wildlife Refuge, Maine (the elusive woodcock and many other birds).

Another whole summer would have to be reserved for such northern-wilderness refuges as Mount McKinley National Park, Alaska (which now has a good system for birdwatching without a car), and Wood Buffalo National Park in Canada's Northwest Territories (hard to reach and best seen if one camps out but very worth it for the rarities. The whooping crane is only one of these, though the largest and scarcest).

Now, for the entries in this book. They show, first, the address, always the mailing address. Sometimes this is the street address, as well. Anything very special about the refuge is stated here. There are telephone numbers for some refuges.

Second, how to reach the refuge (by various means of transportation).

Third, number of species sighted, and qualification of this figure by a count of how many are rare in the refuge. Of course, not all species are seen in any one season. Most are counted in spring and summer, but when a species of special interest appears only in fall or winter, this is noted.

Fourth, which of the birds on the checklist are generally rare, uncommon, or endangered. In other words—the bird may be there, if in season, but you are lucky to see it. There are too many rare birds to name all of them for each sanctuary. Not all rare or uncommon birds are endangered, but to see any bird that is rare is a thrill and stimulates concern for its welfare. The rising popular interest in saving endangered species is good news.

Bird names as given here usually follow local use, especially in the case of the yellow-rumped warbler (myrtle east, Audubon west) and the northern oriole (Baltimore east, Bullock's west).

Fifth, which birds are common and might come into view. A common bird may not be in the area all year round, but is common in some seasons. It is impossible to name them all here, just as it is impossible to name all the rare birds.

Sixth, the look of the land and water. Facilities and sports on the refuge—everything from hot-springs swimming pools to an outdoor theater. Areas with vast caves, or exciting float trips, or interesting archaeology frequently have interesting birds. Some areas have fees. Amounts are not specified here. The $10 "Golden Eagle Passport," good for one year and sold at any Federal recreation area, is a good investment for birdwatchers. It entitles the purchaser and all persons accompanying him in a private vehicle to enter Federal outdoor recreation areas where an entrance fee is applicable. Minimal hunting information is included, but only so that the birdwatcher will know when to stay away.

Seventh, precautions to take. Special note here—insect repellent may come in handy anywhere. Always take it along on birdwatching trips, except in wintertime.

Eighth, checklist date. This is important because birds can change their ranges. Also, more people have been observing and reporting on birds recently, so the later lists are apt to be more complete. Most Canadian lists are very up to date because Canadian lists are being revised to make them bilingual. Other information at the conclusion of the entry: lists of material available on the particular refuge.

Very good state, provincial, and local books about birds are available, but in such numbers that it would be impractical to list them all. However, several very valuable books should be mentioned:

Robert Murphy. *Wild Sanctuaries; Our National Wildlife Refuges—a Heritage Restored.* E. P. Dutton.

Roger Tory Peterson. *A Field Guide to the Birds.* Houghton Mifflin.

———. *A Field Guide to Western Birds.* Houghton Mifflin.

———. *A Field Guide to the Birds of Texas and Adjacent States.* Houghton Mifflin.

Olin Sewall Pettingill, Jr. *A Guide to Bird Finding East of the Mississippi* (another volume also, for west of the Mississippi). Oxford University Press.

Chandler S. Robbins, Bertel Bruun, and Herbert S. Zim. *Birds of North America*; illustrated by Arthur Singer. Golden Press.

Most of the refuges have no overnight accommodations. If they do, it's usually for camping. Usually, no food is available. Some refuges require registration, but it is good sense anyway to stop at the headquarters, look at displays, and pick up information. Some sanctuaries have auto trails but walking trails are more likely, so wear sturdy shoes.

Any refuge manager welcomes documented news of a new bird in his area. "Documented" means exact description, by more than one person, of the bird, where it is, and what it is doing—take a good look and take notes on what you see. Pictures are excellent back-ups if the observers have been quick on the shutter. Before-and-after stops at a refuge headquarters are not only courteous, they also reap dividends: before the visit, in ideas on birds to be seen and places to look and, after the visit, in confirmation of bird identities and often advice on other good birding spots in the neighborhood.

Birders can help their local refuges inaugurate or update their bird lists, and this is an enjoyable and stimulating chore.

By their support of sanctuaries, birders can help preserve these places for both birds and people to enjoy. A wildlife refuge may be the only green area in a desert; the only place for miles where trees grow and birds are abundant; the only place for miles where people may swim or fish or row a boat; the only example within reach to show children what their country used to be like. In particular, the chain of National Wildlife Refuges, stretching from north to south, is necessary shelter and welcome for thousands of migratory wild birds. As this is written, federal budget cuts may curtail essential parts of the chain. The best counter to this is active public support of the refuges.

To send for a bird checklist, write to the refuge you want to know about, considerately enclosing a stamped, self-addressed envelope at least 9″ × 4″.

My thanks to all the refuge managers, education directors, museum staff members, and others who so kindly and helpfully answered my inquiries and sent photographs. My special thanks to Emily S. Jones and Richard R. Frame for their photographs and encouragement.

ALABAMA

UNIVERSITY OF ALABAMA ARBORETUM, Box 1927, University, Alabama 35486. On Loop Road on the University of Alabama campus.

38 species, including such distinctively southern species as the blue grosbeak, Carolina wren, and Carolina chickadee.

60-acre arboretum. No formal checklist available. Birdlist by David T. Rogers, Jr., Associate Professor of Botany.

WHEELER NATIONAL WILDLIFE REFUGE, Box 1643, Decatur, Alabama 35601. 205-353-7243. Stretches 15 miles along the Tennessee River and Wheeler Lake (a reservoir), with its western end in Decatur and its eastern end touching Huntsville. Take Route 31 south from Decatur; turn east on Route 67.

270 species, plus 61 accidental species (each of the latter recorded fewer than four times in the refuge's files). Common birds: waterfowl (especially Canada geese, wood ducks, mallards, black ducks), bobwhite, mourning doves. Rare or endangered: white pelican, wood ibis, peregrine falcon. Greatest concentration of geese: mid-October to early February.

Hardwood bottoms, pine plantations, farmland, pastures, river and reservoir banks. Reservoir fluctuates. Precautions: no guns or dogs except during public hunts and then only by permit. Roads very muddy after rain. Facilities: observation building, picnic tables. Fishing (state license), hunting (permit required), field trials (dogs), pleasure boating (waterskiing in the old river channel only). No overnight camping except by supervised youth groups.

"Accidental Birds" dated April, 1970. Mammal and woody plant lists available.

ALASKA

ALEUTIAN ISLANDS NATIONAL WILDLIFE REFUGE, Pouch #2, Cold Bay, Alaska 99571. A chain of islands stretching 1,100 miles westward from the tip of the Alaska Peninsula to within 500 miles of the Kamchatka Peninsula of the Soviet Union. They are the peaks of a submarine mountain range, the Aleutian Ridge. They house two Aleut villages, some military installations, and great collections of waterfowl. Access by air to some islands.

127 species of regular occurrence; 59 species of casual or accidental occurrence. Rare, uncommon, or endangered: Aleutian Canada goose, Laysan albatross, whooper swan, smew, horned puffin. Foxes, introduced by fur farmers, have depleted bird life on the islands. However, there are still vast numbers of emperor geese, ptarmigans, fulmars, cormorants, and many other kinds of birds.

Sea cliffs, heather-covered hillsides. No trees. Fishing permitted; limited hunting. Weather rainy and windy.

Checklist dated March, 1974.

GLACIER BAY NATIONAL MONUMENT, Gustavus, Alaska 99826. By plane from Juneau, then by boat from Bartlett Cove.

206 species, of which 54 are common or fairly common, and 59 are rare, very rare, or accidental. Rare or endangered: king eider, goshawk, marbled godwit, pomerine jaeger, Thayer's gull, Sabine's gull, parakeet auklet, snowy owl, Vaux's swift. Many birds that are common farther south are rare here, e.g., the starling. Common birds include, among others, the pelagic cormorant, harlequin duck, surf scoter, bald eagle, blue grouse, northern phalarope, glaucous winged gull, mew gull, Arctic

tern, marbled murrelet, varied thrush, and orange-crowned warbler.

Glacier Bay, islands, estuary, brushlands, riverbanks. Glaciers calve majestically into the Bay, a whole sea-cliff of ice collapsing with a roar. Facilities: lodge, foot trail north of Bartlett Cove.

Checklist dated 1973 (send 10¢). Also available: list of extreme migration dates. Guidebook: *Glacier Bay* (paper, Alaska Northwest Pub. Co., Box 4-EEE, Anchorage, Alaska 99509).

IZEMBEK NATIONAL WILDLIFE RANGE, Pouch #2, Cold Bay, Alaska 99571. Near the tip of the Alaska Peninsula. Access by commercial airlines to Cold Bay.

142 species, 48 of them rare in the refuge. Rare, uncommon, or endangered: Leach's petrel, gyrfalcon, peregrine falcon, ancient murrelet, wandering tattler. There are, the checklist says, "spectacular concentrations" of geese, ducks, and shorebirds, especially black brant, emperor geese, Taverner's Canada geese, pintails, mallards, oldsquaws, harlequin ducks, rock sandpipers, Steller's eiders, and yellow warblers.

Izembek has approximately 320,000 acres of volcanic pinnacles, glaciated uplands, low sedge and grass meadows, and, in Izembek Bay, beds of eelgrass. Its climate is rainy and stormy. Fall is the wettest season and spring, the driest. Accommodations (at Cold Bay) are limited.

Checklist dated February, 1973.

KATMAI NATIONAL MONUMENT, P.O. Box 7, King Salmon, Alaska 99613. Reachable by commercial jet from Anchorage to King Salmon, from there to Brooks River by amphibious bush aircraft; from there by four-wheel drive "bus" to the Valley of Ten Thousand Smokes. Accessible only in summer.

Sea birds abound. In the summer, there are more than 40 species of songbirds. Grouse and ptarmigan are common in the uplands. Breeding birds include whistling swans, ducks, loons, grebes, terns, bald eagles, hawks, falcons, and owls.

The monument, covering 2,800,000 acres, centers on the volcanic valley; it also includes lakes, ponds, rivers, volcanic mountains, glaciers, spruce, balsam, poplar, and birch forests, grasslands, and coastline (on Shelikof Strait). Last major eruption, 1912; last minor eruption, 1969. Bring comfortable sport clothes, warm sweater or windbreaker, walking shoes or boots, raingear, insect repellent. Summer temperatures range from 44 to 63 degrees. Use telephoto lens to photograph wildlife. Be wary of animals; do not feed them. When you hike, make noise to warn off large animals. Facilities: Brooks River Lodge, campground at Brooks River (campers should bring in their own groceries), fishing (state license), hiking (get detailed information; plan carefully).

For a price list of maps and books about Katmai and on volcanology, geology, biology, and geography, write Alaska National Parks and Monuments Association, P.O. Box 7, King Salmon, Alaska 99613.

KENAI NATIONAL MOOSE RANGE, Box 500, Kenai, Alaska 99611. In south-central Alaska, 160 miles by road from Anchorage.

146 species and 22 accidental or casual species. Rare or endangered: golden and bald eagles, gyrfalcon, hawk owl, black-backed three-toed woodpecker, other species. Commonly seen: common and Arctic loons, trumpeter swan (on the interior lakes), Barrows goldeneye, common snipe, great horned owl, gray jay, violet-green swallow, varied thrush, water pipit, spruce grouse, many other kinds. Best seasons: late spring and summer. Temperature seldom above 80 degrees in summer.

1,730,000 acres, a contrast between lowland and the Kenai Mountains. Muskeg, rolling hills, hundreds of lakes, and forests of spruce, aspen, willow, and birch. In the mountains there is the Harding Ice Field, and miles of tundra blooming with tiny alpine flowers in season. Bring insect repellent. Facilities: campgrounds, canoe routes, fishing (state license), hunting. Float planes allowed.

Checklist dated January, 1968.

KODIAK NATIONAL WILDLIFE REFUGE, Box 825, Kodiak, Alaska 99615. Constitutes most of Kodiak Island, bordered by Shelikof Strait on the northwest, the Gulf of Alaska to the northeast, and the Pacific Ocean to the south. Reachable by plane from Anchorage. The climate is slightly warmer than the other Alaskan wildlife refuges.

116 species, 27 of these rare or occasional in the refuge. Rare or endangered: gyrfalcon, sandhill crane, golden and bald eagles (about 200 pairs of the latter), hawk owl, other kinds. Common: rock and willow ptarmigans, emperor goose, mallard, scaup, oldsquaw, harlequin duck, golden-crowned sparrow, Lapland longspur, song and fox sparrows, belted kingfisher, common loon, glaucous and mew gulls, kittiwake. On offshore islands, colonies of tufted puffins.

This is the principal habitat of the famed big Kodiak bear (males weigh up to 1,200 pounds). The refuge is 2,780 square miles of the southwest part of Kodiak Island and all 60 square miles of Uganik Island. Vegetation: from Sitka spruce forest in the mountainous north to tundra in the south. Many wildflowers in spring and summer. No roads in the refuge; transport by plane or boat. Hunting is permitted. The annual total take of bears is between 150 and 200, and other kinds of animals may be hunted. Fishing (state license). Commercial fishing boats may be chartered for excursions. Two modern hotels.

Checklist dated September, 1965. Also available: flier about the refuge, with map.

MOUNT MC KINLEY NATIONAL PARK, P.O. Box 9, McKinley Park, Alaska 99755. (Note: there is some discussion about renaming Mount McKinley Denali, its Indian name). Generally open late May to September. Reach via Highway Alaska 3, 120 miles south from Fairbanks, or 240 miles north from Anchorage. Buses run regularly. Or by Alaska Railroad, eight hours from Anchorage, four hours from Fairbanks. Or by plane from principal Alaskan airports.

135 species plus four "hypotheticals." Rare, uncommon, or endangered: golden eagle, harlequin duck, black-backed three-toed woodpecker, gray-headed chickadee, Townsend's soli-

taire. Commonly seen: marsh hawks, short-eared owls, ptar-migans.

McKinley is the highest mountain of the Alaska Range. Below timberline (at 2,700 feet this far north): spruce, paper birch, balsam, poplar, streams, mosses, lichens. Above timber-line: dwarfed shrubs, miniature wildflowers, rocky slopes, glaciers.

Precautions and regulations: Drive slowly. No off-road use of snowmobiles. No motor-powered boats. No destroying, defac-ing, or collecting plants, rocks, and other features. No feeding, capturing, molesting, or killing any animal. Fishing limited. Hunting prohibited. Pets must be leashed and are not permit-ted on backcountry trails. Typical summer weather is cool, wet, and windy. Dress for rough walking and for temperatures ranging from 40 to 80 degrees. Insect repellent is essential. Binoculars, a scope, and a telephoto lens will be useful. If you are hiking (permit required), plan your trip carefully, fol-lowing the park's advice on keeping warm and on avoiding grizzly bears. The park may be toured by bus, with stopoffs. Camping, a lodge, naturalist programs.

Checklist revised July, 1975. Also available: two brochures on the park, one with a large map; schedule of summer events; a "How to Travel" flier; advice on hiking and on animals. For a list of other publications and map, write Alaska National Parks and Monuments Association, McKinley Park, Alaska 99755.

ARIZONA

ARIZONA-SONORA DESERT MUSEUM, P.O. Box 5607, Tucson, Arizona 85703. 602-792-1530. This open-air museum of plants and wildlife of the Sonora Desert houses animals and birds in planned natural-seeming habitats (including a walk-through aviary), but a lot of unplanned bird life goes on, also. Visiting birds include many of those observed in the entire Tucson Mountain area. To reach the Arizona-Sonora Desert Museum, take Arizona 86 from Tucson about six miles to Kinney Road, turn right.

The checklist for this area has 116 species. Of the 116 species, 20 are only rarely seen in this area. Southwestern species fairly commonly seen here: Gila woodpecker, Lucy's warbler, Inca dove, gilded flicker, black-tailed gnatcatcher, Wied's crested flycatcher, hooded oriole, Scott's oriole, pyrrhuloxia, Gambel's quail, roadrunner, Bendire's thrasher, verdin.

Besides the animal and bird exhibits, there are botanical gardens and pleasant shaded places to sit and watch the birds.

Checklist (for the Tucson Mountain area, Pima County Parks and Recreation Department) dated 1964, compiled by Seymour H. Levy.

CABEZA PRIETA GAME RANGE, Box 1032, Yuma, Arizona. Lies along the Mexican boundary in southwestern Arizona. Set aside to be managed as a home for the desert bighorn sheep, this range attracts birds by the thousands. Any water hole in this hot, desert terrain will be crowded with birds such as the white pelican, osprey, and ring-billed gull, many on their way to and from the nearby Gulf of California. However, the area is much used for military purposes. It is suggested that birders

Gambel's quail at the Arizona-Sonora Desert Museum. (*Photo by Emily Jones.*)

wanting to visit the range inquire at refuge headquarters, 356 First Street, Yuma, Arizona.

148 species, plus an additional 50 species of casual or accidental occurrence. Rare, uncommon, or endangered: Lawrence's goldfinch, ferruginous owl, golden eagle, others. Common birds here: screech owl, elf owl, gilded flicker, Gila and ladder-backed woodpeckers, Say's phoebe, verdin, rock wren, black-tailed gnatcatcher, loggerhead shrike, black-throated sparrow, Brewer's sparrow. Best season for visiting: spring—the refuge is directly in the path of bird migrants from the south. Best place to birdwatch: the Growler Valley.

880,000 acres jointly administered by the Bureau of Sport Fisheries and Wildlife and the Bureau of Land Management. Low-lying granitic and lava mountain ranges, none over 3,000 feet high, and desert valleys. Very hot in summer. Some plant life is unique in the U.S. One such plant is the curiously formed elephant tree, appearing to have a trunk buried in sand at its side. Precautions: roads in the area are apt to be mere tracks.

Checklist dated December, 1965. Other information available: folder describing range, with map.

CHIRICAHUA NATIONAL MONUMENT, Dos Cabezas Star Route, Willcox, Arizona 85643. This "island in the sky" is a heaven for birdwatchers. Best reached by driving 36 miles east on Rt. 186 from Willcox. A shorter route from Portal, Arizona, north over the mountains is not recommended for the driver unused to mountain driving.

131 species. Rare, uncommon, or endangered: black-eared bushtit, peregrine falcon, gilded flicker, zone-tailed hawk, Williamson's sapsucker, turkey. Southwestern birds to be seen: Coues' flycatcher (occasional), common bushtit, olivaceous flycatcher, black-headed grosbeak, black-chinned hummingbird, Say's phoebe (this bird likes to take up a post of vantage and sing at 7 A.M.), white-necked raven, painted redstart, white-throated swift, bridled titmouse (very easy to see here), Arizona woodpecker, canyon wren, and others.

A 17-square-mile wilderness of strange rock forms, steep

Chiricahua National Monument. (*Photo by Jessie Kitching.*)

canyons, and glens with many trees and shrubs. A range of elevations, from 5,160 to 7,365 feet, insures a range of bird life. An entrance fee is charged at the visitor center. Several hiking and horseback trails, campgrounds.

Checklist dated March 24, 1970. A new checklist for the Chiricahua Mountains as a whole has just been produced by Dickie Bogle at the Southwestern Research Station, American Museum of Natural History, Portal, Arizona.

DESERT BOTANICAL GARDEN, P.O. Box 5415, Phoenix, Arizona 85010. 602-947-2800. In Papago Park, which is in the Sonoran Desert eight miles east of Phoenix on U.S. 60, 80, and 89. Entrances at 5800 E. Van Buren St. and 6400 E. McDowell Rd.

Many birds are to be seen in the garden. Among the common birds: gilded flicker, vermilion flycatcher, western kingbird, western meadowlark, hooded oriole, burrowing owl, phainopepla, pyrrhuloxia, Gambel's quail, summer tanager, Albert's towhee, Gila woodpecker.

150 acres of plants from the world's deserts. Self-guiding nature walk. Auditorium, library, herbarium, aluminum lathhouse where temperatures are warmer in winter, cooler in summer than the surrounding air. Admission to garden 50¢; children 25¢.

No checklist, but 38 birds commonly seen in the garden are described and pictured in *Birds of the Southwestern Desert* by Gusse Thomas Smith, illustrated by Harriet Morton Holmes (Doubleshoe Publishers, paper, for sale through garden bookstore).

GLEN CANYON NATIONAL RECREATION AREA, P.O. Box 1507, Page, Arizona 86040. Headquarters five miles north of Glen Canyon Dam at Wahweap.

98 species sighted in the Glen Canyon National Recreation Area. 25 of these are water or shore birds and 73 are land birds. The Glen Canyon checklist adds 116 other species known to occur in areas right next to the Canyon. The Glen Canyon staff

points out that desert birds, notably hawks, are comparatively easily seen, and often sit out in the open. Characteristic of this region, and fairly common: red-tailed, sparrow, and Swainson's hawks; western, spotted, and least sandpipers; long-eared owl; broad-tailed hummingbird; western and Cassin's kingbird; Say's phoebe; dusky flycatcher; horned lark; violet-green and cliff swallows; canyon and rock wrens; black-throated gray warbler; Cassin's finch; and others.

Over 1,200,000 acres. The visitor center is on the canyon rim near Glen Canyon Bridge on U.S. 89. Terrain and vegetation: open water in Lake Powell and tributaries, sandbars as the lake fluctuates, marshes in the side canyons, hillsides, cliffs, and terraces. A few cottonwood and juniper trees shelter many owls and wrens. Hunting is allowed in the fall. At Wahweap, five miles north of Glen Canyon Dam, there is camping, a lodge, swimming, waterskiing, and a marina. Guided boat tours of the lake. Warning: the sun is very hot and temperatures can reach 106 degrees in summer.

Checklist dated August, 1974. The Rainbow Bridge National Monument would have many birds that are on the Glen Canyon list.

GRAND CANYON NATIONAL PARK, Box 129, Grand Canyon, Arizona 86023. This vast and splendid area has abundant and interesting wildlife. Access to the South Rim is from Williams and Flagstaff on U.S. 89. Buses run frequently. An airport lies only eight miles south of the park. The North Rim is reached via Jacob Lake, Arizona, and U.S. 89A.

232 species, of which 96 are rare or hypothetical in the park. Rare, uncommon, or endangered: goshawk, Cooper's hawk, golden eagle, peregrine falcon (North Rim), others. Birds characteristic of and common in the park: several hawks, blue grouse, Gambel's quail, belted kingfisher, violet-green swallow, Steller's and pinyon jays, dipper or water ouzel, western and mountain bluebirds, western tanager, and others.

673,575 acres. Visitor Center one mile east of Grand Canyon Village. Yavapai Museum farther east on the South Rim. The park's geology, the record of the ages in its glowing rocks, is overwhelming. The North Rim is forested; the South Rim is more typical of the arid Southwest. Ranger-naturalist trips; hiking trails. Camping (also at the North Rim); lodges, riding; muleback trips to Phantom Ranch 4,500 feet below the South Rim, on the Colorado.

The South Rim is open all year; the North Rim, from mid-May to mid-October. Even in winter, a walk on the level rim trail of the South Rim yields bird sightings, and a stroll partly down Bright Angel Trail in winter, with few other people on the trail, can be a revelation of bird and animal life only a few hundred yards from the hotel.

Checklist dated 1970, compiled by Interpretive Staff, Grand Canyon. Symbols indicate observations from the South Rim, North Rim, inner canyon, or Grand Canyon National Monument.

IMPERIAL NATIONAL WILDLIFE REFUGE, P.O. Box 2217, Martinez Lake, Arizona 85364. About 24 miles above Yuma, Arizona.

205 species; also, 51 species considered casual or accidental. Rare, uncommon, or endangered: Yuma clapper rail, hooded merganser, others. Nesting birds: great blue heron, green heron, least bittern, clapper rail, white-winged dove, red-tailed hawk, great horned owl, and others. Southwestern birds commonly seen here: Abert's towhee, roadrunner, Gila woodpecker, ladder-backed woodpecker, verdin, crissal thrasher, others. Spring and fall have the greatest variety of birds, particularly great concentrations of swallows.

25,765 acres in Arizona and California, and the waters impounded by the Imperial Dam. The land is desert-mountain and some farmland. The wet area is not only the reservoir; there are also lakes, ponds, sloughs, and marshes of various sizes.

Checklist dated September, 1971.

MONTEZUMA CASTLE NATIONAL MONUMENT, Box 218, Camp Verde, Arizona 86322. Twenty miles southeast of

Cottonwood on Arizona 279, then north and east off Rt. 17. Checklist includes territory of Montezuma Wells, a deep lake seven miles away.

157 species, 27 of them of rare or only one occurrence at the monument and the well. Species common here and each a feature of the locality: lesser nighthawk, black phoebe, Gambel's quail, crissal thrasher, bridled titmouse, Abert's towhee, Bell's vireo, Gila and ladder-backed woodpeckers.

The "castle" is a natural fortress built in a limestone cliff by Indians centuries ago. The walk past the cliff winds through a pleasant and surprisingly green semidesert landscape. Picnicking; no camping.

Checklist dated 1974.

ORGAN PIPE CACTUS NATIONAL MONUMENT, Ajo, Arizona 85321. A winter-birdwatching paradise. The several kinds of cacti in this monument provide shelter for many varieties of birds. The monument lies 35 miles southeast from Ajo on Route 85.

248 species, 122 of which are reported as only rare, occasional, or accidental in the monument. Birds fairly commonly seen here, and distinctive to the Southwest: Gambel's quail, white-winged dove, Costa's hummingbird, lesser nighthawk, ladder-backed woodpecker, vermilion flycatcher, verdin, canon wren, rock wren, sage sparrow.

516 square miles of the majestic organ pipe cactus (which can grow as high as twenty feet) and other cacti. Organ pipe cactus blooms in May and June. Other desert flowers bloom even earlier, carpeting the desert with blue, magenta, orange, and gold. The monument's terrain: mountains, outwash plains, rocky canyons, dry washes. Short foot trails. Desert shrubs and paloverde trees line a desert wash near headquarters, and this spot provides good birdwatching. Two scenic drives, evening naturalist talks during winter, year-round campground.

Checklist revised March, 1972.

PETRIFIED FOREST NATIONAL PARK, Holbrook, Arizona 86025. To north entrance, 24 miles east of Holbrook on U.S. 66; to south entrance, 18 miles east of Holbrook on U.S. 160, Interstate 40.

180 species, of which 32 are very rare or accidental. Rare, uncommon, or endangered: Cooper's hawk, golden eagle, Williamson's sapsucker. Special birds of this area, and fairly common here: ferruginous hawk, roadrunner, white-throated swift, Cassin's kingbird, pinyon jay, canyon and rock wrens, Bendire's and sage thrashers, Grace's warbler, Cassin's finch.

94,189 acres featuring not only the colorful petrified rocks of the fossilized forest but many Indian petroglyphs and fantastic Triassic rock formations. Picknicking; no camping. Regulation: no petrified wood may be removed.

Undated checklist based on personal observations in the field by staff members of Petrified Forest National Park.

PRESCOTT NATIONAL FOREST, P.O. Box 2549, Prescott, Arizona 86301. Twenty miles northeast of Prescott on U.S. 89A or one mile southwest on U.S. 89.

237 species, of which eight are only accidental here. Rare, uncommon, or endangered: white-faced ibis, goshawk, Cooper's hawk, golden eagle, Inca dove, flammulated owl, Williamson's sapsucker, hepatic tanager. Southwestern birds to be seen in the forest: roadrunner, calliope hummingbird, gilded flicker, acorn woodpecker, vermilion flycatcher, Mexican jay, pinyon jay, bridled titmouse, canyon wren, several kinds of thrashers, phainopepla, lazuli bunting, others.

Among the scenic regions in this 1,404,215-acre forest are Sycamore Canyon and Pine Mountain Wilderness Areas. Picknicking, camping, hunting, fishing in Granite Basin Lake and Lynx Lake.

Undated checklist.

SABINO CANYON VISITOR CENTER, Coronado National Forest, Santa Catalina Ranger District, Route 15, Box 277-F, Tucson, Arizona 85715. Sabino Canyon is the most popular

Saguaro National Monument. (*Photo by Emily Jones.*)

canyon of this very extensive national forest. It is located twelve miles northeast of Tucson on Tanque Verde Road and Sabino Canyon Road.

191 species, of which 30 are termed "very rare" here. Rare, uncommon, or endangered: Cooper's hawk, golden eagle, Inca dove, groove-billed ani, beardless flycatcher, hepatic tanager, rufous-winged sparrow. In this very good birding area, the birdwatcher is apt to encounter red-tailed hawks, Gambel's quail, roadrunners, white-throated swifts, gilded flickers, Gila and ladder-backed woodpeckers, several flycatchers, verdins, curve-billed thrashers, black-tailed gnatcatchers, phainopeplas, Bell's vireos, Lucy's warblers, hooded and Bullock's orioles, pyrrhuloxias, Abert's towhees. Best bird-observing area: near the stream, particularly the area behind the dam in Lower Sabino Canyon.

Naturalist-conducted hikes, self-guiding auto tours.

A preliminary checklist; the Forest Service says it is continually revising it.

SAGUARO NATIONAL MONUMENT, P.O. Box 17210, Tucson, Arizona 85731. Seventeen miles east from Tucson via Broadway. West section: sixteen miles west of Tucson via Speedway and Gates Pass Road.

188 birds, of which four are only rarely seen at the monument. Birds that are easily seen at the Visitor Center, in the picnic area, or along roads are specially marked on the checklist. Among these: the red-tailed hawk, Gambel's quail, white-winged and western mourning doves, roadrunner, gilded flicker, Gila woodpecker, ash-throated flycatcher, Say's phoebe, verdin, cactus wren, curved-billed thrasher, ruby-crowned kinglet, phainopepla, loggerhead shrike, Audubon's warbler, Wilson's warbler, hooded oriole. Some of the rarest birds are seen only in the Rincon Mountains, over 6,500 feet in elevation. Flickers, wrens, Gila woodpeckers, and other birds nest in the tall saguaro cacti. Saguaros are at peak bloom in late May; the fruit ripens in July.

Rincon-Mountain unit, of 63,360 acres, east of Tucson, has headquarters and Visitor Center with picture windows; nine-mile loop drive; nature trails; picnicking; mountain hiking and riding; guided nature walks in winter. Permit required for camping in the backcountry. The Tucson Mountain unit has 15,360 acres.

Checklist dated 1972. Also available: folder describing monument, with maps; color-illustrated handbook, *Saguaro*.

ARKANSAS

BIG LAKE NATIONAL WILDLIFE REFUGE, P.O. Box 67, Manila, Arkansas 72442. In northeastern Arkansas, two and a half miles northeast of Manila on Rt. 18.

201 species, 38 described as rare. Rare, relatively uncommon, or endangered: bald eagle, Bewick's wren, yellow-throated vireo, worm-eating warbler, dickcissel, others. Common: mallard, blue-winged teal, eastern meadowlark, cardinal, white-throated sparrow, others.

10,974 acres of woods, brush, and cropland, with river bottoms, and open water. This is about half of the area known as the Big Lake "sunken lands," formed by the New Madrid earthquake of 1811, which also formed Reelfoot Lake in Tennessee. Picnicking, fishing, boating, swimming. A levee road from Rt. 18 to the Arkansas-Missouri line is good for bird viewing, but may be muddy in places. Raccoon and squirrel hunting.

Checklist dated July, 1969.

HOLLA BEND NATIONAL WILDLIFE REFUGE, P.O. Box 1043, Russellville, Arkansas 72801. Headquarters in Federal Building, Russellville. Refuge is 14 miles southeast of Russellville via Route 7, then turn left on 155. A relatively new refuge, established in 1957.

158 species, only three described as rare. Rare, uncommon, or endangered: golden and bald eagles, upland plover, Wilson's phalarope, others. Common species: various kinds of ducks, geese, and herons; bobwhite, scissor-tailed flycatcher, mourning dove, turkey vulture, cardinal. Birdwatching is especially varied and interesting here because Holla Bend is in a transition area between eastern and western birds. Best season:

winter—flights of over 100,000 ducks and geese; eagles feeding along the river.

6,367 acres on the Arkansas River. Open water bordered with forest and grain fields. Sport fishing, dove hunting, archery deer hunting.

Preliminary checklist dated March, 1970. A new one is in progress.

HOT SPRINGS NATIONAL PARK, Box 1860, Hot Springs, Arkansas 71901. The city of Hot Springs surrounds the park. Access by car (U.S. 70 and 270, and State Rt. 7), air, or bus. A very beautiful park with good walking trails and a wealth of woodland birds.

107 species, 19 described as rare. Rare, uncommon, or endangered: Bell's and Philadelphia vireos, several kinds of warblers, turkey, others. Common: Carolina chickadee, tufted titmouse, Carolina wren, mockingbird, others.

1,035 acres that yield 47 mineral hot springs. Oak-hickory forests with many flowering trees, wildflowers, and 18 miles of hiking trails. Observation tower, visitor center, campground. Riding. Rules: no disturbing of anything. Careful with fires. No hunting. Pets must be leashed. Speed limit in campground area, 15 MPH. Bicycles, motorcycles, and other vehicles not allowed on park trails.

Undated, duplicated checklist. Also available: folder on park.

WAPANOCCA NATIONAL WILDLIFE REFUGE, P.O. Box 257, Turrell, Arkansas 72384. On the Tennessee border north of Memphis. Headquarters one-quarter mile south of Turrell. A new refuge (established 1961) around a beautiful cypress-edged lake.

205 species, 37 classed as rare. Rare, uncommon, or endangered: Mississippi kite (in spring), turkey (common here), several kinds of warblers. Common species: bobwhite, killdeer, yellow-billed cuckoo, screech owl, chuck-will's-widow, belted kingfisher, several woodpeckers, field sparrow. 1,000 wood

ducks nest here. Best season: this is a wintering area for huge concentrations of waterfowl; more than 30,000 ducks, 10,000 Canada geese.

5,484 acres. Lake, cypress, swamp, and land farmed for wildlife foods. Wildlife drive, nature boat trail through Wapanocca Lake swamp, observation tower. Fishing; managed hunts for squirrel and raccoons.

Checklist dated January, 1970.

WHITE RIVER NATIONAL WILDLIFE REFUGE, P.O. Box 308, DeWitt, Arkansas 72042. For access, check at headquarters, 704 South Jefferson St., DeWitt. Roads may be impassable during floods; some areas accessible only by boat or on foot.

227 species, 30 described as rare. Rare, uncommon, or endangered: turkey, yellow rail, black rail, Sprague's pipit, several kinds of warblers. Nesting birds include: bitterns, gallinules, American coot, cardinal.

113,300 acres. Extends for 54 miles along the lower White River. Lakes, streams, bayous, and bottomlands. Archery and gun hunts, sport fishing, primitive camping.

Checklist dated March, 1972.

Audubon Canyon Ranch. (*Photo by Clerin W. Zumwalt.*)

CALIFORNIA

AUDUBON CANYON RANCH, Shoreline Highway, Rt. #2, Stinson Beach, California 94970. 415-383-1644. A major heronry of great blue herons and American egrets. A joint project of the Marin, Golden Gate, and Sequoia Audubon Societies.

"About 55 species of waterbirds are likely to be seen at the ranch during the year, and 90 species of land birds frequent the watershed. Some 60 species are permanent residents," the Audubon Canyon Ranch flier says. Best season: March 1 through July 4. The ranch is closed Mondays.

1,000 acres of rolling grasslands, chaparral, woodlands, and four rugged canyons. Two canyons are open to the public. Henderson Overlook is a vantage point to see the nesting birds. Display hall, bookstore, trails. Precautions: no smoking, picnic only in ranch yard, no pets, stay on the trails, beware of poison oak, make as little noise as possible at the Overlook.

Checklist (for Point Reyes Peninsula) compiled March, 1973. Also available: flier describing ranch.

BIG BASIN REDWOODS STATE PARK, Big Basin, California 95006. 23 miles northwest of Santa Cruz off Rt. 9.

Around 60 species, eight of which are rare for this park. Particularly notable: marbled murrelet, pygmy nuthatch, sharp-shinned hawk, wood duck, water ouzel, fox sparrow, sparrow hawk.

11,886 acres of redwood groves, luxuriant growths of huckleberries and ferns, mixed woodlands, and chaparral. Hiking, riding, camping, picnicking, summer naturalist program.

Checklist is a habitat study of birds as found in Big Basin Redwoods and Portola State Parks (Portola is 20 miles west of Palo Alto), compiled by Eleanor A. Pugh.

CHANNEL ISLANDS NATIONAL MONUMENT, 1699 Anchors Way Drive, Ventura, California 93003. Two islands, Anacapa and Santa Barbara, off the coast of southern California, reached only by boat from Oxnard and Ventura, California.

138 species plus 28 more for which single or sporadic records exist. Commonest species: western gull, sooty shearwater, double-crested cormorant, Wilson's warbler (as migrant), American kestrel, western meadowlark. Rare or endangered species: brown pelican (locally common), osprey, peregrine falcon.

Island flora has developed some interesting botanical forms. The 1959 fire on Santa Barbara destroyed most of scrubby habitat for birds there. Rangers are resident on Anacapa all year, on Santa Barbara only during the summer. Primitive camping, scuba diving permitted.

Checklist compiled by Lee Jones for forthcoming book on birds of the northern Channel Islands. Revised May 22, 1974.

DEATH VALLEY NATIONAL MONUMENT, Death Valley, California 92328. 70 miles east of Lone Pine via Rts. 136, 190.

307 species, 115 of them rare, accidental, or in a few cases, an unsupported observation, the checklist says. Rare, uncommon, or endangered: black-chinned sparrow, golden eagle. Common birds: Gambel's quail, Costa's hummingbird, cinnamon teal, verdin, lesser goldfinch, rough-winged swallow, yellow warbler, Bullock's oriole, brown-headed cowbird, sage thrasher, sage sparrow, road-runner, LeConte's thrasher. Best season: April. From May to September, Death Valley temperatures are scorching.

3,000 square miles. One point in the monument, Bad Water, is the lowest point in North America (minus 282 feet); Telescope Peak, above it, is 11,049 feet high. Terrain and vegetation: salt beds, borax formations, sand dunes, some springs, desert shrub land, cliffs, canyons, pinyon pine-juniper, with some limber and bristlecone pine at high altitudes. Birding especially good around the golf course and in the date orchard

at Furnace Creek Ranch. Precaution: check with park ranger before venturing off main travel routes.
Checklist dated December, 1971.

DESCANSO GARDENS, 1418 Descanso Drive, La Canada, California 91011. 213-790-5571. A facility of the Los Angeles County Department of Arboreta and Botanic Gardens. Just south of Foothill Boulevard.

111 species. Rare, uncommon, or endangered: Cooper's hawk (resident), osprey (winter), phainopepla (summer). Five hummingbirds: black-chinned, Costa's, Anna's, rufous, Allen's.

150 acres, a native plant garden featuring ornamental camellias in bloom from November to March; azaleas in April; roses in May and June; iris and lilacs in spring; lilies and annuals in summer. A visitors' center, tram tours, oriental tea house.

Checklist dated August, 1974, prepared by Charles H. Bernstein of the San Fernando Valley Audubon Society.

EL DORADO NATURE CENTER, 7550 E. Spring St. (605 Freeway), Long Beach, California 90815. A forest-sanctuary, part of the City of Long Beach Recreation Department.

145 species, 32 described as rare. Rare, uncommon, or endangered: European widgeon, osprey (winter), band-tailed pigeon, wrentit, and others. A very rare sighting, a garganey, a Euro-Asiatic teal, was described as "rare, summer." Common here: green heron, gadwall, cinnamon teal, American widgeon, shoveler, canvasback, ruddy duck, belted kingfisher, common flicker, hermit thrush, and others.

80 acres with two lakes, a stream, and two miles of self-guiding nature trails. A half-mile self-guiding paved nature trail for the handicapped and the unsighted, monthly birdwalks led by the Audubon Society, summer Junior Naturalist programs. Closed Mondays. Regulations: stay on trails, all children under 16 must be accompanied by an adult at least 21 years old. Pets,

food, drinks, radios, and bicycles are not permitted. Shoes must be worn. No collecting.

Checklist, by Barbara W. Massey, dated May, 1975. Also available: information on programs, history of project, regulations.

GRIFFITH PARK, 4730 Crystal Springs Drive, Los Angeles, California 90027. From downtown Los Angeles drive via Glendale Boulevard to Riverside Drive, then left to the park entrance, 5½ miles in all. Entrance is at the north end of Vermont Ave.

About 120 species, divided on the checklist into resident birds, summer visitants, winter visitants, and spring and fall migrants. Rare or endangered: phainopepla (summer), Cooper's hawk. Common birds: Anna's, Costa's, rufous, and black-chinned hummingbirds; western flycatcher; western wood pewee; black-throated gray, Macgillivray's warblers; ringed turtle dove (introduced); Chinese spotted dove (introduced); valley quail; Cassin's kingbird; and many others.

The park has 4,000 mountainous acres; forest; chaparral slopes. Trails, picnicking, horseback riding, golf, swimming pool.

Undated checklist compiled by the City of Los Angeles park rangers with the assistance of the local Audubon societies and the Southwest Bird Study Club.

HAVASU NATIONAL WILDLIFE REFUGE, P.O. Box A, Needles, California 92363. A spectacular waterfowl gathering point, very rich in songbirds and other birds as well. In three sections: Topock Marsh, Topock Gorge, and Bill Williams Delta. The touring birdwatcher really needs a map for this long and narrow refuge, stretched out along the Colorado River. Visitor center is where I-40 (Highway 66) crosses the Colorado River, southeast of Needles, California.

276 species, of which over 64 species nest on the refuge. 67 are rare or accidental at Havasu. Rare or endangered: peregrine falcon, prairie falcon, Ross' goose, Yuma clapper rail (the

latter in Topock Gorge). Many species winter here. Commonly seen migrants: grebes, willets, marbled godwits, avocets, black-necked stilts, northern phalaropes, California gulls, Forster's terns, black terns. Such vivid birds as the vermilion flycatcher, western tanager, yellow-headed blackbird, Costa's humming-bird, violet-green swallow, and yellow-breasted chat may be seen.

Total acreage, including the Needles Peaks: 41,500. The northern part of the refuge is Topock Marsh, then come the eleven miles of Topock Gorge, below that, the Bill Williams River Delta (called Havasu Springs on some maps). Very varied habitats: upland, marsh, lake, canyons. Indian petroglyphs in the Gorge. Precautions: boatmen must observe special boating regulations. Facilities: river float trips, waterfowl feeding area at the Farm at Topock Marsh, observation tower, public hunting in some parts of refuge during specified seasons, fishing, boat ramps, camping.

Checklist dated July, 1973. Also available: brochure on "Know Your Ducks, Field Guide for Hunters," flier describing refuge, flier about 42 species of mammals in refuge, "Conserving Our Fish and Wildlife Heritage," "Cavity-Nesting Birds of Arizona and New Mexico Forests" by Virgil E. Scott and David R. Patton, "Public Use Regulations for Havasu National Wildlife Refuge," "Havasu National Wildlife Refuge, Ducks in the Desert," "Topock Gorge" (flier with map), "Geese of the Havasu National Wildlife Refuge," and information about canoe and float trips.

INYO NATIONAL FOREST, MAMMOTH RANGER DIS-TRICT, Mammoth Lakes, California 93546. Inyo National Forest covers a great area. The Mammoth Lakes section, in the western part of the Inyo Forest, is reached via State Rt. 395 north of Bishop (east of the Sierra Nevada), then west on 203.

249 species in Inyo Forest proper, most of which may be seen around Mammoth Lakes. Rare or endangered: golden eagle, osprey, Williamson's sapsucker. Notable at Mammoth: Hammond's flycatcher, ruddy duck, Wilson's phalarope, common nighthawk, calliope hummingbird, western kingbird, olive-

sided flycatcher, violet-green swallow, kinglets, loggerhead shrike.

In Mammoth (which is a prime gateway to the John Muir Trail over the Sierra Nevada): forests, mountainsides, flowery fields, hot springs. Hiking, camping, naturalist-guided tours, self-guiding walks. Skiing in winter.

Bird checklist dated 1969.

JOAN HAMANN DOLE MEMORIAL SANCTUARY, Box 314, Middletown, California 95461. Middletown is at the junction of Rts. 175 and 29, north of Santa Rosa.

47 species. Rare, uncommon, or endangered: Cooper's hawk, white-tailed kite. Among other species seen: Allen's, Anna's, Costa's, and rufous hummingbirds, tree and violet-green swallows.

Chaparral habitat.

JOSHUA TREE NATIONAL MONUMENT, Twentynine Palms, California 92277. 23 miles east of Indio on U.S. 60, I-10.

261 species, 18 of them rare in the refuge. Rare, uncommon, or endangered: varied bunting, golden eagle, prairie falcon, white-tailed kite, Townsend's solitaire, others. Nesting birds: phainopepla; lesser goldfinch; Anna's, Costa's and rufous hummingbirds; mockingbird; Bullock's, hooded and Scott's oriole; elf owl; great horned owl; Say's phoebe; ladder-backed woodpecker; others. Best season: the Joshua tree, *Yucca brevifolia*, blooms from March through May, and so do other desert flowers.

The monument: more than 870 square miles. The tall Joshua trees and other flora grow among rugged granite formations and with pinyon pine and desert juniper. There are a cholla cactus garden and a few desert springs. Camping in designated grounds, but bring your own firewood and water. Pets on leash only. Picnicking in designated areas. Self-guiding nature trail. Nature walks and campfire talks.

Checklist dated 1972. For it, and other material on the monument, write the Joshua Tree Natural History Association, 74185 Palm Vista Drive, Twentynine Palms, California 92277.

KERN-PIXLEY NATIONAL WILDLIFE REFUGES, P.O. Box 219, Delano, California 93215. In the southern part of California's San Joaquin Valley. Refuge headquarters is on the Kern Refuge, at the intersection of Dairy Avenue (Corcoran Road) and Garces Avenue.

160 species, of which 18 are rare in these refuges. Rare and endangered: Ross' goose, fulvous tree duck, peregrine falcon, Cassin's kingbird. Common birds: coots, pintails, green-winged teal, killdeer, avocets, burrowing owls, horned larks, long-billed marsh wrens, western meadowlarks, Brewer's blackbirds, many others. Best season: September through May (it is hot and dusty from June through September).

The 10,618 acres of the refuges represent an attempt to restore part of a marshland once a home for millions of birds, then drained for farmland until it became semi-desert, and now irrigated again by a complex system of wells, canals, and dikes. Facilities: picnic area near headquarters. Hunting in fall.

Checklist and folder about refuges available.

KLAMATH BASIN NATIONAL WILDLIFE REFUGES, Route 1, Box 74, Tulelake, California 96134. 916-667-2231. Five refuges—Tule Lake, Lower Klamath, Clear Lake, Klamath Forest, and Upper Klamath (the latter two in Oregon) into which millions of waterfowl on the Pacific Flyway funnel in spring and fall. The Bureau of Reclamation manages the reservoir areas, the Bureau of Sport Fisheries and Wildlife controlling the areas designated for wildlife. Refuge headquarters is on Hill Road, south of Rt. 61, which forms the Oregon-California border.

249 species, 180 of which are nesting species. In addition, 25 species are considered to occur casually. Common: white pelican (on Clear Lake), gadwall, redhead, cinnamon teal; cackling, white-fronted, and snow goose. Rare or endangered: great gray owl, red-necked grebe, sandhill crane.

121,158 acres, in all, in the refuges. Open lakes, large marshes, grassy meadows, coniferous forests, sagebrush and juniper, farmlands, and rough lava. Hunting permitted on all of the refuges, fishing on some. Refuge auto trails and tour routes over improved gravel roads.

LASSEN VOLCANIC NATIONAL PARK, Mineral, California 96063. Park headquarters at Mineral on Rt. 36 north of Red Bluff; or enter from north of park, on Rts. 44 or 89. Park road is 30 miles long.

165 species, 37 of them rare at Lassen. Rare or endangered: bald and golden eagles, white pelican, Williamson's sapsucker. Birds to be seen fairly easily: Clark's nutcracker, evening grosbeak, Townsend's solitaire, Steller's jay, green-tailed towhee, others. Main season: mid-June to mid-September.

161 square miles of hot springs, lava, volcanic cones. Last violent eruptions in 1914-1915. Pine forests, lakes, alpine wildflowers. Lodges, camping, fishing, boating (no motors), campfire programs, naturalist-guided walks, skiing in winter, ice skating on Reflection Lake in early winter.

Checklist dated 1969.

LIVING DESERT RESERVE, P.O. Box 390, Palm Desert, California 92260. The Living Desert Association, a division of the Palm Springs Desert Museum, is dedicated to the explanation of the ecology of the natural desert. The checklist of the Living Desert Reserve does not include migratory waterfowl, such as snow geese, which have been sighted passing overhead, but it is intended to be a guide to the common bird species of the Coachella Valley.

86 species, 22 of them rarely seen, 27 of the 86 found nesting on the reserve. Rare, uncommon, or endangered: Cooper's hawk, golden eagle, prairie and peregrine falcons, phainopepla (common here), hermit warbler. Commonly seen more than 50 percent of the time in the reserve: Gambel's quail, mourning and ground doves, roadrunner, white-throated swift, black-

Living Desert Reserve.

chinned hummingbird, western kingbird, western flycatcher, verdin, rock wren, western mockingbird, western bluebird, black-tailed gnatcatcher, starling, yellow-rumped and Wilson's warblers, house sparrow, house finch, white-crowned sparrow.

Checklist by Karen Sausman Fowler, February 10, 1975.

LOS ANGELES STATE AND COUNTY ARBORETUM, 301 North Baldwin Ave., Arcadia, California 91006. 213-446-8251. Six miles north of the San Bernardino Freeway, in an urban area.

177 species. Special notice given in the checklist to "birds declining in all or part of their range": black-crowned night heron, sharp-shinned hawk, Cooper's hawk, red-shouldered hawk, pigeon hawk, sparrow hawk, barn owl, yellow warbler, common yellowthroat. Among other birds reported: red-whiskered bulbul, surely an escapee from a pet shop. (The bulbul has found its way out of Miami pet shops and is living successfully in parts of Miami.)

127 acres of plants from many parts of the world. Peacocks roam the grounds. Greenhouses, library, demonstration home gardens. Conducted tram tours.

Checklist dated 1974 includes a number of injured and hand-raised birds, so indicated on the list.

MODOC NATIONAL WILDLIFE REFUGE, Box 1439, Alturas, California 96101. In northeastern California, at the confluence of the North and South Forks of the Pit River at an elevation of 4,365 feet. Two miles south of Alturas on U.S. 395.

187 species, of which 13 are rare. In addition, eleven species, first noted in recent years. Rare or endangered: trumpeter swan, Ross' goose, golden and bald eagles, osprey. A flock of native Canada geese remains at the refuge throughout the year. Nesting birds include eared grebes, mallards, gadwalls, pintails, ruddy ducks, green-winged teal, cinnamon teal, California quail, and ring-necked pheasants.

8,016 acres. Closed during waterfowl hunting seasons. At

other times, part of Modoc is open for fishing, picnicking, and wildlife observation.

Checklist dated 1966, updated by list from refuge manager.

MOUNT TAMALPAIS STATE PARK, Mill Valley, California 94941. Twenty miles north of San Francisco, seven miles west of Mill Valley on an unnumbered road.

Around 100 species, ten of which are rarely seen. Rare or endangered: white-tailed kite, golden eagle. To be seen fairly easily: western bluebird, pine siskin, white-crowned sparrow, scrub jay, Bewick's wren, rufous-sided towhee, common bushtit, Swainson's thrush, turkey vulture, red-tailed hawk, western meadowlark.

Mount Tamalpais rises 2,605 feet above sea level. In the park, there are chaparral, cliffs and rocky beaches, forests, grassland, and streams. Trails, horseback riding, picnicking, camping, and a natural amphitheater where plays and pageants are presented.

Bird-distribution chart dated January, 1971. Also available: park minifolder.

MUIR WOODS NATIONAL MONUMENT, Mill Valley, California 94941. Seventeen miles north of San Francisco, off Rt. 1.

Between 50 and 60 species. Special bird: pygmy owl (present but rare), spotted owl, western flycatcher, varied thrush. Common birds: Steller's jays, chestnut-backed chickadees, brown creepers, winter wrens, hermit thrushes.

The monument is a beautiful 552-acre grove of redwoods at the foot of Mount Tamalpais. The banks of Redwood Creek offer the best bird-observing. No camping, picnicking, fishing, hunting, firearms, or fire-building. No pets. Stay on trails. There is a Braille trail for the blind.

Checklist now being revised.

Muir Woods. (*Photo courtesy of National Park Service.*)

PINNACLES NATIONAL MONUMENT, Paicines, California 95043. In west-central California, on the San Andreas Fault (the area on which the monument stands has been inching its way north, 1½ inches per year, for millions of years). Enter park only from the east via Rt. 25. The park's western entrance is not a through road.

106 species, 15 of them rarely seen, plus 25 accidental and marginal species. Rare or endangered: peregrine falcon, phainopepla. Special birds: chestnut-backed chickadee, Hutton's vireo, Lawrence's goldfinch. Best season: spring. Summer temperatures can go over 100 degrees.

Chaparral-covered slopes of an ancient volcano. 23 square miles, all in the Upper Sonora Life Zone. Glorious spring wildflowers. Precautions: stay on trails. Rock faces off trails are unstable. Poison oak abounds. So do rattlesnakes. Do not molest rattlesnakes. Don't travel alone. Don't drink from streams; some stream water has been contaminated. Pets must be leashed and may not be taken on trails. Campground available, water and comfort stations, hiking trails.

Checklist dated July, 1967. Also available: flier describing monument, with map.

POINT REYES BIRD OBSERVATORY, P.O. Box 321, Bolinas, California 94924. Take State Rt. 1 north from the Golden Gate Bridge toward Inverness. There is a parking lot at Point Reyes Lighthouse.

361 species, 119 of which are known to breed on the Point Reyes Peninsula. Many pelagic birds, shorebirds. Rare, uncommon, or endangered: black rail, pileated woodpecker, many others. Watch for these birds: pygmy nuthatches, black brant, Brandt's cormorant, red crossbill. Good season: spring— beautiful wildflowers—but winter sees an extraordinary number of migrants.

On the peninsula: bird cliffs, estuaries, grassland, brush, forest. May be rainy or foggy, with strong wind.

Checklist dated March, 1973. Published by Muir Woods-Point Reyes Natural History Association.

RANCHO SANTA ANA BOTANIC GARDENS, 1500 N. College Ave., Claremont, California 91711. North of Foothill Boulevard, on the campus of the Claremont Colleges.

40 common birds, among them the phainopepla (summer), red-shafted flicker, western tanager, rufous-sided and brown towhees. 28 less common birds, among them the California thrasher, screech owl, Cooper's hawk, pine siskin. 25 rare birds (rare to the gardens, that is), among them the golden eagle, white-tailed kite, calliope hummingbird.

A garden of native plants; desert plants, especially cholla cactus; also big trees—conifers, deciduous trees, palms.

Checklist, dated 1974, compiled with help from the Pomona Valley Audubon Society.

SACRAMENTO NATIONAL WILDLIFE REFUGE, Rt. 1, Box 311, Willows, California 95988. Seven miles south of Willows on Interstate 5. No wonder the National Audubon Convention met in Sacramento one year.

This refuge in the Sacramento Valley shelters 175 species, and its bird population may exceed one million at its height in January. Among the most numerous birds are pintails, mallards, widgeons and the snow, white-fronted, and cackling geese. Bitterns, pelicans, herons, and gallinules are attracted to the ponds. Among rare or uncommon species of birds: white-faced ibis, sandhill crane.

A 10,800-acre region of marshes, ponds, and standing fields of rice and wild millet (to draw the birds away from the farms farther south). A few cottonwoods and willows border irrigation ditches.

SALTON SEA NATIONAL WILDLIFE REFUGE, P.O. Box 247, Calipatria, California 92233. 714-348-2323. At the southern tip of Salton Sea in California's Imperial Valley. Refuge headquarters northwest of Calipatria. From State Highway 111, four miles north of Calipatria, turn west on Sinclair Road; drive 5½ miles to the end of the paved road.

258 species plus 44 accidental species. Rare, uncommon, or endangered: white pelican (high water in recent years has erased some of its nesting habitat), brown pelican, roseate spoonbill, pectoral sandpiper. Commonly seen birds: fulvous tree duck, roadrunner, Gambel's quail, cactus wren, verdin. Wintering habitat of Canada, snow, and white-fronted geese and a dozen species of ducks. Heaviest concentrations of waterfowl in December and January, but a good variety of birds at all times of year.

2500 acres with the Sonoran Desert on one side and rich croplands on the other. Winters are mild. Summers are very, very hot, ranging up to 120 degrees. No camping or picnicking. Pets must be leashed. Guided tours can be arranged through refuge. Check with refuge manager about days when hunting is permitted.

Checklist dated June, 1970. Also available: flier and pamphlet describing refuge, sheet of general information on hunting.

SEQUOIA AND KINGS CANYON NATIONAL PARKS, Three Rivers, California 93271. From Grant Grove (reached from Visalia on the south, or Fresno on the north, on Rt. 180) drive on Rt. 180, open in summer, to Cedar Grove, Kings Canyon, or take the Generals' Highway south to Lodgepole in Sequoia. From the south (Visalia), Rt. 198 leads into Sequoia. These are high-country parks. The best way to see them is by hiking along some of the more than 900 miles of trails, from early July into fall. However, Giant Forest (Sequoia), Grant Grove, and Cedar Grove have self-guiding nature trails just off the road.

124 species, ten of these seldom seen, and 15 accidentals. Rare, uncommon, or endangered: golden eagle, California thrasher. Birds to watch for in summer: Clark's nutcracker, mountain quail, blue grouse, gray-crowned rosy finch (at high altitudes), pileated woodpecker, water ouzel, canyon wren, western tanager, fox sparrow, many others.

The two parks embrace more than 1300 square miles of

magnificent wild landscape, from foothills to mountain crest. Precautions: leash pets. Do not smoke while walking. Leave all natural features, include flowers, unharmed. Drive carefully and slowly. Facilities: lodges (reservations needed), hiking trails (permits needed for backcountry travel), horseback riding, camping, fishing, naturalist-guided trips, campfire programs. In winter, skiing in Sequoia.

Joint checklist dated 1974. For further material, write Sequoia Natural History Association, Three Rivers, California 93271.

SILVERWOOD WILDLIFE SANCTUARY, 13003 Wildcat Canyon Road, Lakeside, California 92040. Owned and operated by the San Diego Audubon Society. The distinction of this very interesting sanctuary lies in its variety of wild creatures and plants in a very dry environment, and its preservation of the area in as natural a state as possible, even to the poison oak. Drive east from San Diego on Interstate 8 to the Highway 67 exit in El Cajon and north on 67 to Lakeside. In Lakeside, turn right on Mapleview and left on Ashwood. From this turn, it is five miles to the Sanctuary. Ashwood becomes Wildcat Canyon Road.

161 species, of which 33 species have nested. Notable, and likely to be seen: wrentit, California thrasher, brown and rufous-sided towhee, plain titmouse, bushtit, Nuttall's woodpecker, California quail, Anna's hummingbird, scrub jay, common raven, common crow, Bewick's and canyon wrens, black-headed grosbeak, many others. Rare or endangered: yellow-green vireo, phainopepla, pileated woodpecker, golden eagle, others.

212 acres of chaparral and live oaks in the Holmes Mountains. Low hills and ridges. Sanctuary is closed Mondays. Precautions and regulations: do not smoke. All plants, animals, and rocks are not to be disturbed. Stay on trails. Do not litter. Picnicking only at the tables. No camping or fires. No pets unless locked in the owner's car. Children must remain at all times with the adults who brought them. No motorized vehicles or horses on the trails.

Publications (15¢ each) include "Birds of Silverwood" (May, 1975) and "Bird-Finding in San Diego County."

STRYBING ARBORETUM AND BOTANICAL GARDEN,

Golden Gate Park, San Francisco, California 94222. At South Drive and 9th Avenue.

116 species, of which 46 are rare or uncommon there. 29 birds breed in the arboretum-garden. Among birds commonly seen in spring and summer: mallards, California quail, American coot, killdeer, mourning doves, Allen's hummingbirds, red-shafted flickers, western flycatchers, scrub jays, chestnut-backed chickadees, common bushtits, pygmy nuthatches, brown creepers, wrentits, orange-crowned warblers, Audubon's warblers, yellowthroats, pine siskins.

Checklist dated 1971, compiled by John Kipping. Published by the Strybing Arboretum Society, 9th Ave. and Lincoln Way, San Francisco, California 94122.

TUCKER WILDLIFE SANCTUARY, Star Route, Box 858,

Orange, California 92667. 714-649-2760. A private sanctuary, owned and operated by California State University at Fullerton. 15 miles northeast of Orange via Chapman Avenue, Santiago Canyon Rd.

142 species, 29 of which are incidental (few recorded). Rare, uncommon, or endangered: golden eagle, pigeon hawk, Nuttall's woodpecker (common in western California, but not elsewhere), phainopepla. The sanctuary makes a special effort to attract hummingbirds; six are listed, ranging in frequency from Anna's (common) to the calliope (incidental). Among common birds here: Cooper's, red-tailed and red-shouldered hawk, California quail, acorn woodpecker, scrub jay, house finch, and rufous-sided and brown towhees.

A ten-acre refuge for native wildlife and plants. Observation porch, nature trail, museum displays. A 50¢ donation is requested.

Birdlist appends list of mammals, snakes, and amphibians.

UNIVERSITY OF CALIFORNIA BOTANICAL GARDEN, Berkeley, California 94720. Follow road on north side of Strawberry Canyon on the University campus.

76 species, six unusual for the garden. Characteristic of region: California thrasher, Hutton's vireo, brown towhee, California quail, Anna's hummingbird, scrub and Steller's jay, chestnut-backed chickadee, Bewick's wren, others. Best months: April and May.

Many unusual plants. Picnicking allowed.

Send 15¢ to Botanical Garden for checklist.

WHITTIER NARROWS NATURE CENTER, 1000 No. Durfee Ave., South El Monte, California 91733. 213-444-1872. A facility of the Los Angeles County Department of Parks and Recreation. South of the Pomona River Freeway, just west of the San Gabriel River Freeway.

162 species. Rare, uncommon, or endangered: black-crowned night heron, wood duck, white-tailed kite, sharp-shinned hawk, osprey, phainopepla, yellowthroat. Many riverine birds, such as the great blue heron, green heron, American egret, American bittern, geese, teal, ducks, rails, sandpipers, stilts, the belted kingfisher, swallows.

127 acres of land along the San Gabriel River. Cottonwoods, alders, sycamores, and many shrubs.

Checklist dated 1971. Also available: map showing directions to Whittier Narrows.

YOSEMITE NATIONAL PARK, California 95389. Access from west (Merced) by bus or private car. Eastern entrance (summer only) will scare a driver not used to mountain roads.

223 species in the Yosemite region and slightly beyond the park borders. Of these, 87 are rare to accidental. Rare, uncommon, or endangered: harlequin duck, hooded merganser, bald and golden eagles, osprey, peregrine falcon, Wilson's phalarope, Williamson's sapsucker, black-backed three-toed woodpecker, and hermit warbler (common in tall conifers on the West Coast, but not elsewhere).

The checklist indicates in what life zones, from high to low altitudes, the birds have made themselves at home. From high to low, characteristic birds for each altitude in the park are: Arctic-alpine—gray-crowned rosy finch; Hudsonian—black-backed three-toed woodpecker, mountain bluebird, pine grosbeak, Clark's nutcracker, white-crowned sparrow; Canadian—blue grouse, goshawk, calliope hummingbird, Williamson's sapsucker, Hammond's flycatcher, Cassin's finch, Townsend's solitaire, Lincoln's sparrow; transition—pygmy owl, band-tailed pigeon, solitary vireo, Nashville warbler; Upper Sonoran—brown towhee, Bewick's wren, wrentit, western bluebird; Lower Sonoran—horned lark, American goldfinch, mockingbird.

This magnificent Sierra Nevada park can give delight both to auto visitors (in Yosemite Valley and, higher, at Tuolumne Meadows) and to hikers in the backcountry. Lodges, hotels, campgrounds. A circle of high-altitude camps each at an easy day's hike or ride from the next (early reservations needed). Granite mountains and characteristic Sierra rock domes, flowering alpine meadows, streams, waterfalls, forests of ponderosa pine, lodgepole, and other trees. Field seminars in ornithology. Fishing (state regulations). In winter, ski touring at Badger Pass.

Undated checklist. For this and other publications about Yosemite, write to the Yosemite Natural History Association, P.O. Box 545, Yosemite National Park, California 95389. They issue "Birds of Yosemite National Park" by Cyril A. Stebbins and Robert C. Stebbins (1954, 1974, paper, 84 pages, $1.25). The bird checklist in this is alphabetical. A very helpful color key to birds precedes the checklist. Specific locations where particular birds have been seen are given.

COLORADO

COLORADO NATIONAL MONUMENT, Fruita, Colorado 81521. Ten miles west of Grand Junction off U.S. 70.

116 species. Rare, uncommon, or endangered: sandhill crane, bald and golden eagles, gyrfalcon, peregrine falcon, black rosy finch, beardless flycatcher, Cooper's hawk. Among the other birds to be seen here: many sparrows, many flycatchers, three towhees, three wrens. Best seasons: late spring and late summer. Spring wildflowers are beautiful here.

28 square miles of red sandstone-walled canyon. Weird rock forms. Pinyon pine, juniper, shrubs. Rimrock Drive is a spectacular 22-mile circular drive from either Fruita or Grand Junction. Picnicking, all-year campground, Summer evening programs. Visitor center has geological and natural history exhibits.

Undated mimeographed "Partial List of the Birds of Colorado National Monument."

DINOSAUR NATIONAL MONUMENT, Box 101, Artesia, Colorado 81610. Buried in the quarry at the visitor center in this northwestern Colorado-northeastern Utah park are the bones of dozens of dinosaurs and ancient crocodiles and turtles. The quarry is reachable via Rt. 149 seven miles north of Jensen, Utah, but a better way to see this lovely wilderness park, which stretches for miles along the Yampa and Green Rivers, is by the river trips organized by several experienced companies. Float down the river in a rubber boat, watching banks and sky for birds, stopping for lunch on a sandbar, camping in a side canyon where the only trails are footpaths and the birds are so tame that they sit and watch *you.*

Checklist lists 69 species. The lazuli bunting is the common campground bird in the river canyons, but other very common birds include the Brewer's and red-winged blackbirds, mountain bluebird, mountain chickadee, rosy finch, sparrow hawk, great blue heron, broad-tailed and rufous hummingbirds, pinyon and scrub jays, Oregon junco, western kingbird, black-billed magpie, western meadowlark, common nighthawk, Say's phoebe, western robin, lark sparrow, barn, cliff, and violet-green swallows, turkey vulture, yellow warbler, and house wren.

206,234 acres of hills formed of colorful folded rock layers, narrow valleys carved by mountain streams, some brushy, semidesert vegetation and some very lush green growth. Fishing (Utah or Colorado licenses). Splendid Indian rock paintings on canyon walls. Campgrounds (reachable by car several miles north of the quarry) at Split Mountain Gorge and Echo Park. Visitor center and Split Mountain area open all year, but the rest of the monument probably closed by snow from October 15 to May 15.

Checklist dated 1973.

GRAND MESA-UNCOMPAHGRE-GUNNISON NATIONAL FOREST, P.O. Box 138, Delta, Colorado 81416. Off U.S. 50 south of Grand Junction.

268 species, of which 62 are termed rare or accidental or put down as "possibles." Among those seen from commonly through irregularly in the forests, the rare or endangered species are sandhill crane (common migrant), Williamson's sapsucker (common summer resident), black rosy finch (uncommon winter migrant), goshawk (common resident), Cooper's hawk, golden eagle (common resident), bald eagle (common winter resident). Fairly common birds include the dipper or water ouzel, Wilson's phalarope, black-chinned and broad-tailed hummingbirds, and many others. Early summer is the best season, both for birds and for brilliant wildflowers.

Grand Mesa is the plateau-remains of a great lava cap. It has a forest of scrub oak, pinyon pine, and juniper. Crested Butte Ski Area is active in winter.

GREAT SAND DUNES NATIONAL MONUMENT, P.O. Box 60, Alamosa, Colorado 81101. Thirty miles east of Alamosa via U.S. 160, Colorado Rt. 150.

129 species plus 14 accidentals (one or two sightings only). Fifty of the 129 are rare (sightings unusual). Rare, uncommon, or endangered: goshawk, Cooper's hawk, golden and bald eagles, osprey, flammulated owl, Williamson's sapsucker. Among the bird species that are in abundance here: red-tailed hawk, marsh hawk, sparrow hawk, killdeer, great horned owl, broad-tailed hummingbird, three kinds of woodpeckers, Say's phoebe, horned lark, black-billed magpie, pinyon and Steller's jay, Clark's nutcracker, mountain chickadee, mountain bluebird, several sparrows.

The tall, ever-shifting Great Sand Dunes rise to heights of 600 feet on the western slope of the Sangre de Cristo Mountains. Altitude 8,000 to 9,000 feet. A river pours into the dunes, disappears, and reappears again five miles away as a great spring. Varied habitats: the dunes, grassland, and brush of the San Luis Valley; pinyon-juniper woodland of the valley edges and foothills; stream bottoms, canyons, and cliffs on the western edge of the Sangre de Cristo; ponderosa pine groves on and near the foothills; and aspen groves. Campground, picnic area, self-guiding nature trail.

Checklist, dated December, 1973, compiled by Dana L. Abell, Park Ranger, from an earlier list by Warren H. Hill and George West and from contributions by Maurice Zardus and Ronald A. Ryder.

MESA VERDE NATIONAL PARK, Colorado 81330. A table mountain, the site of hundreds of ancient Indian villages. Access by auto, or by air to Durango and Cortez and by rental car from there. Ten miles east of Cortez, 38 miles west of Durango on U.S. 160 to park entrance, then 16 miles south to Visitor Center. Fee for entrance.

Rare, uncommon, or endangered: golden eagle, spotted owl, flammulated owl. Common: canyon wren, blue grouse, mourning dove, Say's phoebe, other high-desert birds. Best season:

because of its altitude, the park is cooler than the surrounding desert. A summer visit could be very pleasant.

52,074 acres. Altitude, 7,000 feet. Juniper and pinyon forest where the Indians built great cliff houses, which they deserted at the end of the thirteenth century. Museum, ranger-conducted trips into the ruins, picnicking, riding, lodges, campground. Hiking is restricted. No collecting. Interpretive program year-round; accommodations open early May to mid-October.

Checklist dated 1974.

MONTE VISTA NATIONAL WILDLIFE REFUGE, P.O. Box 511, Monte Vista, Colorado 81144. An environment of "greasewood, rush, and water," the checklist says. A prime nesting habitat for migratory birds. Six miles south of Monte Vista via Colorado 16.

172 species, of which 60 are rare in the refuge. Rare, uncommon, or endangered: bald and golden eagles (winter), hooded merganser, Harlan's hawk. Common birds: ducks, rails, wrens, yellowthroats, blackbirds, snowy egrets, black-crowned night herons, black terns, avocets, marsh hawks, and short-eared owls.

Marked visitor tour road; picnicking.

Checklist dated March, 1975.

PAWNEE NATIONAL GRASSLAND, 2009 9th St., Greeley, Colorado 80631. 303-353-5004. In northeastern Colorado, east of the Front Range. Drive north from Greeley on U.S. 85, to seven miles north of Nunn.

193 species, 39 of which are only rarely seen in the grass-lands. Rare, uncommon, or endangered: white-faced ibis, Cooper's hawk, golden and bald eagles, Harlan's hawk, gyrfalcon, prairie falcon, Baird's sandpiper, Hudsonian godwit, Baird's sparrow, McCown's longspur. From the overlook of a low ridge, a waterhole will be seen to hold an exciting variety of shorebirds and waders, notably the avocet and killdeer. Other birds char-

acteristic and common here: rough-legged hawk, Franklin's gull, horned lark, mountain bluebird, lark bunting, others.

775,000 acres. Native shortgrass prairie interspersed with some cultivated land. Precaution: be wary of rattlesnakes.

Checklist dated 1971, compiled by Dr. Ronald A. Ryder of Colorado State University, assisted by Nancy Hurley of the Denver Field Ornithologists.

RIO GRANDE NATIONAL FOREST, RR 3, Box 21, Monte Vista, Colorado 81144. (This now includes Wheeler National Monument.) The forest lies between the Rio Grande and the Saguache Rivers. Route 160 crosses the southeastern corner of the forest. The La Garita Mountains crest in the northern part of the forest.

232 species, 66 of which are occasional or rare in the forest. Rare, uncommon, or endangered: white-faced ibis, Mexican duck, goshawk, Cooper's hawk, golden and bald eagles, sandhill crane, Williamson's sapsucker. Birds to be seen, resident yearlong in the forest: gray (Canada) jay, Clark's nutcracker, brown creeper, ruby-crowned kinglet, pine siskin, Canada goose, green-winged teal, red-tailed hawk, white-tailed ptarmigan, great horned owl, belted kingfisher, red-shafted flicker, black-capped and mountain chickadees, and others.

The Rio Grande National Forest covers a vast expanse of southwestern Colorado, reaching east from the Continental Divide. Elevation can be as high as 11,000 feet.

Checklist taken from "A Checklist of the Birds of the Rio Grande Drainage of Southern Colorado" by Ronald R. Ryder (1965).

ROCKY MOUNTAIN NATIONAL PARK, Estes Park, Colorado 80517. Route 34 traverses the park. This is Trail Ridge Road, 44 miles over the Continental Divide. It is closed in winter and may be snowy even in summer. Enter east or west (Grand Lake).

255 species, of which 93 are rare, casual, or accidental. Of these, and not counting the accidentals, species generally rare,

uncommon, or endangered are goshawk, golden and bald eagles, osprey, and Williamson's sapsucker. Best season: spring. The Colorado columbine blooms June through August. September is a month of fine weather. Winter sports available in winter at Hidden Valley.

262,324 acres of the Front Range, from the lofty heights of Longs Peak (14,256 feet) to the valleys (8,000 feet). Splendid snowy peaks, boulders, upland meadows above and forests of pines, blue spruce, and aspen at lower elevations. Streams, lakes. Trail Ridge Road is about 12,000 feet high. Mountaineering lessons, riding, naturalist program, fishing June 1 through October 31 (state license), camping. Bus tours available from Denver. Precautions: take it easy if you're not accustomed to high altitudes. Don't hike alone. If hiking Longs Peak, register with ranger first.

Checklist dated June, 1970, compiled by Allegra E. Collister in cooperation with the National Park Service.

CONNECTICUT

AUDUBON CENTER IN GREENWICH, 613 Riversville Rd., Greenwich, Connecticut 06830. 203-869-5272. In north Greenwich. Take Exit 28 on the Merritt Parkway; turn left off Johns Street to Riversville Road.

About 190 species, of which 87 nest here. Among the nesting species: green heron; Canada goose; ruby-throated hummingbird; flicker, pileated, hairy, and downy woodpeckers; several flycatchers; cedar waxwing; three kinds of vireos; fourteen kinds of warblers; and other species. The astonishing list of warblers includes all of the most uncommon northeastern warblers. Some of the rare, uncommon, or endangered species: eastern bluebird, Philadelphia vireo, dickcissel (uncommon in this area). Best season: May for warblers, but with habitats this varied and a birdlist this long, any season will provide fine birding.

477 acres of woodland, fields, thickets, lakes, swamps, streams, orchards, and lawns. Self-guiding nature trail, interpretive building with exhibits, summer nature-study camp for adults.

The checklist, revised April, 1975, includes birds seen in the Audubon Fairchild Garden on Porchuck Road. The list indicates habitat (lake, etc.) and expected arrival date.

CONNECTICUT ARBORETUM, Connecticut College, New London, Connecticut 06320. Connecticut College is on Mohegan Ave. (Connecticut 32) one mile north of Main and Williams Streets. The arboretum is west of the campus.

178 species. Rare, uncommon, or endangered: blue-winged warbler, red-necked (Holboell's) grebe, osprey, others. Very

common birds, all breeding here: red-eyed vireo, black and white warbler, ovenbird, wood thrush, veery, catbird, towhee, yellowthroat, bobwhite. The population of Carolina wrens is increasing, as is that of cardinals. Courtship displays of the woodcock have been seen on college property and, the checklist says, "One year a mother was seen leading her brood of four chicks, each about the size of a quarter, across Williams Street into the Arboretum."

350 acres. A pond, woodland, streams, ledges, thickets, open fields (abandoned farmland), swamps. Part of the area was devastated by the 1938 hurricane; it is interesting to see the regeneration.

"A Field List of Birds for Connecticut College" by Richard H. Goodwin and Fleur A. Grandjouan is in *Connecticut College Bulletin*, No. 10 (40¢), which is entirely devoted to the Connecticut Arboretum. The "Field List" includes an occurrence graph and a map of the arboretum. Also in this publication is a report, by Williams A. Niering, on "Birding Bird Studies in Connecticut Arboretum Natural Area," which is a foundation study for long-term research into such topics as the effects of pesticides upon Connecticut's vegetation and wildlife. For other publications about the arboretum, write to the arboretum.

FLANDERS NATURE CENTER, Flanders Road, Woodbury, Connecticut 06798. 203-263-3711. (Van Vleck Farm Sanctuary and Whittemore Sanctuary.) Woodbury is on Route 6, west of Waterbury.

"Flanders Center Spring Bird List," with penciled additions, presumably from later seasons, shows 119 species. Rare, uncommon, or endangered: wood duck, osprey. Typical birds of northeastern meadows, wetland, and woodlands. Four kinds of vireos. Twenty-two species of warblers, including the bluewinged warbler.

Oak woods; at Whittemore Sanctuary, bogs. Nature walks and field trips, apiary, pet shows, nature craft workshop, sales of bird seed. Newsletter available.

DELAWARE

BOMBAY HOOK NATIONAL WILDLIFE REFUGE, R.D. 1, Box 147, Smyrna, Delaware 19977. Headquarters ten miles northeast of Dover, off Rt. 9 and State Route 85.

261 species, 12 described as rare. Rare, uncommon, or endangered: gull-billed tern, Wilson's phalarope, curlew sandpiper, black rail, osprey, bald eagle, and several others. Common: ducks, geese (including the greater snow geese), clapper rail, willet, egrets, plovers, dowitchers, and many others. Best seasons: fall and spring.

15,135 acres of salt marsh, freshwater pools, upland fields, timber, winding rivers, and creeks. Observation towers, trails, and a boardwalk across a part of the salt marsh. Picnic area, toilets, a restored 18th century house. Controlled hunting of waterfowl, upland game, and deer; retriever field trials are held spring and fall. Precaution: in spring and summer, bring mosquito repellent.

Checklist dated September, 1974.

BRANDYWINE CREEK STATE PARK, Delaware Nature Education Center, Greenville, Delaware 19807. Four miles north of Wilmington on State Route 100.

The Center uses a checklist from the Delmarva Ornithological Society, Wilmington, Delaware. This long checklist (not annotated for frequency of occurrence) is very strong on herons, egrets, ducks, geese, gulls, terns, and warblers.

DISTRICT OF COLUMBIA

ROCK CREEK NATURE CENTER, Military and Glover Rds., N.W., Washington, D.C. 20015.

192 species. Rare, uncommon, or endangered: upland plover, Henslow's sparrow, yellow-throated vireo, others. Common: bobwhite, tufted titmouse, turkey vulture, many others.

Rock Creek Park's 1,754 acres wind near the center of Washington. Self-guiding nature trails, riding, bicycling, golf course, tennis courts.

Checklist used is "Bird Checklist of National Capital Parks," undated.

Canoe Trail, "Ding" Darling Reserve. (*Photo by Jessie Kitching.*)

FLORIDA

BOYD HILL NATURE PARK, 1101 Country Club Way, South, St. Petersburg, Florida 33705. Part of a St. Petersburg City Park, Lake Maggiore Park, managed from 1450 16th St., North, St. Petersburg, Florida 33704.

161 species, of which 30 are rare in the park. Rare, uncommon, or endangered: brown pelican, mottled duck, bald eagle, osprey, pileated woodpecker, worm-eating and golden-winged warblers, and others. Among the common birds: double-crested cormorant, magnificent frigate-bird, several kinds of herons, Bonaparte's gull (in winter), screech owl, yellow-bellied sapsucker, black and white warbler, orange-crowned warbler, American redstart, many others.

The park holds both exotic and native flowering plants, shrubs, and trees. Swamp areas, large water areas, and scrubland. Bicycle rentals.

The checklist is compiled by the St. Petersburg Audubon Society and is revised annually.

CHASSAHOWITZKA NATIONAL WILDLIFE REFUGE, Rt. 2, Box 44, Homosassa, Florida 32646. 904-795-2201. 65 miles north of St. Petersburg on the Gulf of Mexico. Headquarters are on U.S. 19, four miles south of Homosassa Springs. Most of the refuge is accessible only by boat from along the Homosassa or Chassahowitzka Rivers or Mason Creek.

234 species, plus 14 species considered out of their normal range. Rare, uncommon, or endangered: Florida sandhill crane, hooded merganser, brown pelican, bald eagle (nests here), osprey, Sandwich tern, black rail, Connecticut warbler, and others. Common here: limpkin, white ibis, mottled duck,

mallard, teal, scaup, shovelers, widgeon, common merganser, wood duck, rails, gallinule, loons, grebes, white pelican (winter), herons, others. Peak populations exceed 20,000 ducks and 25,000 coots. Best seasons: winter and late spring.

30,000 acres of salt bays, estuaries, and brackish marshes, mangrove keys, hardwood swamps, and coastal sandhills. Part of the Homosassa River is included. Fishing, waterfowl hunting.

Checklist dated June, 1970. Also available: folder on refuge.

CORKSCREW SWAMP SANCTUARY, Naples, Florida 33940. Off Route 29, north of Route 84. A National Audubon Society sanctuary, one of the loveliest and most needed bird sanctuaries in North America. The sanctuary was founded to preserve the wood storks, egrets, herons, and other wild creatures of a large and threatened stand of cypress swamp. The wood stork rookery is famous—nests in tall trees, clamorous with young birds.

167 species. 63 species nest in the sanctuary. Rare, uncommon, or endangered: a distinguished long list, among them the wood stork, sandhill crane, wood duck, and eastern bluebird (all of which nest here), and the roseate spoonbill, golden-winged warbler, and Bachman's sparrow, who do not nest but are present occasionally. More common birds here: cardinal, indigo and painted buntings; fish crow; anhinga; white ibis; many herons; the American and least bitterns; and many others. Best season: any time when the weather has not been too dry. Drought can hit hard in this sanctuary.

Boardwalk through cypress swamp, observation points, visitor center, shop, picnic area (frequented by cardinals—have your camera ready).

Undated checklist.

J.N. "DING" DARLING NATIONAL WILDLIFE REFUGE, P.O. Drawer B., Sanibel, Florida 33957. In two sections, each with an observation tower. The larger section is accessible about halfway along the main road through Sanibel Island (Rt.

867) on the north. The smaller section (the Bailey Tract, walking trails only) lies off a side road on the south side of the island. Access to the refuge also at refuge headquarters on the eastern tip of the island. Causeway leads to Sanibel from Fort Myers. "Ding" Darling, for whom the refuge is named, was a famous cartoonist and one of the founders of the National Wildlife Refuge System.

267 species, of which 41 are considered accidental. Rare, uncommon, or endangered: roseate spoonbill, gray kingbird (common here—look on the utility wires), mottled duck, swallow-tailed kite, mangrove cuckoo, bald eagle (breeds here), osprey (breeds here), and others. Common here: Louisiana heron (very easy to get close views of this magnificent bird), ruddy turnstone, cattle egret, turkey and black vultures, black skimmer, prairie warbler, others.

Over 2,500 acres. Auto loop in larger section of refuge, but in dry spells the road may be closed to cars because they stick in the sand. Interpretive program. Canoe trail through mangrove swamps at Tarpon Bay. Note: the shelling on Sanibel (not in the refuge) is justly famous. Shell-hunters and birds do not interfere with each other. The shell-hunters never look up. The birds do; they simply fly around the shell-hunters and settle down on the water's edge again.

Checklist dated October, 1969. Also available: folder on refuge.

EVERGLADES NATIONAL PARK, P.O. Box 279, Homestead, Florida 33030. The "river of grass," an enormous, lovely subtropical park long threatened with the loss (to agriculture in northern Florida) of the water on which it floats. Visitor Center is at Homestead on Route 27. Two miles farther south lies the Anhinga Trail, a boardwalk where it is possible to come quite close to wading birds and other wildlife, including alligators. Thirty miles farther south lies Flamingo, an interpretive center, where there is an extensive marina.

Birds of regular occurrence in the park: 240 species. Birds found in the park no more than ten times: 86 species. Known to have nested in the park: 81 species. Among rare, uncommon, and endangered: brown pelican, wood ibis (stork), reddish egret (Florida Bay), black-whiskered vireo, Cape Sable sparrow, and many others. Interesting local birds common here: boat-tailed grackle, fish crow (it says, "Uh-uh" in a very negative way, thus differentiating it from the common crow), Carolina wren. Thirty warblers have been spotted. The great bird sights of the Everglades are pelicans, roseate spoonbills, egrets, herons, and anhingas. Best seasons: winter and early spring.

2,100 square miles. Botanically and zoologically, the Everglades are fascinating. "Hammocks," grassy clumps with a few trees, grow out of the saw grass. In some places, there are bald cypress and pine forests, or mangroves, or palms. Air plants grow on the trees. Fish and alligators share the many waterways with crabs, shrimp, and other marine organisms. Interpretive centers, boardwalks through the swamps, guided boat caravans, fishing, observation tower, lodge and campgrounds at Long Pine Key and Flamingo. Regulations: smoking forbidden on nature trails, pets must be leashed, do not feed or disturb the wildlife.

Checklist: "Birds Known to Occur in Everglades National Park" by William B. Robertson, Jr. and Richard L. Cunningham, revised February, 1972, by John C. Ogden. For further material on the park, write for the sales catalog of the Everglades Natural History Association, P.O. Box 279, Homestead, Florida 33030. Especially appropriate is "A Checklist of Birds" by John C. Ogden (1969, 28 pages, 30¢).

FLORIDA KEYS NATIONAL WILDLIFE REFUGES, Big Pine, Florida 33040. Three refuges: the National Key Deer Refuge, the Great White Heron Refuge, and Key West National Wildlife Refuge, all made up of scattered islands, all accessible only by boat except those parts of National Key Deer Refuge on Big Pine and Little Torch Keys (on Florida Rt. 940, two miles north of U.S. 1).

185 species and one hybrid, plus eight species considered accidental. Rare, uncommon, or endangered: reddish egret, bald eagle and osprey (both nesting), peregrine falcon, noddy

tern, worm-eating warbler, great white heron, white-crowned pigeon, others. Common: magnificent frigate-bird, yellow-crowned night heron, laughing gull, many others.

About 700 key deer roam in the Key Deer National Refuge. The vegetation is largely palmetto, Caribbean pine, and cacti. Checklist dated May, 1970.

LAKE WOODRUFF NATIONAL WILDLIFE REFUGE, P.O. Box 488, Deleon Springs, Florida 32028.

Along the east side of the St. Johns River, and reachable only by boat—make arrangements with refuge manager.

192 species, 20 of them considered rare. Rare, uncommon, or endangered: mottled duck, bald eagle and osprey (both nest here), sandhill crane, Bachman's sparrow, and others. Nesting on refuge: anhinga, herons, wood duck, swallow-tailed kite, bobwhite, king rail, gallinules, yellow-shafted flicker, great crested flycatcher, fish crow, white-eyed vireo, parula warbler, pine warbler, and others.

18,400 acres of open water, marshes, hardwood swamps, and pinelands.

Preliminary checklist dated October, 1971. Also available: "Mammals of Lake Woodruff National Wildlife Refuge."

LOXAHATCHEE NATIONAL WILDLIFE REFUGE, Route 1, Box 278, Delray Beach, Florida 33444.

Southeast of Lake Okeechobee. Headquarters on east side of refuge, 12 miles west of Delray Beach.

245 species, plus 32 species recorded only once or twice at Loxahatchee. Rare, uncommon, or endangered: Everglade kite, Florida sandhill crane, Bachman's sparrow, bald eagle, osprey (nests here), peregrine falcon, gull-billed tern, pileated woodpecker. Common birds: limpkin, black-necked stilt, chuck-will's-widow, yellowthroat, cardinal, indigo bunting, many others.

145,525 acres of saw grass marshes, wet prairies, sloughs and hammocks. Two access points besides the one mentioned

above, one at north end of refuge, the other at south end. Boat ramps, nature trails, fishing, boating.
Checklist dated August, 1973.

MERRITT ISLAND NATIONAL WILDLIFE REFUGE, P.O. Box 6504, Titusville, Florida 32780. Off the Atlantic coast of central Florida, on Cape Canaveral. Reachable by causeway from Titusville. Headquarters is six miles east of Titusville on S.R. 402.

251 species plus 31 species considered to be of unusual occurrence. Endangered species (research to help these is going on here): dusky seaside sparrow, bald eagle, brown pelican, peregrine falcon (best observed in fall). Common: herons, egrets, white pelican, wood stork, scrub jay, cardinal, mottled duck, red-tailed hawk, red-shouldered hawk, royal tern, black skimmer, screech owl, others. Spectacular migrations of passerine birds, especially warblers, during spring and fall. Wintering waterfowl peaks at 70,000 ducks and 120,000 coots.

Probably the only refuge to share an island with a rocket base. Parts of the refuge are closed to the public. In all, there are 134,143 acres, bounded by the Kennedy Space Center. Saltwater lagoons; marshlands, managed partly to control the mosquito population; mangroves; some uplands, including over 25 miles of barrier beach and sand dunes; some citrus groves leased by private operators. Fishing.

Checklist dated November, 1972. Also available: folder about refuge.

ST. MARKS NATIONAL WILDLIFE REFUGE, Box 68, St. Marks, Florida 32355. The major wintering area for Canada geese in Florida. Twenty miles south of Tallahassee on the shores of Apalachee Bay, this refuge extends from the Aucilla River west to the Ochlockonee River.

263 species (records go back to 1920), plus 41 species which are considered out of their normal ranges. Rare, uncommon, or endangered: Mississippi kite, bald eagle (breeds here), osprey, red-cockaded woodpecker (breeds here), golden-winged war-

bler, and others. Common here, besides the Canada goose: herons, ducks, limpkin, anhinga, turkey, rails, common and purple gallinules, oystercatcher, willet, yellow-billed cuckoo, prothonotary warbler, orchard oriole, summer tanager, and others. Best seasons: fall, winter, and spring.

65,000 acres: freshwater, saltwater, and brackish marshes, ponds, and pine flatwoods. An additional 31,700 acres of the water in Apalachee Bay are included as part of the refuge. Fishing.

Checklist dated August, 1971. Also available: flier about refuge.

GEORGIA

OCMULGEE NATIONAL MONUMENT, Box 4186, Macon, Georgia 31208. Two miles east of Macon on U.S. 80, 129. A very large Indian site, scientifically excavated. It goes back in time to about 8000 B.C., and the history of the site is traced up to the eighteenth-century Creek Indians. Access from U.S. 80 east of Macon.

48 species. Among them: pied-billed grebe; pileated, red-headed and hairy woodpeckers; belted kingfisher; eastern bluebird; cardinal; brown creeper.

Visitor center housing an archaeological museum. Indian craft shop with demonstrations. Nature trail along Walnut Creek, swamp, woods.

Undated birdlist, duplicated.

OKEFENOKEE NATIONAL WILDLIFE REFUGE, P.O. Box 117, Waycross, Georgia 31501. A vast cypress swamp which the Indians called "land of the trembling earth."

210 species, of which 41 are noted as rare. An additional 23 species are very rare or accidental. 76 species breed in the refuge. Rare, uncommon, or endangered: sandhill crane, swallow-tail kite, limpkin, glossy ibis, osprey, red-cockaded woodpecker. Common here: herons, wood stork, barred owl, vultures, parula warbler, Carolina wren, mockingbird, catbird, brown thrasher, others.

377,528 acres of primitive swamp. Wooded peat beds float on the brown waters. Visitor center and interpretive facilities at Suwanee Canal Recreation Area, eleven miles southwest of Folkston via State Rt. 23. Observation tower, swamp tours, picnicking. Also, the north entrance to the refuge at Okefenokee Swamp Park, eight miles south of Waycross via U.S. 1, 23, State Rt. 177, offers guided tours, boardwalks, observation tower, museum, serpentarium, picnic area. Fees. Some parts of the Okefenokee are open to the public for sightseeing, fishing, picnicking, photography, and other recreation. Trips into any other parts of the swamp require guides.

Checklist dated March, 1974. Also available: list of accidental birds of the refuge.

PIEDMONT NATIONAL WILDLIFE REFUGE, Round Oak, Georgia 31080. Headquarters about three miles north of Round Oak off State Highway 11. On the east side of the Ocmulgee River. Outstanding for turkeys and bobwhites.

182 species, including 32 species described as rare. Rare, uncommon, or endangered: Bewick's wren, worm-eating warbler, Bachman's sparrow, red-cockaded woodpecker (a colony can be observed). Common here: turkey, bobwhite, pileated woodpecker, chuckwill's widow, great horned owl, wood duck (in Allison Lake), brown-headed nuthatch.

34,673 acres of pine-hardwood forest. Hilly, with many small streams. Wildlife trail near Allison Lake. Sport fishing in a small lake; managed hunts for deer and other upland game. Only two areas are open to birdwatching; one of these is closed during deer hunts.

Checklist dated April, 1973. Also available: hunting regulations, folder about refuge.

HAWAII

HAWAII VOLCANOES NATIONAL PARK, Hawaii 96718. Access by plane from Honolulu, then rented car. Headquarters off Route 11; check there for current status of roads.

57 species recorded, of which 18 are introduced, six are extinct, 16 are wide-traveling migrants or ocean birds, and only 17 are forms unique to Hawaii. Rare, uncommon, or endangered: apapane (which sucks nectar from the Ohia tree blooms), amakihi (both of these are honeycreepers), elepaio (flycatcher), others. The apapane is commonly found here, but nowhere else. Almost all the birds will be rarities to the birder from continental North America but he will also see a few familiar birds, such as the barn owl, American cardinal, and house finch. Best season: summer has the best weather.

220,345 acres that include Kilauea and Mauna Loa. Lava formations, Thomas A. Jaggar Memorial Museum, visitor center, eleven-mile crater rim drive, tree fern forest, nature trail at Bird Park (Kipuka Puaulu), arboretum. Several backcountry trails. Lodge, cabins, campgrounds. Precaution: bring raingear. Rules: stay on trails. Hikers must register at headquarters. Permits are required to collect specimens of any kind. Pets must be leashed. Auto speed limit: 45 mph. No hunting or trapping.

Undated checklist. Also available: folder about park. For list of other publications, write Hawaii Natural History Association, Hawaii Volcanoes National Park, Hawaii 96718.

HAWAIIAN ISLANDS NATIONAL WILDLIFE REFUGE, a chain of eight islands and reefs reaching from Hawaii almost to Midway. Write: Refuge Manager, 337 Uluniu St., Kailua,

Hawaii 96734. Landing on islands only by permit from refuge manager.

30 species (besides accidentals). Most are pelagic birds. Rare or endangered: Nihoa millerbird, Nihoa finch, Laysan teal, Laysan finch. Best seasons: spring and winter. Breeding birds: most of the observed birds nest on the islands. Common birds: sooty terns, Bonin Island petrels, red-tailed tropic birds.

Some islands are volcanic, some, coral. Fragile vegetation. Landing hazardous and rough, and only with permit; storms frequent and severe. No facilities available.

Checklist dated 1971. Also available: folder describing islands, with list of mammals.

IDAHO

CAMAS NATIONAL WILDLIFE REFUGE, Hamer, Idaho 83425. In southeastern Idaho, 38 miles north of Idaho Falls.

166 species, six described as rare, plus 12 species which are very rare or formerly occurred in this area. Rare, uncommon, or endangered: pectoral sandpiper, ferruginous hawk, golden and bald eagles (in winter), others. Common: several kinds of ducks, Canada goose, whistling swan, sage grouse, pheasants, long-billed curlew, willet, avocet. Concentrations of pintail migration in late March or early April. Best seasons: spring and fall for the migrations.

Altitude, 4,700 feet. 10,471 acres of water, marsh, cropland, and grassland. Camas Creek flows through the refuge. A road borders the willow-lined creek, and roads run along most of lakes and marshland, giving the birdwatcher good views. Hunting permitted.

Checklist dated July, 1963.

CRATERS OF THE MOON NATIONAL MONUMENT, Box 29, Arco, Idaho 82313. 208-527-3257. Twenty miles southwest of Arco on U.S. 93A.

140 species. Rare, uncommon, or endangered: golden eagle, prairie falcon, Williamson's sapsucker, others. Common: common raven, blue grouse, saw-whet owl, horned lark, rock wren, fox sparrow, others.

53,545 acres in an area seared and blasted by volcanoes about 2,000 years ago. It is supposed to resemble the surface of the moon. Visitor center, seven-mile loop drive, interpretive program, guided auto caravan in summer. Wildflowers bloom colorfully and abundantly in spring. Campground (no hook-ups) open April 15 to October 15.

Checklist, dated April 12, 1970, compiled by Dennis L. Carter, Park Naturalist.

MINIDOKA NATIONAL WILDLIFE REFUGE, Rupert, Idaho 83350. On the Snake River in south-central Idaho, 12 miles northeast of Rupert.

204 species, 24 described as rare. 83 species nest on the refuge. Rare, uncommon, or endangered: ferruginous hawk, white-faced ibis, sandhill crane, others. Common: western grebe (a large handsome grebe that is locally abundant), Canada goose, ducks of several kinds, sage grouse, coot, willet, avocet, California and Franklin's gulls, Swainson's hawk. Best season for birding: winter, viewing from access roads the concentrations of up to 250,000 waterfowl. Best way to see waterfowl in summer is by boat.

25,630 acres. Altitude, 4,545 feet. Two principal water resources: Lake Walcott, formed by Minidoka Dam, and the Snake River. Marshy land around lake; on higher ground, grasses and desert vegetation. Camping, picnicking and boat ramp at Minidoka Dam. Fishing, swimming, boating, water-skiing.

Checklist dated April, 1969.

ILLINOIS

CHAUTAUQUA NATIONAL WILDLIFE REFUGE, R.R. 2, Havana, Illinois 62644. Nine miles east of Havana on Manila Road. Major feature—wood ducks.

246 species of birds, 53 of which are rare on the refuge. Seventy species nest here. Wood ducks have happily nested in special boxes erected for their use. Rare, uncommon, or endangered: bald eagle, red-headed woodpecker, osprey, others. Common: wood duck, mallard, black duck, bobwhite, towhee, Bell's vireo, sora, prothonotary warbler, many others. Best seasons: mid-March to April and mid-November to December for staggering concentrations of ducks—more than a million mallards alone.

5,114 acres. A very large pool, forested river bottoms, and sand-dune bluffs. The Illinois Natural History Survey maintains the Quiver Creek Laboratory for waterfowl research (especially on the wood duck) on the refuge. Sport fishing from boats March 15 to September. Hunting permitted in specified areas. Picnicking, boat ramp, observation tower, toilets.

Checklist dated May, 1967. Also available: folder about refuge, with map.

CRAB ORCHARD NATIONAL WILDLIFE REFUGE, P.O. Box J, Carterville, Illinois 62918. 12 miles east of Carbondale on Rt. 13, then south on Rt. 148. Great flocks of Canada geese in winter.

238 bird species, of which only nine are listed as rare. 97 species nest. Rare, uncommon, or endangered: bald eagle (especially in winter), red-headed woodpecker (nests here),

Bachman's sparrow (nests here). Common: Canada goose, snow goose, dickcissel (nests here), turkey vulture, barred owl, eastern bluebird (nests), parula warbler, Louisiana waterthrush.

42,825 acres. Two large shallow lakes, freshwater marshes, deciduous forests, evergreen groves, and open farmlands. This area is a transition zone between north and south plant and animal species, so it is rich in wildlife. Nature trails, boat ramps, picnic areas, swimming, camping, riding, fishing, hunting, trapping. Annual national field trials for hunting dogs.

Very good graphic checklist dated June, 1973.

FOREST GLEN PRESERVE, R.R. 1, Westville, Illinois 61883. East central Illinois, eight miles southeast of Danville.

199 species. Rare, uncommon, or endangered: sandhill crane, goshawk, others. Common: several kinds of woodpeckers; many kinds of warblers. Both the scarlet and the summer tanager. Other summer birds here: Bell's vireo, orchard and Baltimore orioles.

Nature center, observation tower overlooking Vermilion River, picnicking, camping.

"Field Checklist of Illinois Birds" annotated for birds observed at Forest Glen Preserve since 1969.

MARK TWAIN NATIONAL WILDLIFE REFUGE, P.O. Box 225, Quincy, Illinois 62301. This is the Tom Sawyer-Huckleberry Finn area. More to the point for birders, the refuge harbors and astonishing number of bald eagles, up to 300 in winter. The refuge borders the Mississippi River at scattered points for 250 miles from Rock Island to Grafton, taking in land in Iowa and Missouri as well as Illinois. Eight management divisions, totalling 24,000 acres. One division is the Clarence Cannon National Wildlife Refuge—3,670 acres near Elsberry, Missouri. Access to the divisions varies from road to boat. Before visiting, contact the refuge manager (address above).

221 species, eight of which are rare. Common: wood duck

raising their young in summer. Among other breeding birds: great blue heron, green heron, bobwhite, yellow-billed cuckoo, several woodpeckers, purple martin, and others.

Checklist dated 1967, prepared by W. D. Vasse and Dr. T. E. Musselman.

MISSISSIPPI PALISADES STATE PARK, Savanna, Illinois. North of Savanna on Rt. 84.

249 species, 29 of which are rare or accidental. Rare, uncommon, or endangered: hooded merganser, bald eagle, peregrine falcon, Wilson's phalarope, red-headed woodpecker. Common: house wren, Swainson's thrush, nighthawk, several kinds of woodpeckers, yellow warbler, ovenbird, several kinds of ducks.

1,717 acres. Interpretive program, visitor center, trails, striking rock formations, Indian mounds. Fishing, boating, picnicking, camping.

Undated checklist prepared by the park naturalist in cooperation with the Illinois Audubon Society and the Upper Mississippi Wildlife Refuge Manager.

MORTON ARBORETUM, Route 53, Lisle, Illinois 60532. 25 miles west of Chicago. State Rt. 53 passes through the arboretum.

Common birds: Cooper's hawk, long-eared owl, screech owl, saw-whet owl (winter), woodpecker, tufted titmouse, brown creeper, others. Many kinds of warblers.

800 acres. Ponds, nature trails, flowering trees in bloom from May through August, a prairie restoration, library.

Checklist, "Birds of the Morton Arboretum," is out of print and probably will not be available again until 1977.

INDIANA

HAYES REGIONAL ARBORETUM, 801 Elks Rd., Richmond, Indiana 47374. A project of the Stanley W. Hayes Research Foundation, Inc. Two miles east of Richmond on U.S. 40.

A list of bird arrival and departure dates in spring for the entire Whitewater Valley (the arboretum is in the northern part of the valley) is rich in woodpeckers, swallows, sparrows, warblers, and vireos. Rare, uncommon, or endangered: pileated and red-headed woodpeckers, Henslow's sparrow, blue-winged, golden-winged, and worm-eating warblers, Connecticut and mourning warblers.

The arboretum holds 130 specimens of trees and shrubs native to the region. 30-acre beech-maple forest, fern garden, children's gardens, walnut research area. Closed Mondays.

MC CORMICK'S CREEK STATE PARK, Nature Center, R.R. 1, Box 28, Spencer, Indiana 47460. Star Route 46 passes the entrance four miles east of Spencer.

At least 85 species have been seen, largely land birds.

1,753 acres in the scenic limestone canyon of a creek, which is lined with slopes of beech and pine. Some shrubby growth. Interpretive services, field trips, foot trails, bridle paths, camping, picnicking, playground, cabins. Bicycling, tennis, fishing, swimming pool.

Checklist in progress. Basic checklist: Winter bird populations in the park, 1952-1973, by Dr. William Overlease and a team of helpers, plus later additions of bird species at other seasons.

POKAGON STATE PARK, R.R. 2, Box 29C, Angola, Indiana 46703. On the shores of Lake James in northern Indiana. Six miles north of Angola on U.S. 27.

In summer, 62 species. Among the more common birds in summer: woodcock, eastern kingbird, wood thrush, Baltimore (northern) oriole, yellow warbler, scarlet tanager, cardinal, indigo bunting, field sparrow, and sora rail.

1,175 acres. Deciduous forests, old farmlands, marshes. Interpretive services, wildlife exhibit, swimming (lifeguard on duty), waterskiing, boating, fishing, riding, archery, camping. In winter, skiing, ice-skating, iceboating, and tobogganing.

No formal checklist, but a personal census of summer birds by the park naturalist.

IOWA

DE SOTO NATIONAL WILDLIFE REFUGE, Route 1-B, Missouri Valley, Iowa 51555. In two states, Iowa and Nebraska, on the Missouri River. Geologically, this is a cutoff oxbow of the winding river. U.S. 30 goes past the refuge. 195 species, of which 16 are rarely seen. 79 species nest. Rare, uncommon, or endangered: piping plover (nests here), least tern (rare inland), bald eagle. High banks in three sites provide ideal nesting for bank swallows. Other common birds: Traill's flycatcher, bobwhite, yellow warbler, American redstart, others. Best seasons: March and April, October and November, for up to 400,000 snow geese and up to one million ducks.

7,800 acres of open water, flood plains, and freshwater marshes. 3,700 acres are farmed for bird food. Swimming, fishing (state permit), boating, waterskiing, picnicking, mushroom picking in May, hunting. No camping, no pets.

Checklist dated October, 1968. Also available: folder about refuge, with map.

EFFIGY MOUNDS NATIONAL MONUMENT, Box K, McGregor, Iowa 52157. Three miles north of Marquette on Rt. 76. The mounds, preserving Indian civilization of centuries ago, were built in the shape of animals or birds.

130 bird species. Rare, uncommon, or endangered: turkey, bald eagle, osprey, glaucous gull. Common: woodpeckers, great crested flycatcher, upland plover, indigo bunting, yellow warbler, others. Best seasons: spring and fall.

Self-guiding trail and visitor center. Scenic bluffs overlooking the Mississippi and Yellow Rivers. The bluffs are fine points for observing hawks.

Checklist dated 1973. Tells where to look for specific birds.

UNION SLOUGH NATIONAL WILDLIFE REFUGE, P.O. Box AF, Titonka, Iowa 50480. Two miles north of Burt on U.S. 169, turn east, drive for four miles.

219 species, of which 17 are only rarely seen. 96 species breed here. Rare, uncommon, or endangered: bald eagle, Le-Conte's sparrow, Wilson's phalarope. Common: pied-billed grebe, Virginia rail, blue-winged teal, Franklin's gull, Western meadowlark, yellow-shafted flicker, tree swallow, others. Best seasons: shorebird concentrations in late summer and early fall.

2,074 acres. Large marsh, cropland, grazing land. Swimming, fishing, picnicking on a 30-acre public use area.

Checklist dated 1969.

KANSAS

KINGMAN COUNTY GAME MANAGEMENT AREA, Pena-
losa, Kansas 67121. Off U.S. Highway 54, eight miles west of
Kingman, Kansas. Area managed by Kansas Forestry, Fish and
Game Commission.

327 species of regular or fairly regular occurrence at various
times during year. 50 other species occur as vagrants, accidentals, or occasionals. Rare or endangered: burrowing owl, golden
and bald eagles, osprey. Common: doves, quails, and sandpipers among many others.

4,462 acres with a 185-acre shallow lake. In 1974, designated
a Natural Area by the Soil Conservation Society of America.
Precautions to take: insect repellent needed. No lifeguards—
swim at own risk. Be alert for deer on roads while driving.
Careful about fires. Facilities: Camping, fishing, hunting in
season, toilets, bath house, wells, boat ramps.

Checklist: Kansas Ornithological Society Field Check List,
"Birds of Kansas," dated January, 1968. Available from Museum of Natural History, University of Kansas, Lawrence,
Kansas 66044, 3¢ each. Also available: folder about game management area. Inside it is a double-page map.

KIRWIN NATIONAL WILDLIFE REFUGE, Kirwin, Kansas
67644. Five miles south of Phillipsburg on U.S. 183 to Glade,
then six miles east on Route 9.

186 species, of which 17 are noted as rare. Rare, uncommon,
or endangered: sandhill crane, whooping crane, Mississippi
kite, ferruginous hawk, golden and bald eagles. Common:
white-fronted goose, Canada goose, Mallard, green-winged
teal. Because of its location, this refuge gets both eastern and

western representatives of different kinds of birds: horned and eared grebes, red-shafted and yellow-shafted flickers, eastern and Say's phoebes, and eastern and western kingbirds and meadowlarks. On one day in mid-March, as many as 130,000 ducks and 42,000 geese might be observed.

10,778 acres. Marshes, grasslands, croplands, and open water. An impoundment of the North Fork of the Solomon River. Camping, fishing, boating, swimming, waterskiing, picnicking. Hunting in some parts of the refuge.

Checklist dated March, 1972. Also available: folder about refuge; folder on mammals of the refuge.

QUIVIRA NATIONAL WILDLIFE REFUGE, P.O. Box G, Stafford, Kansas 67578. 12 miles northeast of Stafford.

245 species, of which 27 are rare or accidental. Rare or endangered: bald and golden eagles, Swainson's hawk, sandhill crane, whooping crane, prairie falcon, peregrine falcon. Common: Franklin's gull; bobwhite; king, Virginia, and sora rails; many other kinds of birds. September-December: flights of thousands of Canada geese, mallards, and other migratory birds. Among breeding birds: Mississippi kite, snowy plover, avocet; 56 species nest on the refuge. Best season: spring or fall.

1900 acres of wheat and sorghum, 13,000 acres of grassland, 4,700 acres of marsh. Creek, canals, ditches. Part is an example of the original bluestem prairie. Precautions: travel on township roads. Facilities: no camping, no picnic area, no toilets or drinking water. No hunting, fishing, or boating.

Checklist dated April, 1969. Endangered and rare species in reverse print. Also available: general folder about refuge, with map.

KENTUCKY

CLYDE E. BUCKLEY WILDLIFE SANCTUARY, R.R. 3, Frankfort, Kentucky 40601. 606-873-5711. Privately funded; operated by the National Audubon Society. Donated by Mrs. Clyde E. Buckley of Lexington, Kentucky. Access: Route 60 from Frankfort toward Versailles. Turn right at Jett Road. Bear right again after the Millville School.

251 species. Rare, uncommon, or endangered: Philadelphia vireo, golden and bald eagles, Wilson's phalarope, others. Common: bobwhite, several kinds of owls, belted kingfisher, three kinds of grebes, least and American bitterns, others.

The Ray Harm House, a converted farmhouse, serves as a nature museum. Library, bookstore, herbarium. 285 acres of hill land, six miles of trails and a birdwatching shelter overlooking a wildlife pond. Regulations: stay on trails, no pets, no disturbing anything, no collecting, no picnicking. Closed Mondays and Tuesdays. Undated checklist.

DANIEL BOONE NATIONAL FOREST, 27 Carol Road, Winchester, Kentucky 40391. Extends north-south from Morehead on U.S. 60 to Whitley City on U.S. 27. Spectacular sandstone formations and scenery, including Red River Gorge and the Natural Arch Scenic Area.

195 species. Birdlist does not indicate how frequently each species is seen. Rare, uncommon, or endangered: Bewick's wren, red-cockaded woodpecker, Henslow's and Bachman's sparrows, golden and bald eagles, osprey, others. Also present in forest: many flycatchers, vireos, 35 kinds of warblers.

636,000 acres. Lakes, waterfalls, natural arches, cliffs. Camping, picnicking, boating, hunting.

Birdlist compiled by William D. Zeedyk as reported or inferred in "The Birds of Kentucky" by Dr. Robert M. Mengel.

LAND BETWEEN THE LAKES, Golden Pond, Kentucky 42231. 502-924-5602. A peninsula forty miles long and eight miles wide nearly surrounded by two man-made lakes and offering dozens of kinds of outdoor recreation. Access west from Cadiz, Kentucky.

224 species, of which 59 are rarely seen. Rare, uncommon, or endangered: golden and bald eagles (especially in late February), others. Characteristic birds of this region, fairly commonly seen: wild turkey, common merganser, great blue and little blue herons, American egret, bobwhite, red-tailed hawk, ring-billed gull, mourning dove, red-bellied woodpecker, mockingbird, red-eyed vireo, yellowthroat, rufous-sided towhee.

170,000 acres between Kentucky Lake and Lake Barkley in western Kentucky and Tennessee. Environmental Education Center, several nature trails, observation tower (a converted silo), an educational farm, a herd of buffalo. Three major campgrounds; other camping sites. Archaeological lectures; arts and crafts festival. Trail for wheelchairs. A 2500-acre tract in the Turkey Bay area is designated for off-road vehicles, which are not supposed to be used elsewhere. Riding, swimming, fishing (floating fish pier), boating, ramps, picnicking.

Checklist dated December, 1967, compiled by members of the Kentucky Ornithological Society. Also available: pamphlet, folder.

MAMMOTH CAVE NATIONAL PARK, Mammoth Cave, Kentucky 42259. In south-central Kentucky. Access from Rt. 70 south from Rt. 62. The caves are fascinating, and the land around is green and full of birds.

192 birds, of which 93 are noted as rare. Especially interesting because there are remnant populations of the former farmland birds, but the increasing amount of wild food (and picnic food) have attracted increasing numbers of such varied birds as woodpeckers and tufted titmice, while the farmland birds,

which prefer open to forest land, are diminishing in number. Rare, uncommon, or endangered: green heron, black vulture, purple martin, Bewick's wren, pine siskin, others. Common: prairie and prothonotary warblers, tree sparrow, wood thrush, Carolina chickadee, eastern bluebird, indigo bunting, many others. Best season: late spring or early summer.

51,354 acres. The Green River winds through the park. Visitor center. Cave trips—fees (it's cool; bring a jacket). Special cave tour for persons in wheelchairs. Seven miles of hiking trails outside the caves. Guided walks. Boating, fishing. Hotel, motor lodge, campground, craft shop, picnic area. No swimming (river unsafe).

Checklist, 1968, adapted from *Birds and Their Habitats in Mammoth National Park* by Gordon Wilson (Eastern National Park and Monument Association, Mammoth National Park, paper, $2.00).

LOUISIANA

DELTA-BRETON NATIONAL WILDLIFE REFUGES, Venice, Louisiana 70091. Delta is on the east bank of the Mississippi River, seven miles below Venice. Breton is one of the Gulf Islands. Both points can be reached only by boat.

239 species at Delta, plus an added nine species that are very rare or accidental. Rare, uncommon, or endangered: Brown pelican, magnificent frigatebird, groove-billed ani, Sandwich tern, others. Common: snow geese, black skimmer, ducks (especially the mottled duck), others. Best seasons: late winter and early spring. 100,000 snow geese are normally present in Delta in winter.

Delta: 48,799 acres. Breton: 48,800 acres of channelled, very watery land. Timber only along the banks of the channels where the Mississippi has deposited mud.

Checklist dated August, 1967.

LACASSINE NATIONAL WILDLIFE REFUGE, Route 1, Box 186, Lake Arthur, Louisiana 70549. Headquarters eleven miles southwest of Lake Arthur off State Highway 14. The largest concentration of white-fronted geese in the Mississippi Flyway.

203 species, of which 21 are described as rare. 43 species breed here. Rare, uncommon, or endangered: roseate spoonbill, olivaceous cormorant (common in southern Louisiana but not elsewhere in North America), white ibis, white-faced ibis, others. Common: fulvous tree duck, ibises, anhinga, yellowthroat, egrets, gallinules, Forster's tern, long-billed marsh wren, others.

31,766 acres. A 16,000-acre freshwater pool, sawgrass. Fishing. Part of the refuge is open to waterfowl hunting. Checklist dated December, 1972.

SABINE NATIONAL WILDLIFE REFUGE, M.R.H. Box 107, Hackberry, Louisiana 70645. Headquarters six miles southwest of Hackberry on State Highway 27. Highway 27 is a good viewpoint over the marshes.

250 species, of which 32 are described as rare. Rare, uncommon, or endangered: roseate spoonbill, white-faced ibis, yellow rail, others. Common: snow goose, mottled duck, yellowlegs, herons, anhinga, egret, vultures, marsh hawk, clapper rail, black-necked stilt. Best season: winter.

142,845 acres. Three freshwater impoundments. Two large brackish lakes on the boundaries. Wildlife trail in Pool 1B.

Checklist dated April, 1974.

MAINE

ACADIA NATIONAL PARK, Bar Harbor, Maine 04609. Reachable by air or bus or by car (Route 1; turn east on Route 3). Headquarters three miles northwest of Bar Harbor at Hulls Cove.

314 species, of which 120 are termed "rare visitors." Rare, uncommon, or endangered: red-necked grebe, sooty and Manx shearwaters, harlequin duck, king eider (winter), bald eagle, osprey, peregrine falcon, merlin, puffin (winter), several kinds of warblers, and other species. Common: fulmar (summer), great blue heron, green-winged teal, Virginia rail, ruby-throated hummingbird, eastern phoebe, cliff swallow, winter wren, blackpoll warbler and other warblers, scarlet tanager, American goldfinch, white-throated sparrow, and others.

A rocky park surrounded by the sea and dominated by the bold range of the Mount Desert Mountains. Here, the flora of the Northern and Temperate Zones meet and overlap. Trees are mainly fir, pine, and spruce. More than 30,000 acres. The largest section is on Mount Desert Island, with smaller sections on Schoodic Peninsula, Isle au Haut, Little Cranberry Island, Baker Island, and Little Moose Island.

Interpretive service in summer, nature walks, guided car caravans and boat cruises. Park roads and many miles of foot trails, from easy to strenuous. Visitor center. Special attractions (not at headquarters): Abbe Museum of Archaeology and Isleford Historical Museum. Park facilities open only in summer, though park is accessible all year. Regulations: observe rules about fire, do not disturb wildlife, leash dogs or cats, camping permitted only in campgrounds, do not litter.

Checklist compiled by Paul G. Favour, Jr., 1969, amended by William C. Townsend, 1974. Based chiefly on *Birds of*

Mount Desert Island, Acadia National Park, Maine by James Bond and C. S. Tyson (American Academy of Natural Sciences, 1941, paper).

MOOSEHORN NATIONAL WILDLIFE REFUGE, P.O. Box 285, Calais, Maine 04619. Headquarters, Baring, six miles south of Calais, off U.S. Rt. 1, and Charlotte Rd. Another unit of the Refuge, Edmunds, farther south, on Cobscook Bay.

207 species, 36 of them rare or occasional. Rare or endangered: red-necked grebe, wood duck, American woodcock, Arctic tern, boreal chickadee, parula warbler. The unusual mating performance of the woodcock, a soaring flight and plummeting fall, with whistling notes, may be seen in late April or early May. 138 species of breeding birds. Among abundant birds: the ring-necked duck (the neck ring is inconspicuous—better identification is the two white rings around the bill).

22,666 acres, from the shore of Cobscook Bay to spruce-fir forests. Upland; also ponds, marshes, sphagnum bogs. Facilities: visitor center open May to September, ten-mile self-guided auto tour in summer, hiking trails.

Checklist dated 1970. Also available: flier about refuge; mammal list (many mammals but few moose).

MARYLAND

BLACKWATER NATIONAL WILDLIFE REFUGE, Route 1, Box 121, Cambridge, Maryland 21613. On the eastern shore of Chesapeake Bay, ten miles south of Cambridge.

250 species, 15 described as rare. Nesting species: Canada goose, black duck, blue-winged teal, mallard, wood duck, bald eagle, bobwhite, king and Virginia rail, barn owl, osprey, Henslow's sparrow, many others. The brown-headed nuthatch is here, near the northern limit of its range. Best seasons: November and December—many thousands of Canada geese and ducks.

About 17½ square miles (11,627 acres) of marsh, freshwater ponds, brushy and timbered swamps, and cropland (for bird food). Visitor center, 2½ mile wildlife drive, picnic area, rest rooms.

Checklist dated February, 1970

CATOCTIN MOUNTAIN PARK, Thurmont, Maryland 21788. Three miles west of Thurmont on Rt. 77. A northern spur of the Blue Ridge Mountains. This is the area of the U.S. President's Camp David.

Long birdlist, very strong on warblers, hawks, sparrows, thrushes, vireos, flycatchers. Rare, uncommon, or endangered: Henslow's sparrow, worm-eating warbler, white-winged crossbill, others. Common birds: scarlet tanager, American goldfinch, eastern wood pewee, nighthawk, many others.

5,765 acres. Craft demonstrations, self-guiding nature trails, auto drive, picnicking, camping, fishing.

Undated checklist compiled from *Birds of Maryland and the District of Columbia* (U.S. Dept. of the Interior, Fish and Wildlife Service).

MASSACHUSETTS

ARNOLD ARBORETUM, The Arborway, Jamaica Plain, Massachusetts 02130. In southwest Boston off Route 1.

154 species seen in the arboretum by the Children's Museum Bird Club during the period 1939-1968. Of these, 50 are infrequent or no longer seen (as of 1971). Rare, uncommon, or endangered: Cooper's hawk, Cape May warbler. Good representation of warblers, thrushes (wood, hermit, Swainson's, grey-cheeked), sparrows. Black-capped chickadee very common. Nesting birds: 23.

265 acres containing 6,000 varieties of trees and shrubs. Bonsai display, horticultural library, herbarium.

Birdlist from *Arnoldia*, 31-349-365, 1971.

BARTHOLOMEW'S COBBLE, Ashley Falls, Massachusetts. On a winding loop of the Housatonic River, in southwestern Massachusetts, south from Great Barrington, off U.S. 7, through Sheffield. The Cobble is supervised by a Massachusetts organization, the Trustees of Reservations. It has been designated a National Natural Landmark. Primarily a gorgeous place for wildflowers and ferns but rich in birdlife and small mammals as well.

Rare, uncommon, or endangered: osprey, black-backed three-toed woodpecker, other birds, especially warblers. Common species: rose-breasted grosbeak, scarlet tanager, towhee, black-capped chickadee. Best season: April and May for birds and wildflowers.

More than 200 acres of rocky knobs, cedar and hemlock woods, bogland. Many different kinds of ferns, growing everywhere. Look up—ferns are tucked into the pockets of the rock. Lichens and mosses are also abundant. The Cobble itself is on

Great Meadows National Wildlife Refuge. (*Photo by Tim Doyle.*)

one side of the road. On the other side, a trail climbs through woods to a high grassy meadow. Bring sunflower seeds. The chickadees will feed from your hand. Children (and adults!) love this.

The best recent material on the Cobble is an article, "Rock Garden in a Cow Pasture," by Hal Borland, with paintings by Francis Golden, in *Audubon*, May, 1975.

CAPE COD NATIONAL SEASHORE, South Wellfleet, Massachusetts 02663. The Cape Cod Seashore is crowded in summer, but on a sunny weekday (too much traffic weekends) there are few places lovelier, with Cape Cod's wide sweep of sand, sky, and water, and the seabirds calling. Winter here can have a beauty all its own, but the winter wind is cutting.

Summer birds, 78 species. Rare, uncommon, or endangered: piping plover, Arctic tern, roseate tern, others. Common: American goldfinch, herring gull and other gulls, semipalmated plover, song sparrow, others.

26,666 acres, 40 miles long, on the outer edge of the Cape: long stretches of sand beaches; marsh and a beech forest in one section, sandy bluffs and the famous Nauset Marsh. Interpretive services, guided walks, picnicking, swimming, surf fishing.

Undated checklist, "Common Summer Birds of the Cape Cod National Seashore." For further material, see Wellfleet Bay Wildlife Sanctuary.

GREAT MEADOWS NATIONAL WILDLIFE REFUGE, 191 Sudbury Road, Concord, Massachusetts 01742. Twenty miles west of Boston, in the neighborhood of Thoreau's Walden Pond. The Concord unit of the refuge is off Monsen Road, two miles northeast off Mass. 62. The Sudbury section of the refuge is four miles south of the Concord section. Great Meadows also administers Monomoy National Wildlife Refuge.

214 species, of which 46 are classified as rare. An additional list of accidental species seen only once or twice on the refuge is available on request. 88 species are known to have nested here. Rare, uncommon, or endangered: glossy ibis (this pic-

turesque bird is still rare, though increasing in numbers), hooded merganser (nests here), goshawk, bald eagle, osprey (nests here), merlin, white-rumped and Baird's sandpipers, pileated woodpecker, others. Species abundant here in some seasons: mallard, black duck, wood duck, herring gull, tree and barn swallows, blue jay, red-winged blackbird, swamp sparrow, others.

3,800 acres of open water, freshwater marshes, and bottomlands along the Concord and Sudbury Rivers. Trails, bicycle paths, observation tower, canoeing, boating, fishing.

Checklist dated February, 1975.

IPSWICH RIVER WILDLIFE SANCTUARY, Perkins Row, Topsfield, Massachusetts 01983. 617-887-2241. In two units, Topsfield and Wenham. To Topsfield: from Rt. 128 and Boston, take Rt. 1 north (toward Newburyport). Turn right on Central Street, just past the Ipswich River and a railroad. Central Street becomes Perkins Row. Topsfield is on the right. To Wenham, the same route, except after turning right on Central Street, turn right (south) again on Rt. 97, then left on Cherry Street.

221 species, 74 of which are termed rare. 94 species nest in the refuge. Rare, uncommon, or endangered: greater scaup, hooded merganser, bald eagle, osprey, merlin, northern and loggerhead shrike, Philadelphia vireo, Henslow's sparrow, and others. Common species here: Canada goose, mallard, black duck, wood duck, mourning dove, blue jay, common crow, white-breasted nuthatch, gray catbird, brown thrasher, American robin, veery, starling, yellow warbler, yellowthroat, common grackle, brown-headed cowbird, American goldfinch, song sparrow, and others.

2,500 acres of marsh and upland. Facilities: Topsfield— regional offices of Massachusetts Audubon, trailside natural history museum, library, auditorium, shop, wild animal care services. 15 miles of trails, canoeing, snowshoeing, wilderness camping on Perkins Island by reservation. Wenham—nature center, workshop, three miles of trails. Admission fee of $2 per car for non-members. Closed Mondays.

Checklist dated March, 1975. Also available: calendar of events.

LAUGHING BROOK NATURE CENTER, 789 Main St., Hampden, Massachusetts 01036. Southeast of Springfield, east of Longmeadow.

90 species. Rare, uncommon, or endangered: Cooper's hawk, eastern bluebird, blue-winged warbler. Among other bird species to be seen: wood duck, broad-winged hawk, ruffed grouse, screech owl, belted kingfisher, eastern phoebe, tufted titmouse, brown creeper, several warblers, scarlet tanager, rose-breasted grosbeak, others.

Checklist is by the Allen Bird Club of Springfield, Mass., marked for birds occurring in the Laughing Brook Nature Center by Mrs. M. R. Bates.

MONOMOY NATIONAL WILDLIFE REFUGE, Morris Island, Chatham, Massachusetts 02633. On Monomoy Island, an eight-mile-long island extending into the Atlantic Ocean at the elbow of Cape Cod. The headquarters building in Chatham is manned during the summer months. The refuge is administered from Great Meadows National Wildlife Refuge, 191 Sudbury Rd., Concord, Mass. 01742; inquiries should be directed there. Monomoy Island can be reached only by boat, in a one-mile crossing that can be made dangerous by winds and riptides.

252 species, of which 75 are termed rare. Rare, uncommon, or endangered: harlequin duck, king eider, hooded merganser, bald eagle, osprey, peregrine falcon, Hudsonian godwit, Wilson's phalarope, Arctic tern, Philadelphia vireo, Cape May warbler, other species. Species abundant here: Canada goose, black duck, common eider (this is the best place on the East Coast to see the common eider, in great rafts), white-winged scoter, red-breasted merganser, great black-backed gull, herring gull, common tern, red-winged blackbird, song sparrow.

2,700 acres. Surf fishing. Dogs on leash only.

Checklist dated August, 1974. For other relevant material, see Wellfleet Bay Wildlife Sanctuary.

PARKER RIVER NATIONAL WILDLIFE REFUGE, Northern Boulevard, Plum Island, Newburyport, Massachusetts 01950.

Two very rare birds, the Ross's gull and the ivory gull, have turned up at Newburyport as single accidentals in the past two years. Don't count on seeing them, but this whole region is a superb place to view sea-birds. To reach the refuge, drive three miles east on Plum Island turnpike to the north end of the island.

268 species, 36 of which are recorded as rare. 61 nesting species. Among rare, uncommon, or endangered species: hooded merganser, osprey, pigeon hawk, Hudsonian godwit, dovekie, northern and loggerhead shrikes, Philadelphia vireo, Ipswich sparrow (a subspecies of the savannah sparrow). Species that are abundant here in some seasons: Canada goose, black duck, semipalmated sandpiper, herring gull, myrtle warbler, redwing blackbird, white-throated sparrow, others. Notable bird traffic here is: shorebird migrations in summer, concentrations of waterfowl in fall, winter, and early spring, and periodically heavy concentrations of swallows.

The 4,650 acres which make up the Parker River National Wildlife Refuge include 1,000 acres of sand dunes, 3,287 acres of salt marsh and tidal waters, 272 acres of freshwater marsh, and 91 acres of glacial upland. The refuge has six miles of sandy ocean beach. Picnicking, swimming, surf fishing (by permit), beach plum and cranberry picking. Pets must be leashed. Entrance fee.

Checklist dated 1972, prepared in cooperation with the Massachusetts Audubon Society, the Brookline Bird Club, and the Peabody Museum.

WELLFLEET BAY WILDLIFE SANCTUARY (Massachusetts Audubon Society), South Wellfleet, Massachusetts 02663. On west side of U.S. 6.

258 species, 57 of which are "accidental." Rare, uncommon,

or endangered: sooty shearwater, greater scaup, common (black) scoter, Cooper's hawk, osprey, white-rumped and Baird's sandpipers, Hudsonian godwit, Iceland Gull, Arctic tern, Philadelphia vireo, blue-winged and Cape May warblers, and others. Breeding birds: 23 species. Common: redwing blackbird, yellowthroat, rufous-sided towhee, black-capped chickadee, myrtle warbler, mallard, semipalmated and least sandpipers, greater yellowlegs, tree swallow, whimbrel (almost exterminated in the 1880's but recovered in numbers now), and others. All seasons, including winter, provide interesting bird-watching here.

700 acres of saltmarsh and upland. The Austin Ornithological Research Station, a large private bird-banding station, is part of the property; anyone interested in bird-banding should see this station. Sanctuary facilities: wildlife tours, guided walks, natural history day camp, rest room. Regulations: no dogs, no hunting or firearms, no open fires.

Checklist is an attractive 28-page booklet, "Goose Pond Trail." Also available at the sanctuary: "Birds of Cape Cod National Seashore" (annotated checklist, 120 pages, $1.50) and "Monomoy Wilderness" (brief annotated checklist of Monomoy records, 48 pages, $2.00). For the latter two, add 50¢ for tax and handling.

MICHIGAN

FOR-MAR NATURE PRESERVE AND ARBORETUM, G
2252 N. Genesee Rd., Flint, Michigan 48506. Maintained by the
Genesee County Parks and Recreation Commission.

125 species, the most common birds sighted on the preserve.
Rare, uncommon, or endangered: dickcissel, green heron,
hooded merganser, Henslow's sparrow, red-headed woodpecker. Particularly interesting birds of the region: red-bellied
woodpecker, rusty blackbird, warbling vireo, grasshopper sparrow.

380 acres. Nature trails, indoor and outdoor exhibits, interpretive building.

Typewritten checklist revised as of December, 1975.

ISLE ROYALE NATIONAL PARK, Houghton, Michigan
49931. On the biggest island in Lake Superior. Reachable by
boat from Copper Harbor, Michigan, or Houghton, Michigan,
or Grand Portage, Minnesota, or by seaplane from Houghton.
Primarily a refuge for moose and wolves, which originally
swam across from the mainland or came across on the winter
ice.

208 species. Rare, uncommon, or endangered: bald eagle,
osprey, pileated woodpecker, black-backed three-toed woodpecker, others. Particularly interesting regional species: gray
jay, Swainson's thrush, sharp-tailed grouse, boreal chickadee,
palm and mourning warblers.

The main island, 45 miles long and five to eight miles wide
(539,347 acres), is surrounded by more than 200 islets. Isle
Royale has inland lakes; forests, beaver ponds. More than 163
miles of foot trails. No roads and no wheeled vehicles. Camp-

grounds with lean-tos, lodges. Fishing inland (Park Service regulations) or in Lake Superior (State permit). Precautions: bring warm clothing and insect repellent. Don't plan to swim. Only larger boats should try to cope with the choppy lake waters. Park open May to October.

Typewritten, duplicated checklist complete as of 1975.

KALAMAZOO NATURE CENTER, 7000 North Westnedge Ave., Kalamazoo, Michigan 49007.

185 species, of which 51 are rare or accidental. In the beautifully printed and well-planned checklist, most likely trails for observation of each species are noted. Species usually seen only in flight over the area are marked with an asterisk. Rare, uncommon, or endangered: wood duck, Cooper's hawk, Henslow's sparrow, osprey, Cape May warbler, others. Particularly interesting local birds: clay-colored sparrow, screech owl, ring-necked pheasant, gray-cheeked thrush, others.

Interpretive center, nature trails, domestic animal barnyard (summer), arboretum, fern valley, ridge (a lookout for hawks), beechwoods, marsh, river. Admission fee.

Checklist dated 1974, compiled by Raymond Adams.

OTTAWA NATIONAL FOREST, Watersmeet, Michigan 49969. In the northwest tip of Michigan, east of Ironwood via U.S. 2, State Route 28. Visitor center in Watersmeet is 50 miles southeast of Ironwood.

Checklist helpfully notes in what habitats the individual species of birds are likely to be found. 238 species, of which 32 are termed rare. An additional 18 "irregular visitants and accidental stragglers" are noted. Also, the list mentions that three birds—double-crested cormorant, peregrine falcon, and greater prairie chicken—have been "extirpated" from this area, and that the passenger pigeon, once here in vast numbers, is extinct. Rare, uncommon, or endangered: black-backed three-toed woodpecker, Philadelphia vireo, mourning and Connecticut warblers. Particularly interesting local species: giant

Canada goose, whistling swan, wood duck, common goldeneye, northern horned lark, boreal chickadee, others.

915,000 acres. Lakes, streams, waterfalls, a tree nursery, and recreation areas. Picnicking, camping, fishing, hunting.

Checklist, Forest Service Handbook 2609.21, "Ottawa Wildlife Surveys Handbook" (Ottawa Supplement no. 2), includes amphibians, reptiles, and mammals, dated March, 1975.

SENEY NATIONAL WILDLIFE REFUGE, Seney, Michigan 49883. On the Upper Peninsula. On Highway M-77 about five miles south of Seney and two miles north of Germfask. This region was once known as the Great Manistique Swamp. After heavy lumbering and set fires, the region is being restored for wildlife use, with outstanding success.

201 species observed since 1935, plus another 31 species very rarely seen, or accidentals. Rare, uncommon, or endangered: sandhill crane, Le Conte's sparrow (in marsh grass), goshawk (breeds), others. Nesting species: Canada goose (including a flock established by captive geese), mallard, black and ring-necked ducks, spruce grouse, ruffed grouse, common merganser, blue-winged teal, wood duck, bobolink, grosbeaks, swamp sparrow, others. Best season: September and October for sandhill cranes.

95,455 acres of freshwater sedge marshes, open water in 21 impoundments, sand ridges, and stands of red pine and jack pine. The Manistique River flows through the refuge. Visitor center open April to October, picnic areas (with toilets), nature trails, guided auto tours in summer over marked auto loop, observation tower. Fishing and hunting allowed. No camping. Crops are grown as supplemental food for wildlife. Regulations: No boating except on Manistique, dogs must be leashed.

Note: Five islands (147 acres) in Lake Superior near Big Bay make up the Huron National Wildlife Refuge, administered from Seney Refuge.

SHIAWASSEE NATIONAL WILDLIFE REFUGE, 6975 Mower Rd., Saginaw, Michigan 48601. Special feature—the many whistling swans in spring. Six miles southwest of Saginaw, one-half mile west of Michigan Highway 13. The Shiawassee River Estate Game Area is directly to the west—much of this is open to hunting.

187 species, plus an additional ten considered rare or accidental. Rare, uncommon, or endangered: bald eagle (permanent resident), sandhill crane, red-headed woodpecker, others. Birds common here: bobwhite, ring-necked pheasant, snow goose, snow bunting (in winter), others.

8,850 acres of cropland (for birds), freshwater marshes, bottomland hardwoods, pools, and ponds.

Checklist dated September, 1967. Also available: folder about refuge.

MINNESOTA

AGASSIZ NATIONAL WILDLIFE REFUGE, Middle River, Minnesota 56737. 218-446-2110. Eleven miles east of Holt in northwestern Minnesota. A refuge in the Mississippi Flyway. Formerly called Mud Lake National Wildlife Refuge.

245 species, of which 26 are rare or accidental. Rare, uncommon, or endangered: red-necked grebe (common here), goshawk, golden and bald eagles, greater prairie chicken, sandhill crane, Wilson's phalarope. Common: geese, ducks, sharp-tailed grouse (which "dance" on open lands during April), swallows, yellow-headed blackbird. A flock of giant Canada geese nests here.

61,500 acres. Freshwater marshes (25,000 acres), woodland, and spruce bogs. State Highway 7 gives a good general view of the refuge.

Checklist dated May, 1970.

ITASCA STATE PARK, Lake Itasca, Minnesota 56460. In northwest Minnesota, on U.S. Route 71, 22 miles north of Park Rapids.

141 species, of which 111 "are regarded as breeding in recent years," according to the booklet mentioned below. Rare, uncommon, or endangered: osprey, bald eagle (one nest), black-backed three-toed woodpecker, Cape May warbler. Nesting here: flycatchers, warblers, grosbeaks, finches, sparrows. Common: red-eyed vireo, ovenbird, American bittern, ring-necked duck, broad winged hawk, woodpeckers, flycatchers, swallows, wood warblers. Best month: June—birds are singing and easy to find.

32,214 acres. 17-mile park drive. Fine stands of red and

white pine; other trees, deciduous and evergreen. Lake Itasca is the source of the Mississippi River. Interpretive program, self-guiding and guided hikes, auto tours, campgrounds, picnic areas. In Lake Itasca: swimming, boating (with ramp), fishing. Indian mounds exist in the park. The University of Minnesota forestry school and biological station operate in the park; the school has an arboretum.

Checklist; also booklet, "Early-Summer Birdlife of Itasca State Park" by Joseph J. Hickey, John T. Emlen, Jr., and S. Charles Kendeigh (Minnesota Dept. of Conservation, St. Paul; reprint from *The Loon*, vol. 37, no. 1, March, 1965).

PIPESTONE NATIONAL MONUMENT, Box 727, Pipestone, Minnesota 56164. In southwestern Minnesota, near Sioux Falls, South Dakota. The monument preserves the sacred quarry from which, for three centuries, Indians have cut the special red stone to make their ceremonial pipes. The stone is called catlinite, after the artist, George Catlin, who first described the quarry.

41 species. Rare or uncommon: long-billed curlew (east of its range), sandhill crane, Baird's sparrow, red-headed woodpecker.

283 acres. Visitor center, store selling Indian artifacts, self-guiding trail, waterfall.

No formal checklist: typewritten list.

RICE LAKE NATIONAL WILDLIFE REFUGE, McGregor, Minnesota 55760. South from McGregor; take State Route 65 five miles to East Lake, then turn right.

212 species, of which nine are rare or accidental on the refuge. Geese and other water birds like island nesting sites, plentiful here. Nesting species here: great blue heron, black duck, wood duck, others. Common: ruffed grouse, sharp-tailed grouse, ring-necked pheasant, snipe, American woodcock, Virginia rail. Rare, uncommon, or endangered: white pelican, green heron, whooping crane, Caspian tern, black-billed magpie, western bluebird.

17,000 acres, 4,000 of which are water. Indians still harvest the rice in Rice Lake (in mid-September). There are four other smaller lakes, bogs, freshwater marshes—an ideal habitat for beaver, and there are beaver. Old logging trails facilitate birding in this forest refuge. Indian burial mounds. Fishing, picnic area north of Rice Lake. Some fur-bearers are trapped, by permit, but there is no hunting on the refuge.

Note: Mille Lacs National Wildlife Refuge, two small islands in Lake Mille Lacs, is a purple martin nesting site and is administered from Rice Lake Refuge.

Checklist dated March, 1964. Also available: folder about refuge, with map.

SUPERIOR NATIONAL FOREST, Voyageur Visitor Center, Box 149, Ely, Minnesota 55731. A very large national forest. On the north shore of Lake Superior. The visitor center is ¼ mile east of Ely on Minn. 169. Best access to the forest is by canoe. Good outfitters in Ely can send the canoeist off with the right supplies and wise advice.

207 species, 41 of which are rare or occasional. Rare, uncommon, or endangered: goshawk and Cooper's hawk (both breed here), bald and golden eagles, osprey, peregrine falcon, pigeon hawk (breeds here), sandhill crane. Among breeding birds: common loon, great blue heron, Canada goose, teal, wood duck, other ducks, mergansers (three species), black tern, cuckoos, woodpeckers, flycatchers (several kinds), Philadelphia vireo, warblers (many kinds), and others. The common loon and its ringing cry are what any canoeist will best remember from these lakes.

Over a million acres. More than 2,000 lakes. This and Quetico Provincial Park in Ontario (see Canadian entries) are known to canoeists as the Boundary Waters Canoe Area (permit required for canoe travel). Fishing, boating, swimming. Camping, picnicking. Be *sure* to bring insect repellent. Visitor center has historical, geological, and natural history exhibits; open May to September. Deer hunting under Minnesota game regulations. Winter sports.

Checklist dated October, 1973.

TAMARAC NATIONAL WILDLIFE REFUGE, Rochert, Minnesota 56578. From Detroit Lakes in west-central Minnesota, drive nine miles northeast on State Route 34; turn left on Route 71 and drive north for another nine miles.

221 species, 35 classified as rare. An additional nine species have been recorded once or twice. Rare, uncommon, or endangered: Holboell's grebe, bald and golden eagles, pileated woodpecker, osprey, grey partridge, shrikes. Common: Common goldeneye, ruddy duck, ruffed grouse, mallard, blue-winged teal, Canada goose.

43,000 acres. Lakes, marshes, wet lowlands, and uplands. Prairies, northeastern evergreen forests, and southern hardwoods meet here. Wild rice is harvested by Indians—a bumper crop exceeds 90,000 pounds. Picnic area, trails, some fishing and hunting on parts of the refuge.

Checklist dated December, 1970. Also available: folder on refuge, with map.

UPPER MISSISSIPPI RIVER NATIONAL WILDLIFE REFUGE, P.O. Box 226, Winona, Minnesota 55987. Great birding on a major flyway. Minnesota holds only about 33,000 of the 195,000 acres that make up this refuge. Wisconsin, Iowa, and Illinois have the rest. The refuge extends for 284 miles along the Upper Mississippi River from near Wabasha, Minnesota, to near Rock Island, Illinois.

291 species, of which 28 are rare (present only in some years) and 26 have had only one or two recorded observations. In addition, seven species formerly occurring on the refuge site (two of them now extinct) are listed. They are: trumpeter swan, swallow-tailed kite, greater prairie chicken, whooping crane, passenger pigeon, Carolina parakeet, sharp-tailed grouse. Rare, uncommon, or endangered species now are: red-necked grebe, black scoter, hooded merganser, surf scoter (out of its range), bald eagle, peregrine falcon, osprey, merlin, turkey, white-rumped and Baird's sandpipers, pileated woodpecker, yellow-throated vireo, Henslow's sparrow (breeds here).

Marshlands, wooded bottomlands, open water, sandbars,

sand prairie, and wooded bluffs. The refuge is rich in sand-pipers; bring a scope to get good views of these small shore-birds. Some roads parallel the river; birding can also be done by boat.

Checklist dated February, 1975.

MISSISSIPPI

NATCHEZ TRACE PARKWAY, TUPELO ENVIRONMEN-
TAL STUDY AREA, RR 1, NT-143, Tupelo, Mississippi 38801.
Five miles north of Tupelo, at the junction of Natchez Trace
Parkway and U.S. 45.

Wayside stops and walks along the parkway's self-guided
trails might reveal some of the 24 birds on a list of the more
common species for the Tupelo area. Of special interest:
barred owl, chuck-willow's-widow, purple martin, red-tailed
hawk.

The parkway's Tupelo Center has Indian artifacts, a working
farm, a crafts center.

NOXUBEE NATIONAL WILDLIFE REFUGE, in east central Mississippi, southeast of Starkville off State Rt. 25.

216 species, of which nine are noted as rare. Twelve additional species are accidental or very rare. Rare, uncommon, or
endangered: bald eagle, red-cockaded woodpecker, yellow-
throated vireo, Bachman's sparrow, turkey, brown-headed
nuthatch. Common: coot, anhinga, dickcissel, bobwhite, orchard oriole, blue grosbeak, several kinds of warblers. Any
month will offer much of interest to birdwatchers.

46,000 acres of impounded water (Bluff Lake), brushy
fields, and woods (largely loblolly and short-leaf pines). Some
crops are raised for wildlife. Fishing from March to October,
hunting from October to April.

Checklist dated October, 1972.

YAZOO NATIONAL WILDLIFE REFUGE, Rt. 1, Box 286, Hollandale, Mississippi 38748. Thirty miles south of Greenville and twelve miles south of Hollandale in west central Mississippi.

140 species plus seven species of accidental or rare occurrence. Rare, uncommon, or endangered: Mississippi kite (common here), upland plover. Common: cattle egret, mourning dove, Carolina chickadee, mockingbird, blue-grey gnatcatcher, prothonotary warbler, indigo and painted buntings, others. Best seasons: fall and winter.

Over 12,000 acres of open water, cropland, marshes, and woods. Walking and driving trails.

Checklist dated August, 1971.

MISSOURI

BENNETT SPRINGS STATE PARK, Lebanon, Missouri 65536. Twelve miles west of Lebanon on State Rt. 64.

110 species. Rare, uncommon, or endangered: upland plover, red-headed woodpecker, Bewick's wren, yellow-throated vireo (summer), several warblers (summer), osprey, bald eagle (winter), turkey, and others. Among the year-round birds: sharp-shinned hawk, kingfisher, prairie horned lark, brown thrasher, robin, bobwhite, and others.

Picnicking, trout fishing, swimming pool, cabins, camp-grounds (trailer hookups), fish hatchery, and nature museum.

Special typewritten list from George A. Kastler, museum naturalist.

MINGO NATIONAL WILDLIFE REFUGE, Route 1, Box 9A, Puxico, Missouri 63960. One and a half miles northeast of Puxico on State Route 51.

207 species, of which 26 are noted as rare. An additional 24 species are accidental or extremely rare. Rare, uncommon, or endangered: Harlan's hawk (fall and winter), bald eagle (fall and winter), Bewick's wren, others. Common: Canada goose, mallard, pintail, red-headed woodpecker, mockingbird, song sparrow, others. Best season: fall migration.

21,650 acres of wooded swamp, rolling forested hills, crop-land, and limestone bluffs. Self-guiding auto tour in the fall.

MISSOURI BOTANICAL GARDEN, ARBORETUM AND NATURE RESERVE, 2101 Tower Grove Ave., St. Louis, Mis-

Ozark National Scenic Riverways. (*Photo by Gregg Bruff, National Park Service.*)

souri 63039. U.S. 66 west of St. Louis to Gray Summit. Arboretum is on left.

302 birds on St. Louis checklist, but birds seen in arboretum will be mainly land birds. Among more common birds: pileated, red-bellied and red-headed woodpeckers, woodcock, blue-grey gnatcatcher, prairie warbler, rose-breasted and blue grosbeaks, lark sparrow, five species of thrush, chickadees.

70 acres of forest and fields. Emphasis on Missouri flora, rose and herb gardens, flower shows, a geodesic dome greenhouse. Fee for garden admission.

Use St. Louis Audubon Society's "Checklist of Birds of the St. Louis Area" compiled by Earl Comfort and others (1970). Also available: "Guide to Finding Birds in the St. Louis Area" (44 pages, $1.25).

OZARK NATIONAL SCENIC RIVERWAYS, P.O. Box 490, Van Buren, Missouri 63965. Alley Spring Visitor Center: five miles west of Eminence on Rt. 106. Open May to October.

168 species. Rare, uncommon, or endangered: red-headed woodpecker (common here), yellow-crowned night heron, osprey, Bewick's wren (common here), bald and golden eagles (winter), others. Common here: (year-round) wood duck, great horned owl, Carolina chickadee, barred owl, and others; (in summer) green heron, killdeer, whippoorwill, and others; (in winter) tree sparrow, kinglets, others; (as migrants) pied-billed grebe, Canada goose, teal, and others.

White waters. Limestone bluffs. More than 57,000 acres along the Current and Jacks Fork Rivers. Sinkholes from collapsing caves are sources of springs. Interpretive services and summer evening programs. Except for Big Spring, Alley Spring, and Round Spring areas, hunting is permitted. Fishing, float trips (canoes, John Boats—long, flat-bottomed boats), craft demonstrations, canoe demonstrations, camping, Round Spring cavern tours (by reservation). Precautions: observe water safety rules, be careful with fire, stay out of caves unless you check the cave with a park ranger.

Duplicated undated list.

SQUAW CREEK NATIONAL WILDLIFE REFUGE, Box 101, Mound City, Missouri 64470. Northwestern Missouri. South from Mound City (which is on U.S. 275), take Bluff Road.

253 species, of which 39 are noted as rare here. Another 23 species are accidental or very rare. 94 species breed here. Rare, uncommon, or endangered: white faced ibis, Harlan's hawk, osprey, white-rumped sandpiper (common here), LeConte's sparrow, others. Common: white pelicans (several thousand in spring and fall), snow geese, ducks (especially American widgeon, green-winged teal, and gadwall), tree swallows, pied-billed grebe, many others. And from mid-November to January —up to 50 bald eagles! Great concentrations of waterfowl in spring—200,000 to 250,000 snow geese and blue geese (a form of snow geese) in later February and early March. The fall buildup of waterfowl is tremendous.

6,809 acres. Mississippi bottomlands: freshwater marshes, farmland, loess-bluff woodland, and pools. Intensive bird-banding program for ducks and geese with interesting results in returns of bands from distant places. Picnic area, rest rooms at headquarters. Auto or bicycle touring roads, fishing (April 1 to December 31 with State permit). Trapping of muskrats. Mushroom picking in May.

Checklist dated March, 1975. Also available: calendar of events, folder about refuge, folder about mammals there.

SWAN LAKE NATIONAL WILDLIFE REFUGE, Sumner, Missouri 64681. 90 miles east of Kansas City.

216 species, 41 of them occasional or rare. Rare or endangered: golden and bald eagles. Best seasons: spring and fall. Fall migration flock of over 100,000 Canada geese. Breeding birds: mourning doves, cardinals, indigo buntings, others.

Marsh, water, and old farmland. "Most of the refuge is restricted to public traffic from late October to early January because of the managed public hunting season," the checklist says.

Three-page 8″ × 11″ checklist and refuge description, dated 1966.

MONTANA

BENTON LAKE NATIONAL WILDLIFE REFUGE, P.O. Box 2624, Great Falls, Montana, 59401. Twelve miles north of Great Falls via U.S. 87.

142 species. 55 species nest here. Rare, uncommon, or endangered: McCown's longspur, burrowing owl, Baird's sparrow, others. Common: ring-necked pheasant, horned lark, lark bunting, Swainson's and marsh hawks (in fall), barn and cliff swallows, others. Best season for quantities of birds: late August through fall. Best seasons for just watching bird behavior, courtship, nesting, rearing of young: spring and summer.

12,383 acres of open water, marshes, and grassy uplands.

Checklist dated May, 1973.

CHARLES M. RUSSELL NATIONAL WILDLIFE RANGE, P.O. Box 110, Airport Road, Lewistown, Montana 59457. 406-538-8707. Access via Rt. 191 north from Lewistown.

218 species, 22 described as rare. Rare, uncommon, or endangered: burrowing owl, mountain plover, peregrine falcon, golden and bald eagles, others. Common: Canada goose, sharp-tailed and sage grouse, mourning dove, great blue heron, white pelican, others. The sharp-tailed grouse dance their mating dance in April. Best season: spring and fall for migratory waterfowl.

910,000 acres, stretching for 220 miles along the Missouri River. High plateaus, areas of shrubs and evergreens, and marshes and open water. 21-mile auto tour. Regulations: no off-road vehicles, aircraft may not fly below 1,000 feet, ice houses (for fishing) are permitted only from December 1 to March 31.

Checklist dated February, 1972. Also available: separate fliers on wildlife species of the region, folder on wildlife auto tour route.

GLACIER NATIONAL PARK, West Glacier, Montana 59936. Montana, "The last of the big time splendors," as its official highway map says, has the southern half of one of the most rugged, splendid wilderness parks in the world, Glacier. The northern part of this big area is Waterton Lakes National Park in Canada. Glacier Park is on U.S. 2 and 89.

216 species. Rare, uncommon, or endangered: osprey, bald eagle. Common: dipper (water ouzel), Clark's nutcracker, several kinds of thrushes and sparrows, white-tailed ptarmigan.

1,013,029 acres of mountains, valleys, alpine meadows and flowers, waterfalls, lakes. Interpretive services; three information centers. Boating (motors not permitted on some lakes), boat cruises, riding, bicycling (restricted to special areas), fishing, camping, lodges. Rules: Be very careful with fire. Overnight backcountry hikers need permit. No pets on trails; pets must be leashed everywhere. Don't feed animals; no vehicles allowed on trails. On roads, wide vehicles sometimes prohibited (this is true for the spectacular Going-to-the-Sun Road). Precaution: bring insect repellent, sun cream, and rain gear.

MEDICINE LAKE NATIONAL WILDLIFE REFUGE, Medicine Lake, Montana 59247. In northeastern Montana. Headquarters, one mile south of the town of Medicine Lake and two miles east of State Highway 16. In two tracts, the north tract very watery, including Medicine Lake, smaller lakes and many potholes, the southern end around Homestead Lake.

204 species, 19 described as rare. 92 species breed on the refuge. Rare, uncommon, or endangered: whooping crane (in spring), peregrine falcon (in summer), sandhill crane, burrowing owl, Sprague's pipit, Baird's and Le Conte's sparrows, McCown's longspur. Common: Canada goose, various kinds of ducks, double-crested cormorant, white pelican, great blue heron, California and ring-billed gulls. Best seasons: spring,

fall, and summer. Not winter—temperatures can plummet to 57 degrees below zero, all water areas freeze, and all the waterfowl go south.

31,457 acres. Open water and upland grassy areas, and a small percent in cropland. A good place to see the native grasses. Picnic area, bathhouse, rest rooms. Boating, swimming, waterskiing, fishing. Hunting of deer and upland birds in eastern part of refuge.

Checklist dated June, 1966.

NEBRASKA

CHET AGER NATURE CENTER, Pioneers Park, Lincoln, Nebraska 68522. 402-435-6147. Southwest of Lincoln, one-half mile south of junction of Burlington Ave. and Van Dorn.

213 species. Rare or endangered: Louisiana waterthrush, black-headed grosbeak.

Many pine trees, some small ponds. Pioneers Park has golf, picnicking, a zoo, and an outdoor theater.

Checklist: a three-column sheet, printed on both sides. Also available: field checklist of Lancaster County birds.

NEVADA

DESERT NATIONAL WILDLIFE RANGE, 1500 North Decatur Blvd., Las Vegas, Nevada 89108. 28 miles northwest of Las Vegas just north of U.S. 95. Administered jointly with Pahranagat National Wildlife Refuge.

245 species, 34 of which are described as rare. Rare, uncommon, or endangered: Williamson's sapsucker, flammulated owl, sandhill crane, white-faced ibis, others. Common: Gambel's quail, mourning dove, pinyon jay, Clark's nutcracker, mountain chickadee, rock wren, water pipit, Cassin's finch, others.

1,588,000 acres. Desert, mountains, outwash plains. Elevation varies from 2,500 feet to nearly 10,000 feet. Desert bighorn sheep refuge. Limited hunting (for deer and bighorn sheep) and fishing. Precautions: roads on the range are primitive, not for ordinary passenger cars.

Checklist dated December, 1970.

LAKE MEAD NATIONAL RECREATION AREA, 601 Nevada Highway, Boulder City, Nevada 89005. Partly in Nevada, partly in Arizona. Main area with interpretive program: Boulder Beach, seven miles northeast of Boulder City. Access by plane to Las Vegas, by car or bus from there.

272 species, of which 95 are rare or accidental. Rare, uncommon, or endangered: white-faced ibis, ferruginous hawk, golden eagle, others. Common: mourning dove, eared and western grebes, cinnamon teal, American avocet, crissal thrasher, gray vireo, others.

3,000 square miles along the Colorado River. With two principal lakes: Lake Mead is a man-made reservoir, impounded by Hoover Dam; Lake Mohave formed behind Davis Dam. Interpretive program. Swimming, fishing (Nevada or Arizona license), boating, camping, waterskiing. Precaution: wear a hat and sunglasses for protection against the very strong sunlight.

Checklist dated November, 1970. Also available: folder on recreation area; boating regulations.

PAHRANAGAT NATIONAL WILDLIFE REFUGE, 1500 North Decatur Blvd., Las Vegas, Nevada 89108. In Southern Nevada, six miles south of Alamo. Administered jointly with Desert National Wildlife Range.

193 species, of which twelve are rare. Rare, uncommon, or endangered: golden eagle, Townsend's solitaire, burrowing owl. A rookery at the north end of the refuge is used by great blue herons and double-crested cormorants. Common or fairly common birds: warblers, finches, sparrows (especially the black-throated), orioles, meadowlarks, blackbirds, killdeer, Gambel's quail, roadrunner, crissal thrasher.

About 5,380 acres. Two water impoundments, desert country around them.

Checklist dated July, 1968.

RUBY LAKE NATIONAL WILDLIFE REFUGE, Ruby Valley, Nevada 89833. Sixty miles south and east of Elko. Good opportunities here to see and photograph sandhill cranes and trumpeter swans.

195 species, of which 14 are described as rare. Rare, uncommon, or endangered: greater sandhill crane, trumpeter swan (successfully introduced), peregrine falcon. Among the ducks here in quantity in summer: canvasback, redhead, mallard, gadwall, pintail and cinnamon teal. Other common species: sage grouse, avocet, turkey vulture.

37,191 acres of marshes, ponds, and grassy islands between the rugged Ruby Mountains on the west and the Butte Range on the east. Fishing (state license), waterfowl hunting, picnicking.

Undated checklist. Also available: list of "accidentals" seen, folder about refuge.

STILLWATER WILDLIFE MANAGEMENT AREA, Box 592, Fallon, Nevada 89406. The place to see canvasbacks and other ducks in vast numbers in late fall. Headquarters is 18 miles east of Fallon.

155 species, including 13 described as rare. 80 species breed here. Rare, uncommon, or endangered: burrowing owl, golden eagle. Common: whistling swans, several kinds of ducks, northern phalarope, barn owl, horned lark, snowy plover, many others. Best seasons: March and April for ducks and the desert flowers; August and September for tremendous flights of shore birds; October and November for ducks again.

24,203 acres of desert land, sand dunes, marshes and saline ponds. 24 mile loop tour. Camping (no water provided), boating, fishing, and waterfowl hunting.

Note: Anaho Island National Wildlife Refuge in Pyramid Lake seven miles northwest of Nixon is administered from Stillwater. Anaho holds a very large white pelican nesting colony.

Checklist dated May, 1972. Also available: checklist for Anaho Island, annotated List of Accidental Bird Sightings on Stillwater Wildlife Management Area and Vicinity, folder about Stillwater, list of mammals.

NEW HAMPSHIRE

WAPACK NATIONAL WILDLIFE REFUGE, New Hampshire (under administration of Parker River National Wildlife Refuge, Northern Blvd., Plum Island, Newburyport, Massachusetts 01950) Wapack Refuge is between the towns of Peterborough, Greenfield, and West Hilton, off Route 202.

Nesting species: tree sparrow, winter wren, Swainson's thrush, magnolia warbler, white-throated sparrow, and others. A hawk migration and nesting area.

738 acres of the Pack Monadnock Mountain. Bogs and swamps, mountain peaks, ledges and cliffs, blueberry bushes. Three-mile nature trail. No camping; no open fires.

NEW JERSEY

BATSTO NATURE CENTER, Batsto R.D. 1, Hammonton, New Jersey 08037. On N.J. 542 off U.S. 30 from Hammonton. This area is in the very extensive Wharton State Forest, through which runs the Mullica River.

84 species listed as breeding birds in the Wharton Tract (largely synonymous with the Wharton State Forest). Rare, uncommon, or endangered: Cooper's hawk, Henslow's sparrow. Birds especially characteristic of this area: green heron, red-tailed and broad-winged hawks, woodcock, prothonotary and chestnut-sided warblers, meadowlark.

Batsto State Historic Site is a restored late eighteenth-century village, with sawmill, gristmill, and other buildings. The countryside around it is good for birds and excellent for rare plants. White cedar swamps nearby. Canoeing a very popular activity around here—ideal small streams. If driving, beware of getting stuck in the local sand roads.

Undated (1962?) list, "Breeding Birds of the Wharton Tract," compiled by David Fables. A very good book on the area is *Exploring the Little Rivers of New Jersey* by James and Margaret Cawley (Rutgers University Press, 1971). There is a fine description of birdlife in the Pine Barrens in *The Birds of New Jersey* by Charles Leck (Rutgers University Press, 1975). This book also is informative on Brigantine and Great Swamp National Wildlife Refuges and other prime birding spots in New Jersey.

BRIGANTINE NATIONAL WILDLIFE REFUGE, P.O. Box 72, Great Creek Road, Oceanville, New Jersey 08231. Headquarters eight miles west and north of Atlantic City, off Route

119

Turnstones and horseshoe crabs, Brigantine. (*Photo by Richard Frame.*)

9, near Oceanville on Great Creek Road. One of the great bird sights of the East Coast.

269 species, 45 of them noted as rare. Rare, uncommon, or endangered: yellow-crowned night heron, blue goose (uncommon on East Coast), hooded merganser, golden and bald cagles, osprey, peregrine falcon, white-rumped and curlew sandpipers, Hudsonian godwit, Wilson's phalarope, roseate tern, eastern bluebird, and others. Breeding birds include: yellow, pine, prairie, and black and white warblers, clapper and Virginia rails, sora, several kinds of swallows, many species of duck, teal, and many others. Best time to visit: depends on what you want to see: mid-March to mid-April—waterfowl migration. Around April 28—glossy ibis. First week in May—warblers. May and June—ruddy turnstones. September—teal. First week in November—spectacular concentrations of ducks, geese, and brant in pools.

20,237 acres of salt marsh, tidal bays, freshwater marsh, barrier beach, and coniferous brushland. Seven-mile interpretive auto tour route. Observation towers, foot trails. The 250-acre Holgate Unit on Long Beach Island supports nesting colonies of skimmers, terns, and oystercatchers. Bring insect repellent. Photo blinds available by permit. Waterfowl hunting only under special regulations.

Checklist dated 1974. Also available: "Calendar of Wildlife Events," information sheets for self-guiding auto tours.

GREAT SWAMP NATIONAL WILDLIFE REFUGE, R.D. 1, Box 148, Basking Ridge, New Jersey 07920. Headquarters on Pleasant Plains Road, off Route 202, through New Vernon and Lee's Hill Road. Wildlife Observation Center (with blind) is on Long Hill Road. Grounds around the Center have been planted to attract many species of wildlife. The refuge was established in 1960, by a great united effort on the part of local citizens' groups and conservationist organizations. Most of the refuge is managed as a breeding and resting area for migratory waterfowl and as a center for environmental education. All this is just 26 miles west of New York City's Times Square.

205 species, of which 23 are noted as rare. Rare, uncommon,

Boardwalk through the marsh, Great Swamp National Wildlife Refuge. (*Photo courtesy of Dept. of the Interior, U.S. Fish and Wildlife Service.*)

or endangered: yellow-crowned night heron, glossy ibis, goshawk, bald eagle, osprey, yellow-throated vireo, several species of warbler, Henslow's sparrow, and others. Breeding birds include the long-billed marsh wren, wood duck, veery, ruffed grouse, turkey, white-eyed vireo, and blue-winged warbler. Best times to visit: early spring—May for warblers. Not Sunday afternoons—the wild creatures retreat from the large number of visitors.

5,891 acres (two miles long and five miles wide) of hardwood swamp, upland timber, marsh, water, brush, and open fields. Stands of mountain laurel and rhododendron, a beautiful sight in June. 3,600 acres, composing the eastern two-thirds of the refuge, are a Wilderness Area, access limited to foot travel. Two foot trails. Rest rooms. Canoeing on Great Brook and the Passaic River (get permits from the Somerset County Lord Sterling Park on Lord Sterling Road). For hiking in the refuge, waterproof footgear, protective clothing, and insect repellent are recommended. Regulations: foot travel only on all trails, all pets must remain in parking areas, park only in designated areas, no collecting or disturbing natural objects, smoking only in parking area, drinking not permitted, no picnicking or camping, don't litter.

Checklist dated August, 1973. Much of the list is from records of the Summit Bird Club. Also available: folder "A Great Place to Know."

SANDY HOOK UNIT, GATEWAY NATIONAL RECREATION AREA, P.O. Box 437, Highlands, New Jersey 07732. 201-872-0115. At the eastern end of Route 36, off the Garden State Parkway, south of Perth Amboy. Spermaceti Cove Visitor Center is near the swimming beach.

267 species, of which 49 are recorded as unusual. Rare, uncommon, or endangered: red-necked (Holboell's) grebe, gannet, Wilson's phalarope, Hudsonian godwit, osprey (nests here), peregrine falcon, black rail (unusual), white-rumped sandpiper, glaucous gull, roseate tern, others. Breeding birds: fish crow, clapper rail, great horned owl, whippoorwill, common flicker, barn swallow, brown thrasher, robin, towhee.

This literally is a long sandy hook reaching into New York's Lower Bay. All-year interpretive services, guided car caravans, marsh trail, Sunday birdwalks at 9:00 A.M. Fishing (observe rules). Food is sold, change and shower rooms. Regulations: pets on leash only, keep off the dunes (walking loosens the sand, breaks down dunes), don't litter, don't disturb anything (no picking of plants), don't swim in unguarded areas.

Checklist dated October, 1975.

SCHERMAN WILDLIFE SANCTUARY (New Jersey Audubon Society), P.O. Box 693, Bernardsville, New Jersey 07924. From Interstate 287 (Bernardsville exit), drive west past Rt. 202 (traffic light) on Childs Road, turn right on Scrabble Road. Museum is just past bridge.

125 species, 60 of which are resident. For a checklist, the sanctuary uses the excellent booklet, "Checklist for Birds of New Jersey" (New Jersey Nature Study Series, No. 1, N.J. Dept. of Conservation and Economic Development and N.J. Audubon Society, 1964, 25¢).

100 acres of hilly woodland with a stream. Marked nature-study trails. Next to the sanctuary, just across the Morris County line, is another New Jersey Audubon Society sanctuary, the 140-acre Hoffman Wildlife Sanctuary. Scherman Sanctuary is open Tuesday through Saturday (possibly Sunday as well).

New Jersey Audubon Society members receive *New Jersey Nature News*, a quarterly. Address of the Society is 790 Ewing Ave., Franklin Lakes, New Jersey 07417.

NEW MEXICO

BANDELIER NATIONAL MONUMENT, Los Alamos, New Mexico 87544. Though the main feature of this canyon-country preserve is the cliff and open-pueblo ruins, there are 60 miles of walking trails through forests and gorges. 46 miles west of Santa Fe, reachable from Santa Fe north on U.S. 285 to Projoaque, then west on New Mexico 4.

130 species, 41 of them only rarely seen in the monument. Rare, uncommon or endangered: Cooper's hawk, golden eagle, flammulated owl, Williamson's sapsucker. Common birds here: turkey vulture, sparrow hawk, mourning dove, common night hawk, white-throated swift, several kinds of hummingbirds and flycatchers, Steller's and scrub jays, pygmy nuthatch, Grace's warbler, and others.

29,000 acres, much of it wilderness. About 7,000 feet in altitude. Interesting geology in the backcountry, especially a caldera created when a volcano collapsed thousands of years ago. Forests (pinyon-juniper, ponderosa pine, spruce, fir, and aspen) and beaver dams in the Upper Frijoles region. Museum in the Visitor center, evening campfire programs in summer. Large all-year campground in Frijoles Canyon with tent and trailer sites but no utility hookups; lodge open in summer. Regulations: do not disturb or deface any object, whether wildflower, rock, tree, or Indian artifact; register with rangers before departing on hikes.

Checklist dated July, 1971, compiled by James R. Travis and Bruce P. Panowski. Also available: a guide booklet describing the Indian ruins; general description of monument, with map.

BITTER LAKE NATIONAL WILDLIFE REFUGE, P.O. Box 7, Roswell, New Mexico 88201. Thirteen miles northeast of Roswell off U.S. 70.

293 species, among which 78 are rare or accidental on the refuge. Rare, uncommon, or endangered: white-faced ibis, Ross' goose, Mexican duck, golden eagle, osprey, lesser sandhill crane (common in spring), Baird's sandpiper, Sprague's pipit. Among breeding birds: the snowy plover, least tern, Virginia rail, sora, American bittern, pied-billed grebe, American avocet, scaled quail. Southwestern birds commonly seen here: eared grebe, roadrunner, rock wren, Cassin's sparrow.

Over 23,000 acres of the Pecos River Valley. In the valley, tamarisk and cottonwood. On the low hills rising around the valley, desert and semidesert vegetation. Small lakes and impoundments attract great numbers and varieties of water birds and waterfowl. Picnicking, fishing and hunting in season (State license.)

Checklist dated December, 1972, with typewritten list of additional sightings through May, 1974.

BOSQUE DEL APACHE NATIONAL WILDLIFE REFUGE, P.O. Box 278, San Antonio, New Mexico 87832. Bosque del Apache is off Route 85 south of Socorro. A promising experiment in nurturing whooping cranes is going on in this enormous marshy refuge. Canadian and U.S. authorities are cooperating in removing surplus eggs of whooping cranes from their Canadian nests and depositing them with greater sandhill cranes in order to have this somewhat similar species act as foster parents. The sandhills nest at Grays Lake National Wildlife Refuge in Idaho. They migrate to Bosque del Apache in winter. The joy of the experts was great when six of the young whoopers which sandhills had raised migrated with them. If this experiment succeeds in establishing Bosque del Apache as a wintering spot for one offshoot family of whoopers, and Grays Lake as the breeding spot for the offshoot, there will be an extra colony of the great birds (besides the famous Aransas colony) and all their eggs will not, literally, be in one basket. Scientists followed the cranes' moves—the six young whoopers are color-banded—and noticed that they stopped off en route at Monte Vista National Wildlife Refuge in Colorado.

281 species, of which 48 are rare or accidental, in the refuge. Rare, uncommon, or endangered: Mississippi kite, golden and bald eagles, osprey, peregrine falcon, greater and lesser sandhill cranes, purple gallinule, Baird's sandpiper, Williamson's sapsucker, hepatic tanager, Wilson's phalarope, pyrrhuloxia, others. Common in the area but not elsewhere: white-necked raven. 98 species nest in the refuge. Best season: fall.

57,191 acres of bottomland and desert upland. The bottomland roads may be used for sightseeing by car.

Checklist dated September, 1973.

SAN ANDRES REFUGE, P.O. Box 756, Las Cruces, New Mexico 88001. This isolated refuge is entirely within the White Sands Missile Range and is closed to public entrance except by special permission. For entry permission and instructions on reaching it, apply at refuge manager's office, 1480 N. Main St., Las Cruces, New Mexico. The original purpose of the refuge was to protect the desert bighorn sheep. The area is rich in semidesert birdlife.

142 species, of which fifteen are rare or occasional in the refuge. Rare, uncommon, or endangered: Cooper's hawk and golden eagle (both common here), Lawrence's goldfinch, peregrine falcon. Species seen only in this general southwestern area: zone-tailed hawk, harlequin quail, black phoebe, white-necked raven, crissal and curve-billed thrashers, phainopepla, pyrrhuloxia. Best season: April 20 to November 1. Best place for birdwatching: Ash Canyon.

57,217 acres, a 21-mile-long narrow strip of the southern San Andres Mountains, extending from San Augustine Pass northeast of Las Cruces in Dona Ana County to Mockingbird Gap in Socorro County. Upper Sonoran life zone, with semidesert or desert plants such as pinyon, juniper, scrub oak, ocotillo, cactus, buckthorn, and grama grasses. Some waterholes.

Checklist dated January, 1968. Also available: map.

NEW YORK

ARTHUR W. BUTLER MEMORIAL SANCTUARY, Chestnut Ridge Rd., Mount Kisco, New York 10549. Drive south from Bedford Village on Rt. 22, turn right on State Rt. 172 for about two miles, then left on Chestnut Ridge Road.

123 species. Rare, uncommon, or endangered: pigeon hawk, pileated woodpecker, osprey (summer), Philadelphia vireo, blue-winged and Cape May warblers. Particularly interesting birds of the region: pine grosbeak (winter), eastern meadowlark (summer), eastern wood pewee, ringnecked pheasant, rufous-sided towhee, cedar waxwing, tufted titmouse.

225 acres of marsh and swampy woodland.

Alphabetical checklist. Also available: checklist of mammals.

CONSTITUTION ISLAND AUDUBON SANCTUARY, RFD #1, Rt. 9D, Garrison, New York 10524. Just off the east shore of the Hudson River across from West Point. Visit only by prearrangement with the Sanctuary Department, National Audubon Society, 950 Third Ave., New York, New York 10022. 212-832-3200.

122 species. Sightings of two of these are "somewhat questionable." Rare, uncommon, or endangered: golden and bald eagles, osprey, Carolina wren (to the north of its normal range here), three uncommon warblers (worm-eating, golden-winged, and blue-winged), white-winged crossbill, and others. A great place to see vireos, finches, and wrens. The Hudson River is also a flyway for raptors, among other birds. The rocky heights and deep valleys around here set up wind currents on which turkey vultures can easily be seen soaring.

No formal checklist, but the sanctuary manager keeps a record.

CORNELL LABORATORY OF ORNITHOLOGY, 33 Sapsucker Woods Road, Ithaca, New York 14850. A famous center of research on birds, and a nature preserve. The laboratory is located about three miles northeast of the Cornell campus, two miles north of the village of Varna, via Hanshaw Road.

Ducks, other water birds, and thrushes are outstanding here, both in numbers and varieties. The woods in springtime are full of melodious birdsong. The entire area, Sapsucker Woods, is named for a bird very common here, the yellow-bellied sapsucker. In summer, resident birds include the brown creeper, hermit thrush, Canada warbler, and northern waterthrush. If the day is stormy, the pond birds may be observed through plate glass windows and telescopes at the laboratory center. Sounds of the birds outside are piped into the room. The center also has an excellent bookstore and displays of original Louis Agassiz Fuertes bird paintings and sketches. The laboratory's phonograph records of bird songs and calls are classics.

Four miles of winding trails through woods and marshes (boardwalks here) and past a large pond. In summer, bring insect repellent. Stay on trails, do not pick or disturb anything, close gates behind you.

The laboratory *Newsletter* is available to members. Also, an annual journal, *The Living Bird*.

HIGH ROCK PARK, 200 Nevada Ave., Staten Island, New York 10306. A very active teaching center in environmental education. It has both private and public funding. In east-central Staten Island, south of Richmond Parkway. Access is by Nevada Avenue.

66 species. Common: red-winged blackbird, grackle, woodpeckers, screech owl, goldfinch, song sparrow, others.

A 72-acre forested site in the Staten Island greenbelt. Swamp, forest, hill. Visitor center, trails, shop, toilets.

Checklist dated September 22, 1967. Other material available: "Swamp Trail; a Trail Guide to the Loosestrife Swamp," trail map, flier.

IROQUOIS NATIONAL WILDLIFE REFUGE, RFD #1, Basom, New York 14013. Fifteen miles northwest of Batavia between Rochester and Buffalo. On State Rt. 63, eight miles north of Oakfield and seven miles south of Medina. Thruway Exit 48 is convenient. Formerly called Oak Orchard National Wildlife Refuge. The refuge was established to provide nesting, resting, and feeding grounds for ducks, geese, and other water-loving birds.

211 species, including 46 classified as rare or accidental. Nesting species: 97. Rare or endangered: wood duck (common here, and nests here), hooded merganser (uncommon here, but known to nest), bald eagle, osprey, pileated woodpecker, northern shrike, golden-winged warbler (nests), others. Common: pied-billed grebe, herons, turkey vulture, red-tailed hawk, Virginia rail, sora, American woodcock, screech and great horned owls, belted kingfisher, yellow-shafted flicker, eastern phoebe, swallows, robin, warbling vireo, ovenbird, eastern meadowlark, rose-breasted grosbeak, others. Best birding: March to November. Peak migrations of waterfowl in mid-April and early October, but birding here is interesting in any month.

10,784 acres of marsh, swamp, wet meadows, pasture, and cropland. Regulated fishing and hunting.

Checklist dated March, 1970.

JAMAICA BAY WILDLIFE REFUGE, New York City. Address inquiries to: Jamaica Bay Unit, Gateway National Recreational Area, Floyd Bennett Field, Brooklyn, New York 11234. This refuge, astonishingly rich in birds, is directly across Jamaica Bay from Kennedy Airport. On most days, you can see the towers of Manhattan from the outer walks of the refuge. Jamaica Bay Refuge was formerly Jamaica Bay Park, a New York City park, managed and planted from scratch to suit the food tastes of birds by Herbert Johnson. Now it is under

Federal ownership and management. Reachable by subway (IND to Broad Channel; then walk west to Cross Bay Blvd. and north three-quarters of a mile). By car on Woodhaven Blvd. in Queens; Woodhaven becomes Cross Bay Blvd.

A 1968 checklist (a collector's item, edited by Phyllis Sternau with maps and other illustrations by Richard Edes Harrison) lists 257 species, with 53 additional species that are rare or have occurred accidentally. Among the rare, uncommon, or endangered species: glossy ibis, European widgeon, greater scaup, hooded merganser, osprey, white-rumped sandpiper, glaucous and Iceland gulls, roseate tern, several kinds of rare warblers, summer tanager (north of its range here), and Lapland longspur. Rare winter birds in 1975 included peregrine falcon, black-headed gull. Spring birding at Jamaica Bay has produced hermit thrushes (almost as tame and plentiful as robins on one lovely spring day here) and Cape May warblers. In summer, bobwhites scurry among the bushes. A spot of vivid color in a small tree turns out to be a rose-breasted grosbeak. In various seasons, egrets, ruddy ducks, snow geese, white-crowned sparrows, and many other birds are likely to be seen.

The refuge has shrubby woodland fringed by a grassy expanse known as the North Garden; extensive marshes; a large freshwater pond; a beach area sometimes closed because of birds' nesting. The North Garden took the brunt of a freak windstorm in the fall of 1975, but the damage is largely repaired. Any trees that were not killed have been propped up, and new trees planted. Walks extend around the refuge, with benches at observation points. The headquarters building has a lecture room, information desk, and toilets, but no food facilities. No picnicking; no collecting, or disturbing plants, animals, or birds; stay on trails.

MONTEZUMA NATIONAL WILDLIFE REFUGE, R.D. #1, Box 232, Seneca Falls, New York 13148. 315-568-5987. 32 miles west of Syracuse at the north end of Cayuga Lake. Five miles east of Seneca Falls on U.S. 20. Thruway Exit 41 is the most convenient. On the north, the Cayuga River and the New York

Montezuma National Wildlife Refuge. (*Photo courtesy of U.S. Fish and Wildlife Service.*)

State Barge Canal; on the east, the Cayuga and Seneca Canal. 236 species, of which 34 are rare on the refuge. 110 species breed on the refuge. Among rare, uncommon, or endangered species: Holboell's grebe, European widgeon, common scoter, bald eagle, osprey, peregrine falcon, Baird's sandpiper, Hudsonian godwit, eastern bluebird, Cape May warbler (common here in spring and fall). Commonly seen: redhead, canvasback, ringnecked duck, lesser scaup, common goldeneye, bufflehead, hooded and common mergansers. Peak migration: 70,000 geese (in spring) and 100,000 ducks (in fall).

6,334 acres of cattail marshes, impoundments fringed with woodlands, and winter wheat meadows planted as food for migrating Canada geese. Five-mile self-guided auto tour, nature trail, hiking, picnic area, rest rooms, two observation towers. Hunting permitted in certain seasons in accordance with special regulations—trappers take between 1,000 and 8,000 muskrats annually. Fishing. Entrance fee.

Checklist dated August, 1971. Also available: folder about refuge with map, "Mammals of Montezuma National Wildlife Refuge," and "A Tour through Montezuma National Wildlife Refuge."

MORTON NATIONAL WILDLIFE REFUGE, R.D. 359, Noyac Road, Sag Harbor, New York 11963. Near the junction of Millstone Road, Long Island, off Route 27, between Little Peconic Bay and Noyac Bay. A resting area for waterfowl and shorebirds.

222 species, of which 23 are accidental and eight, rare. Rare, uncommon, or endangered: great cormorant, greater scaup, common scoter, hooded merganser, osprey (nests), Wilson's plover, white-rumped sandpiper, glaucous gull, roseate tern, several rare warblers, snow bunting (all seasons except summer). Among common birds: herring gull, black-capped chickadee, cardinal, sanderling, great black-backed gull, yellowthroat. Greatest use by waterfowl: November and December. Winter ducks in the surrounding waters: scaup, goldeneyes, and black ducks.

187 acres. The northern two-thirds of the refuge is a penin-

sula known as Jessups Neck. A two-mile trail leads to the north
tip of the peninsula. Sandy, gravelly, and rocky beaches with
thickets of beach plum; wooded bluffs; a three-acre brackish
pond. Interpretive facilities. Photography, painting, nature
study encouraged.

Checklist dated July, 1972. Also available: folder about
refuge.

TEATOWN LAKE RESERVATION, Spring Valley Road,
Ossining, New York 10562. Off Taconic State Parkway, west on
Rt. 134; to Spring Valley Road, to lake.

Water and woodland birds.

Information center, nature study classes, in connection with
the Brooklyn Botanic Garden, New York City.

Checklist not available because it is being revised.

WARD POUND RIDGE RESERVATION, Cross River, New
York 10518. About four miles northwest of Pound Ridge on
N.Y. 137, then 3½ miles north on N.Y. 121, at junction of 35 in
Cross River.

151 species, 52 of which are noted as rare. Rare, uncommon,
or endangered: bald eagle (winter), osprey (migrant), goshawk, northern shrike (winter). Some particularly interesting
regional birds: pine siskin, evening and pine grosbeaks (in winter), black-billed cuckoo, many warblers, including several
that are uncommon anywhere. Best season: spring, but a walk
in the reservation is rewarding for birders anytime.

Upland woods (Meyer Arboretum—170 acres), hills, meadows. Nature trails, trailside nature museum, camping, picnicking. Maple sugar demonstrations in early spring. In winter:
skiing, toboggan trails. Closed Mondays.

Checklist dated May, 1973.

NORTH CAROLINA

CAPE HATTERAS NATIONAL SEASHORE, P.O. Box 675, Manteo, North Carolina 27954. Access from Cedar Island via ferry or from south of Nags Head via bridge.

248 species, 28 described as rare. Rare, uncommon, or endangered: brown pelican, peregrine falcon, piping plover, roseate tern, others. Common: ducks, geese, black-bellied plover, loons, grebes, herons, pheasants, gulls, coot, whistling swan, dunlin, black skimmer, others.

28,500 acres, a barrier beach in three sections—70 miles long in all. Freshwater ponds on Bodie Island and Pea Island. Observation platforms, nature trails. Visitor center on Ocracoke. A hard-surfaced road runs the length of the barrier beach, except at Hatteras Inlet, where a free ferry is the connection. Sport fishing, swimming, boating, sailing, picnicking, camping. Toilets. Precaution: swim only where lifeguards are on duty.

Note: within the seashore, Pea Island National Wildlife Refuge is maintained as a refuge.

Undated checklist.

MATTAMUSKEET NATIONAL WILDLIFE REFUGE, New Holland, North Carolina 27885. Headquarters one-half mile north of New Holland on U.S. 264.

227 species, of which 32 are termed rare. Rare, uncommon, or endangered: osprey, glossy ibis, oystercatcher, red-cockaded woodpecker, and others. Common: ducks, whistling swan, redwinged blackbird, turkey vulture, clapper rail, bobwhite, others.

50,179 acres dominated by shallow Lake Mattamuskeet. Cypress trees on the north, marsh and low swampland elsewhere. Adjacent parts of Pamlico Sound have been closed to migratory waterfowl hunting. Precaution: when first arriving, check at headquarters on road conditions.

Note: Swanquarter National Wildlife Refuge is nearby.

Checklist dated October, 1970. Also available: folder about refuge, with map.

NORTH DAKOTA

ARROWWOOD NATIONAL WILDLIFE REFUGE, Pingree, North Dakota 58476. On the James River in east-central North Dakota, about 14 miles north of Jamestown. Headquarters at the south end of Arrowwood Lake about six miles east of Edmunds.

251 species, 67 of them considered rare on the refuge. Rare, uncommon, or endangered: bald eagle, osprey, peregrine falcon, greater prairie chicken, sandhill crane, Hudsonian godwit, Cape May warbler. Common: white pelicans, redheads, canvasbacks, Canada geese, sharp-tailed grouse. Principal nesting species: mallard, gadwall, American widgeon, shoveler, blue-winged teal, pintail. In all, 106 species nest here. Waterfowl peak: October.

15,934 acres of lakes (Arrowwood Lake, Mud Lake, Jim Lake), marshes, prairie grasslands, wooded coulees, cultivated fields, and shelterbelts. Some trapping, some grazing allowed; fishing in season from boats without motors. Some fields farmed for wildlife food. Swimming and picnicking at the south end of Arrowwood Lake. No camping except for supervised scout troops. No bird hunting, but some areas may be open for deer hunting.

Checklist dated April, 1972. Also available: flier about refuge.

AUDUBON NATIONAL WILDLIFE REFUGE, Coleharbor, North Dakota 58531. This is the south half of the Snake Creek Reservoir area on the east end of Lake Sakakawea. The north half of the area is managed by the North Dakota Game and Fish Department, primarily for hunting and fishing.

159 species, plus ten species (among them the Ross' goose) observed only once on the refuge. Rare or endangered: sandhill cranes (hundreds in migration), whooping cranes (four observations in recent years), burrowing owls, peregrine falcon, golden and bald eagles. The giant subspecies of Canada goose is present as a nesting species. Common nesting birds (59 species nest): ducks, white pelicans, double-crested cormorants, common terns, western grebes (which perform a spring courting dance, walking on the water).

13,498 acres of short-grass prairie on hilltops and moraine knobs, reservoir shoreline and marsh, many prairie potholes and salt-grass marshes, and shelterbelts.

Checklist dated June, 1968.

LONG LAKE NATIONAL WILDLIFE REFUGE, Moffit, North Dakota 58560. 701-673-4403. Headquarters four miles south and east of Moffit.

193 species (53 are rare here), plus six species that are considered out of their normal range. Rare, uncommon, or endangered: Cooper's hawk, golden and bald eagles, greater prairie chicken, Baird's sandpiper, others. 75 nesting species. Abundant kinds of birds: avocet, house sparrow, red-winged blackbird, western meadowlark, others. Four principal nesting ducks: gadwall, pintail, blue-winged teal, and mallard. Best seasons for birds: spring, summer, and fall. Peak flight of waterfowl, mid-April, but a greater variety of waterfowl in fall. In September, the number of sandhill cranes builds up to several thousand. Fall duck populations average 50,000 birds.

22,310 acres of prairie grasslands, ravines, cultivated fields (for bird food), and small tree and shrub plantings. No sizable trees. Long Lake is a long shallow lake separated into three units by dikes. The refuge was established partly for the control of botulism in waterfowl. Fishing and hunting permitted at various times and places and under Federal and State regulation. Ice fishing from December 16 to March 15.

Checklist dated September, 1967. Also available: flier about the refuge.

SLADE NATIONAL WILDLIFE REFUGE, Dawson, North Dakota 58428. Dawson is on Interstate 10, halfway between Bismarck and Jamestown.

197 species (of these, 26 are rare on the refuge) plus five other casual or accidental species. 88 species nest on the refuge. Rare, uncommon, or endangered: sandhill crane, greater prairie chicken, peregrine falcon, Hudsonian godwit, Lapland longspur. Abundant kinds of birds: besides the ducks, killdeer, mourning dove, western meadowlark, red-winged blackbird. Best season: fall—10,000 to 15,000 ducks; for sandpipers, May and September. In general, the birdwatching is not as good in spring, because the ice is late in melting.

3,000 acres of prairie pothole habitat. Five semipermanent lakes and marshes and many small potholes. Many small wetland areas have been deepened mechanically to provide additional nesting habitat for waterfowl.

Checklist dated May, 1968.

SOURIS LOOP NATIONAL WILDLIFE REFUGES. Under this umbrella name there are four refuges: Des Lacs (18,881 acres, Kenmore, North Dakota 58746), Lostwood (26,747 acres, Lostwood, North Dakota 58724), J. Clark Salyer (58,695 acres, Upham, North Dakota 58799), and Upper Souris (32,096 acres, Foxholm, North Dakota 58738).

262 species, of which 98 are only rarely or occasionally seen on the refuges. About 140 species nest on the refuges. Rare, uncommon, or endangered: sandhill crane, Baird's and Le Conte's sparrows (the latter seen on tall-grass meadows), European widgeon, Harlan's hawk, golden and bald eagles, peregrine falcon, whooping and sandhill cranes (the latter abundant here), greater prairie chicken, Baird's and buff-breasted sandpipers, Hudsonian godwit, Philadelphia vireo, mourning warbler, sharp-tailed grouse (its spring mating dance is noisy and spectacular), and others. The Canada geese include the subspecies, the giant Canada. A double-crested cormorant colony is located on the southern part of the J. Clark Salyer refuge.

The Souris Loop Refuges are a reclamation project that is

restoring the ducks (once heavily shot for the market) and the land drained for agriculture in the early years of this century. With the aid of dams, the marshes are functioning again and the waterfowl are abundant. Most of the land is flat, but it rolls gently along the Souris River, with shelterbelts of trees. Lostwood Refuge is lake-and-pothole country, traditionally a happy home for ducks.

J. Clark Salyer Refuge permits some haying, grazing, and trapping, and has a bee colony. Ten oil wells are operated along the refuge boundaries. Salyer Refuge can be reached by turning off U.S. 2 at Towner, North Dakota, and driving 26 miles north on State Highway 14. Recreation at Salyer: two auto trails, hunting, fishing (state license), picnicking. Canoe trail on Souris River.

Des Lacs Refuge extends from the Canadian border to eight miles south of Kenmare. Spring bird migration peak: April 12 to 25. The refuge is closed during the waterfowl hunting season.

Precautions on all Souris refuges: be wary of poison ivy, check with refuge headquarters on road conditions.

Checklist dated September, 1969, compiled with the aid of Dr. and Mrs. R. T. Gammell. Other materials available: J. Clark Salyer Refuge descriptive folder (with map) and "Scenic Trail Guide"; Des Lacs National Wildlife Refuge descriptive folder; a pamphlet, "Waterfowl Identification in the Center Flyway."

SULLYS HILL NATIONAL GAME PRESERVE, Fort Totten, North Dakota 58335. Headquarters: off Rt. 57, southwest of Sweetwater Lake.

163 species. Rare, uncommon, or endangered: golden and bald eagles, osprey, peregrine falcon, sharp-tailed grouse, sandhill crane, Hudsonian godwit. Abundant kinds of birds: Canada, snow and blue geese, whistling swans, others. Giant Canada geese nest. Peak bird populations: from late April to early June and from late August to mid-October.

1,674 acres of wooded glacial moraine hills and grassland. In two parts: 994 acres with a 700-acre big game enclosure on the south shore of Devils Lake in the Fort Totten Sioux Indian Reservation, and 680 acres southwest of Fort Totten. Open May through October, at other times as conditions permit. Auto tour routes, one-mile-long nature trail, native grass planting display, picnic area and toilet facilities on southwest side of Sweetwater Lake. Regulations: no camping, no firearms, dogs must be leashed.

Checklist dated June, 1970.

TEWAUKON NATIONAL WILDLIFE REFUGE, Cayuga, North Dakota 58013. On the Wild Rice River in the southeastern corner of North Dakota. Headquarters five miles south of Cayuga.

235 species, plus seven other species considered very rare or accidental (21 of the 235 species are only rarely encountered on the refuge). Rare or endangered: Cooper's and Harlan's hawks, golden and bald eagles, peregrine falcon, greater prairie chicken, sandhill crane, Baird's and white-rumped sandpipers, Hudsonian godwit, Sprague's pipit, Philadelphia vireo, others. "Principal bird attractions include nesting colonies of western grebes and double-crested cormorants, a late August and early September buildup of white pelicans (up to 1500 birds), about 200,000 Franklin's and ring-billed gulls during August and September, and up to 30,000 snow, blue, and Canada geese during mid October. Fall concentrations of ducks have numbered 60,000. Bitterns, herons, and egrets are most numerous in the late summer," the checklist says. Best seasons: spring and fall, but other seasons can be rewarding for birdwatchers, too.

7,869 acres. Gently rolling terrain, bordered on the south by the Sisseton Hills. Open water, marsh, smaller pools, and potholes. The area had been farmed, but has been seeded back to native grasses as much as possible. 1700 acres are now farmed to provide bird food. No camping.

THEODORE ROOSEVELT NATIONAL MEMORIAL PARK, Box 7, Medora, North Dakota 58645. Headquarters of the three units of this park, in Peaceful Valley at Medora, off

Interstate 94. The middle unit, the Elkhorn Ranch site, is reachable only by dirt roads—check on their condition at Medora. The northern unit of the park is reached via U.S. 85 from Watford City.

116 species, of which 33 are only rare or occasional in the park. 90 species nest in the park. The golden eagle has been reported seen during every month in the year. Other rare, uncommon, or endangered birds: the sandhill crane (abundant here), boreal owl, Sprague's pipit, Baird's sparrow, McCown's longspur.

70,436 acres; three separate units of Federally owned land, a memorial to Theodore Roosevelt on land that greatly appealed to him when, in the 1880's, he was a rancher in the Badlands. Rugged buttes, gorges, and canyons. Prairie-dog towns, petrified forest, peculiar lignite layers of ground which are sometimes ignited by lightning and burn for years. Nature trails, camping, picnicking, campfire programs from June to September. Precautions: yield right of way to buffalo on highway, staying in your car for safety.

Checklist published by the Theodore Roosevelt Nature and History Association in cooperation with the National Park Service, U.S. Department of the Interior.

OHIO

CALIFORNIA WOODS OUTDOOR EDUCATION CENTER, 5400 Kellogg Ave., Cincinnati, Ohio. Part of the Cincinnati Recreation Commission, Division of Outdoor Education. East from downtown Cincinnati on Rt. 52.
156 species. 66 species nest in the preserve, among them: wood duck, bobwhite, barred owl, belted kingfisher, Acadian flycatcher, wood thrush, yellow-throated vireo, prothonotary and worm-eating warblers, ovenbird, scarlet tanager, goshawk.
60 acres. A small creek, and woods of beech, oak, and maple.
List (typed) dated November, 1971, with additions.

HUESTON WOODS STATE PARK, Route 1, College Corner, Ohio 45003. More of a sports-vacation spot, but still interesting for birders. Four and a half miles north from Oxford on State Rt. 732.
248 species (on Miami University, Ohio, checklist). 35 warblers; also ten sparrows, 23 ducks.
3,596 acres. Fishing, swimming, boating, golf course, riding trails, picnicking, camping, lodge, interpretive nature program.
No specific checklist for the Hueston Woods. Use "Field Check List, Ohio Birds" (Ohio Dept. of Natural Resources) or "Checklist of Birds (Oxford, Ohio)" (Miami University).

MILL CREEK PARK, Ford Nature Education Center, 816 Glenwood Ave., Youngstown, Ohio 44502. A fine place for birding, but the only available list is old. The park is in the southwestern part of the city, bounded by Mahoning Avenue,

143

U.S. 224, Lockwood and Mill Creek Boulevards. Park established 1891; part of Youngstown Township Park District.

270 species, including four accidentals (as of 1941). Rare, uncommon, or endangered: Cooper's hawk, bald eagle, red-headed woodpecker, and others.

2,383 acres of gorges, ravines, and hills from the Mahoning River to Lake Newport Dam. Three lakes and interconnecting Mill Creek. Fine wildflowers near Lake Newport. 15 miles of foot trails. Picnicking, boating, six acres of formal gardens, three recreation areas, golf course, fishing.

Bird checklist is from the book *Mill Creek Park* by Edward Galaida (published by the author, 1941).

OTTAWA NATIONAL WILDLIFE REFUGE, 14000 West State Rt. 2, Oak Harbor, Ohio 43449. 419-897-2521. Fifteen miles east of Toledo, via Rt. 579, on Lake Erie. Established in 1961.

288 species, 61 of which are rare or accidental. The Kirtland's warbler, one of the rarest North American birds, has been seen in the vicinity of the refuge, but not on it. 133 birds nest locally. Bird species common here: black duck, mallard, American widgeon, blue-winged teal, redhead, scaup, Canada goose, whistling swan; in summer, great blue heron, black-crowned night heron, and great egret. Best seasons: spring (especially for whistling swans) and fall migration.

4,800 acres of open water and freshwater marshes. Included in this refuge: Darby Marsh (480 acres), Navarre Marsh (533 acres), Cedar Point National Wildlife Refuge (a 2,250-acre marsh lying six miles west of Ottawa), and West Sister Island National Wildlife Refuge (an 82-acre island nine miles offshore in Lake Erie), all managed by the Ottawa Refuge.

Checklist dated December, 1970. Also available: folder about refuge, trail guide.

OKLAHOMA

PLATT NATIONAL PARK, Box 201, Sulphur, Oklahoma 73086. A small national park distinguished by mineral springs. 25 miles north of Ardmore on I-35, then ten miles east on Rt. 7 to Sulphur, then south off U.S. 177.

136 species. Rare, uncommon, or endangered: Townsend's solitaire, golden eagle, osprey, others. Common: Carolina wren, red-eyed vireo, hairy and downy woodpeckers, red-tailed hawk, others.

912 acres of freshwater and cold mineral springs, woods, wildflowers, streams, and waterfalls in the foothills of the Arbuckle Mountains. Travertine Nature Center open in summer, nature walks, self-guiding nature trails, aquatic nature walk—wading a short section of rock creek or Travertine Creek, bison range, campgrounds, motels, hotels, fishing, boating, waterskiing. Pets must be leashed. No collecting.

Undated checklist. Also available: folder about park and the nearby Arbuckle Recreation Area.

SALT PLAINS NATIONAL WILDLIFE REFUGE, Jet, Oklahoma 73749. 405-626-4794. One mile west of State Highway 38 and two miles south of State Highway 11.

256 species. In addition, 18 rare or accidental species. Rare or endangered: bald and golden eagle, Mississippi kite. Best season: fall. The refuge description says, "It is not uncommon for 30,000 geese and 90,000 ducks to be present in the fall." Fall concentration, also, of over three million Franklin gulls. Birds especially common: mallard and pintail duck, green-winged teal, avocet, yellowlegs, sandpiper, dowitcher, godwit, bobwhite, snowy plover. Many species breed in the refuge.

Salt flats, upland, farm fields, and ponds and marshes. Many plantings for wildfowl. Precautions to take: stay on roads. Salt flats are dangerous (quagmire under crust). Wear sunglasses and protective clothing against sunburn. Picnic areas, limited-stay camping (seven days), observation tower, fishing.

Checklist dated April, 1968. Also available: description and map of refuge: description of 30 mammals; folder on selenite crystals, which may be dug in specified places in the refuge.

TISHOMINGO NATIONAL WILDLIFE REFUGE, P.O. Box 248, Tishomingo, Oklahoma 73460. Six miles southeast of Tishomingo on the Washita Arm of Lake Texoma.

252 species, 34 described as rare or accidental. 77 species nest on the refuge. Rare, uncommon, or endangered: ferruginous hawk, golden and bald eagles, sandhill crane, black rail, others. Common: several kinds of geese, ducks and herons; bobwhite, scissor-tailed flycatcher, Franklin's gull, blue grosbeak, painted bunting, coot, others. Best season: August on, for waterfowl migration.

16,500 acres of open water (the lakes), marsh, cropland, and grassland. Picnicking, camping.

Undated checklist.

WICHITA MOUNTAINS WILDLIFE REFUGE, P.O. Box 448, Cache, Oklahoma 73527. Twelve miles north of Cache. A fenced refuge for big game.

241 bird species, 94 described as rare or accidental. Rare, uncommon, or endangered: turkey, Mississippi kite, Bewick's wren, upland plover, black-capped vireo, others. Common: bobwhite, chuck-will's-widow, painted bunting, dickcissel, rufous-crowned sparrow, others.

59,020 acres. Oak slopes, valleys, grassland (a feature of this park is a good sample of native mixed-grass prairie), lakes, ponds. Good roads, scenic highway. Trails, camping, fishing, swimming, boating, picnicking.

Checklist dated August, 1972.

OREGON

CRATER LAKE NATIONAL PARK, Box 672, Medford, Oregon 97501. The lake is in an extinct volcano, Mount Mazama, last heard from violently 10,000 years ago. Access by bus or auto in summer, from Klamath Falls or Medford.

191 species. Rare, uncommon, or endangered: bald and golden eagles, peregrine falcon, white-winged crossbill. Common: California gull, common raven, gray and Steller's jays, Clark's nutcracker, mountain bluebird, red crossbill, Oregon junco, Steller's and gray jays, others. Best months, for birds and accommodations: July and August.

Very blue lake. All around it, evergreens, pines, hemlocks, and firs; meadows. Exhibit building in Rim Village, 33-mile Rim Drive, hiking trails, naturalist-guided launch trip, rowboats for rent (no motors), marked wildflower garden and many wildflowers everywhere, firetower, lodge, campgrounds (no hookups), fishing. In winter, skiing.

Undated checklist.

OREGON CAVES NATIONAL MONUMENT, Cave Junction, Oregon 97523. Twenty miles east of Cave Junction on Rt. 46.

76 species, a count which the checklist author feels does not fully represent the wealth of birds in the area. More observers would see more birds, and more kinds of birds. Rare, uncommon, or endangered: Townsend's solitaire, golden eagle, others. Common: pileated woodpecker, Steller's jay, chestnut-backed chickadee, red-breasted nuthatch, winter wren, pine siskin.

480 acres of the Siskiyou Mountains, including the caves. Guided tours of the caves, which are cool and damp. The tour

is strenuous. Children under six are not admitted; there is a nursery for them (for a fee). Hotel open from the end of March to beginning of September, Forest Service campgrounds nearby, trails.

Checklist, revised in 1960 by Roger J. Contor.

SHELDON, HART MOUNTAIN ANTELOPE REFUGES,

P.O. Box 111, Lakeview, Oregon 97630. Two refuges administered from the same office. Both are very large, isolated, and with rare and interesting birds—if you can get there.

Hart Mountain National Antelope Refuge in south-central Oregon is a steep volcanic ridge 8,065 feet high, well-watered by streams, and surrounded by desert range, 240,000 acres in all. It is 45 miles northeast of Lakeview on an unpaved road.

In Hart Mountain: 213 species. Rare, uncommon, or endangered: Ross' goose, golden eagle, ferruginous hawk, sandhill crane, others. Common: several raptors, western sandpiper, avocet, common raven, canyon wren, sage grouse, loggerhead shrike, green-tailed towhee, others. Best season: summer. Undated checklist.

Sheldon National Antelope Refuge is high mesa, semidesert country. The sparse tree growth is mostly juniper and mountain mahogany. Canyons shelter many birds. Area of refuge: 543,898 acres. Refuge is 45 miles northeast of Cedarville, California, and 30 miles southwest of Denio, Nevada. Inquire at Lakeview, Oregon, about road conditions.

In Sheldon: 147 species, eight defined as rare. Rare, uncommon, or endangered: golden and bald eagles, ferruginous hawk, Wilson's phalarope, black swift, others. Common: avocet, rock wren, western and mountain bluebirds, green-tailed towhee, others. Best seasons: summer and early fall. Checklist dated March, 1963.

PENNSYLVANIA

BOWMAN'S HILL STATE WILDFLOWER PRESERVE, Washington Crossing State Park, Washington Crossing, Pennsylvania 18977. 215-862-2924. From New Hope, take Rt. 32 south for two and a half miles.

144 species (no indication of how frequently seen). Many kinds of hawks, woodpeckers, flycatchers, swallows, thrushes, vireos, sparrows. 34 warblers. Rare, uncommon, or endangered: osprey, six species of warblers, white-winged crossbill. Best viewpoints: feeding area near headquarters; Parry Trail along Pidcock Creek. Best season: April and May, not only for the birds but for the flowers, which are extraordinarily lovely, varied, and abundant.

100 acres of varied habitat. Pidcock Creek, dammed at one point to make a pond. Plants are all native to Pennsylvania. Headquarters building has a shop, picnic area. Gate is open every day from 10:15 A.M. to 4:30 P.M. unless driving conditions are hazardous, in which case park outside the gate and walk in.

Checklist from 1972 or later. Also available: trail maps and plant lists with approximate blooming times.

ERIE NATIONAL WILDLIFE REFUGE, R.D. #3, Box 13, Guys Mills, Pennsylvania 16327. 814-789-3585. In northwestern Pennsylvania. Headquarters is on State Rt. 173, two miles south of Mt. Hope, and 14 miles east of Meadville.

223 species, of which 13 are noted as rare. Rare, uncommon, or endangered: hooded merganser (breeds here), goshawk, Cooper's hawk, bald eagle, osprey, pigeon hawk, turkey, white-rumped and Baird's sandpipers, black tern (locally common;

breeds here), eastern bluebird (nests here), yellow-throated and Philadelphia vireos, Connecticut warbler (in fall). Abundant or common: whistling swan, horned grebe, killdeer, tree swallow, catbird, robin, yellowthroat, redwinged blackbird, and others.

4,967 acres. A long narrow valley through which run Lake and Woodcock Creeks. Swamp woodland, marsh, wet pasture and cropland, and abandoned farmland. Beaver ponds. Two large impoundments and five upland ponds. Pool 9 Overlook and Beaver Run Trail are the best places to see birds. Picnic area overlooking Pool 9. Hunting and fishing permitted under special regulations from September 1 through March 15.

Note: Seneca Unit, a division of the Erie Refuge, is a 3,027-acre area eight miles north of Erie Refuge along the north side of Route 408 between the towns of Teepleville and Cambridge Springs. It shelters migrating waterfowl and other wildlife.

Checklist dated July, 1969. Also available: hunting and fishing regulations; list of mammals; folder about refuge, with map.

HAWK MOUNTAIN SANCTUARY, Kempton, Pennsylvania 19526. Eleven miles east of Hamburg, on U.S. 22, then turn north on Rt. 143. The most famous East Coast viewing spot for hawk flights. On the bare top of this mountain in the Kittatinny Ridge, it is possible to get very close views of the soaring birds, even to see them from above.

Rare or endangered: bald eagle, osprey. Common: broad-winged hawk, sharp-shinned hawk, other kinds of hawks, turkey vulture, Canada goose, golden-crowned kinglet, others. In the woods below the crest, many birds smaller than hawks may be seen. Best season: fall for big flights of hawks. It's a matter of luck for the viewer: wind and weather might bring hundreds, or dozens, or just a few hawks past the crest.

New visitor center. For the trail to the mountain top, wear sturdy shoes.

A rewarding and delightful book about the sanctuary's founding and its early days is *Hawks Aloft; the Story of Hawk Mountain* by Maurice Broun (1960, © 1948, 1949).

HERSHEY ROSE GARDENS AND ARBORETUM, Hershey, Pennsylvania 17033. 717-534-3531. Reachable from east and west via Pennsylvania Turnpike; from south via Interstate 83. Arboretum is near Hotel Hershey.

104 species seen. Rare or endangered: prothonotary warbler. Best season: not summer—apt to be crowded.

22 acres of roses, azaleas, other flowers, trees and shrubs. Admission charge. No picnicking inside arboretum; picnic area just outside. Facilities in Hershey: taped and self-guided tours, free parking, rest rooms, Hershey factory tour, museum of Pennsylvania Dutch artifacts, amusement park, sports arena, hotels and golf, daily carillon concerts.

Checklist dated 1972-1975. Also available: three brochures: "Welcome to Chocolate Town U.S.A.," "Hersheypark," and "Guided Tour, Hershey Rose Gardens and Arboretum" (map of gardens).

LONGWOOD GARDENS, Kennett Square, Pennsylvania 19348. 215-388-6741.

188 species, of which 48 are termed rare or very rare. Rare, uncommon, or endangered: hooded merganser, Cooper's hawk, osprey, Cape May warbler (common here in fall), and others. Common: Canada goose, turkey vulture, sparrow hawk, ring-necked pheasant, killdeer, mourning dove, downy woodpecker, mockingbird, bluebird, golden-crowned kinglet, ovenbird, red-winged blackbird, northern oriole, scarlet tanager, cardinal, indigo bunting, song sparrow, and others.

Admission fee. Gardens open daily, outdoors 9 to 6, conservatories 10 to 5. Organ concerts: Sundays 3 to 5.

No formal checklist. Checklist of birds seen at the gardens, dated July, 1975, compiled by Jesse Grantham III for course, "Amateur Field Ornithology."

RACCOON CREEK STATE PARK, R.D. 1, Hookstown, Pennsylvania 15050. West of Pittsburgh near the Ohio border. North on Rt. 30 to Harshaville, then south on Rt. 16.

155 species. Rare birds: goshawk, osprey. Birds common

here: sparrow hawk, red-tailed hawk, ruffed grouse, red-bellied woodpecker, yellow-bellied sapsucker, winter wren, kinglets, song sparrow, many others.

Thickets; wooded hillsides.

No formal checklist; typed list of records since 1964.

READING NATURE CENTER (Ferndale Museum and Trails), c/o Bureau of Recreation, City Hall, Reading, Pennsylvania. In southeastern Pennsylvania, at Lake Antietam.

106 species. Rare or uncommon: hooded merganser, several warblers (Cape May, worm-eating, blue-winged—the latter nests here). Among nesting species: green heron, broad-winged hawk, spotted sandpiper, screech owl, ruby-throated hummingbird, yellow-shafted flicker, eastern phoebe, eastern wood pewee, white-breasted nuthatch, and many others.

Marked nature trail. Ten fern species have been noted. Nature trail for the blind. Note: there are no poisonous snakes on or near the nature trail. Beware of ticks in high grass. Regulations: do not disturb wildlife, stay on trails.

Checklist in descriptive sheets, dated 1971.

RHODE ISLAND

NINIGRET NATIONAL WILDLIFE REFUGE, Box 307, Charlestown, Rhode Island 02813. Refuge established in 1970. Ninigret also administers the Block Island National Wildlife Refuge, a thrilling place for a birder to be during spring and fall migrations; and the Nantucket National Wildlife Refuge.

Ninigret: A 27½ acre barrier beach, on which no vehicles are permitted. To reach it, turn south from U.S. 1 onto East Beach Road. Hiking, fishing, photography. Birdlists not yet available for any of these three refuges. Ninigret uses the "Check-list of Rhode Island Birds, 1900-1973" published by the Audubon Society of Rhode Island, 40 Bowen Street, Providence, Rhode Island 02903.

Block Island National Wildlife Refuge: To reach it, take the ferry at Galilee, south of Wakefield which is on U.S. 1. Block Island is about 15 miles from the mainland. Refuge is on the northern tip of the island. Sand dunes in large part.

Nantucket National Wildlife Refuge: 40 acres (surplus from U.S. Coast Guard land) on the northernmost tip of Nantucket Island, about 25 miles south of Cape Cod (via all-year passenger-and-car ferry from Woods Hole, Massachusetts). Sea ducks, Canada geese, black ducks; a tern nesting site.

The Rhode Island bird list contains well over 300 species, not all of which would be found at Ninigret or even on Block Island. However, the waves of warblers on Block Island in May or in mid-September are famous. At any time of year seabirds will be seen (especially on the trip out and back).

Black skimmers at Cape Romain. (*Photo by Richard Frame.*)

SOUTH CAROLINA

CAPE ROMAIN NATIONAL WILDLIFE REFUGE, Rt. 1, Box 191, Awendaw, South Carolina 29458. 803-928-3368. Headquarters is three miles east of U.S. 17 (about 20 miles north of Charleston) at Moore's Landing. Take refuge boat from there. (Romain Tours, McClellanville, S.C. 29458. 803-887-3380. Fees.) The refuge is a prime place to see American oystercatchers and black skimmers.

251 species plus 36 species considered rare or out of their normal range. Rare, uncommon, or endangered: brown pelican, peregrine falcon (in winter), oystercatchers, others. Common: rails, terns, teal, ducks, Wilson's plover, willets, yellowlegs, parula warbler, others. Best season: April, fall, or winter.

34,197 acres of islands, waterways, beaches, marshes, including Bull's Island—a virgin forest of live oaks, magnolias, pines, and palmettos (no food on island; bring your own lunch; no overnight accommodations). Cape Romain is a resting area for the loggerhead turtle in June. Fishing, swimming, boat ramps, picnic areas. Hunting permitted for deer, upland game, and rails. Precautions: bring rain gear, insect repellent. No camping. No pets. No weapons.

Checklist dated November, 1972. Also available: map, information sheet, calendar, and folder about refuge.

CAROLINA SANDHILLS NATIONAL WILDLIFE REFUGE, McBee, South Carolina 29101. Headquarters four miles northeast of McBee on U.S. 1.

184 species, 56 of them described as rare, plus twelve species that are accidental or extremely rare. Rare, uncommon, or endangered: turkey, red-cockaded woodpecker, osprey, others.

Common: bobwhite, wood duck ("very good response" from the wood duck to man-made nesting boxes put up for their benefit), mallard, black duck, American widgeon, ring-necked duck, teal, pine warbler. Best season: November-December (concentrations of waterfowl).

46,000 acres. Land that was almost a desert when it was turned over to the Federal government in 1939 is now a green and watery shelter for many kinds of birds and mammals. Rolling hills. Impoundments. Forests of longleaf pine and scrub oak, fields of grasses for bird food. Picnic area, toilets. Sport fishing. Hunting. Precaution: maximum speed is 35 MPH.

Checklist dated October, 1973. Also available: folder about refuge, information sheets for self-guiding auto route.

SANTEE NATIONAL WILDLIFE REFUGE, P.O. Box 158, Summerton, South Carolina 29148. Headquarters eight miles southeast of Summerton on U.S. 301. Wintering place of the southernmost major Canadian geese flocks.

In four separate units, 234 species, 22 described as rare, plus seven species that are of extremely rare occurrence. Rare, uncommon, or endangered: glossy and white ibis, Mississippi kite, osprey (breeds here), others. Common: herons, coot, geese, bobwhite, cattle egret, blue jay, others. Best seasons: fall and spring.

74,352 acres on the Santee-Cooper Reservoir which includes Lakes Marion and Moultrie. Marshy area, upland forest. To attract birds for observation, an area near refuge headquarters is planted to small grains, lespedeza, and sunflowers. Other fields are farmed for bird food. Foot trail, observation tower, picnicking, boat ramps, waterskiing. No camping. Fishing. Hunting in the Pinopolis unit of the refuge.

Checklist dated October, 1972.

SAVANNAH NATIONAL WILDLIFE REFUGE, Route 1, Hardeeville, South Carolina 29927. Partly in Georgia, partly in South Carolina. A refuge reclaimed from abandoned rice fields.

Ten miles north from Savannah, Georgia. Route 17 passes through the refuge.

213 species, 11 marked as rare, plus 11 recorded only once or twice. Rare, uncommon, or endangered: osprey, brown pelican, glossy ibis, white ibis, others. Common: wood duck (nesting here), herons, egrets, bitterns, king rail, snipe, fish crow, loggerhead shrike, pine warbler, yellowthroat, others.

13,173 acres of flatland on the Savannah River.

Note: Savannah Refuge administers Wassaw Island National Wildlife Refuge—10,242 acres of marsh and timbered dunes near Savannah, with public day access to trails and beaches. Shorebirds and wood species. Blackbeard Island (scaup, introduced chachalacas, painted buntings, others) and Harris Neck (Canada geese, willets, clapper rails, others) are also administered from Savannah. Blackbeard Island is accessible only by boat. Harris Neck is accessible from Rt. 131, 20 miles north of Darien, Georgia, on Rt. 17.

Checklist for Savannah Refuge dated March, 1970.

SOUTH DAKOTA

BADLANDS NATIONAL MONUMENT, P.O. Box 72, Interior, South Dakota 57750. From Interstate 90, 62 miles east of Rapid City. A boundary area between eastern and western birds.

195 species. Rare, uncommon, or endangered: white pelican, sharp-shinned and Cooper's hawks, golden and bald eagles, prairie falcon, whooping crane, Baird's and buff-breasted sandpipers, others. Birds fairly easy to see: Say's phoebe (the eastern phoebe has been seen, too), mountain bluebird, rock wren, horned lark, western meadowlark, lark sparrow, cliff swallow.

Over 100,000 acres watered by the White River and its tributaries. Fantastic vari-colored rock formations, ridges, low hills, and cliffs. Visitor center with exhibits and an audiovisual program, foot trails, summer evening programs, campgrounds.

Undated checklist with nine handwritten additions to the list.

LACREEK NATIONAL WILDLIFE REFUGE, Martin, South Dakota 57551. In the Pine Ridge Sioux Reservation region near the Nebraska border. From Martin, travel five miles south on State Highway 73, then nine miles east on a graded road.

235 species, 22 of them rare on the refuge. Rare or endangered: American and bald eagles, prairie falcon, trumpeter swan, western burrowing owl, Hudsonian godwit. Fairly commonly seen: cliff swallows, sharp-tailed grouse, lark buntings, mallards, common golden-eyes, common mergansers. Nesting birds: white pelicans, double-crested cormorants, grebes, terns, black-crowned night herons, American bitterns, long-billed

marsh wrens, yellow-headed blackbirds, willets, avocets, Wilson's phalaropes, long-billed curlews, upland plovers. Best seasons: early spring and late summer. At these times, there are concentrations of songbirds and shorebirds.

9,825 acres in the valley of the South Fork of the White River. A series of dammed man-made lakes and marshes plus rolling grassland with some willow thickets and stands of cottonwoods and elms. Prairie dog colony. Self-guiding tours.

Checklist dated September, 1969.

SAND LAKE NATIONAL WILDLIFE REFUGE, Columbia, South Dakota. 605-885-6320. Seven miles east of Aberdeen in northeastern South Dakota, turn north at Bath Corner onto County Road 16 and drive about 20 miles north.

226 species plus an additional 15 species sighted only once or twice on the refuge. Rare, uncommon, or endangered: Cooper's hawk, golden and bald eagles, buff-breasted sandpiper. Common in migration: blue geese, snow geese, Canada geese, mallards, pintails, and many other ducks, white pelicans, double-crested cormorants, catbirds. Principal nesting species of waterfowl: Canada goose, mallard, gadwall, pintail, blue-winged teal, redhead, and canvasback. Spring gatherings of geese may number from 250,000 to 500,000.

21,451 acres of marsh, grass-covered uplands, fields cultivated for the wildfowl feeding, and shelterbelt. Two low dams impound water. An active waterfowl banding program. The entire refuge may be closed during the waterfowl hunting season. Precaution: stop at headquarters for latest news on road conditions.

Checklist dated March, 1970. Also available: flier about refuge.

WAUBAY NATIONAL WILDLIFE REFUGE, R.R. 1, Waubay, South Dakota 57273. 605-947-4695. Turn north one mile east of Waubay, then drive eight miles north.

232 species, plus 13 accidentals. Rare or endangered: osprey, burrowing owl. Common: Franklin's gull, ring-necked pheas-

ant, willet; warblers and other songbirds in spring and early fall. Best season: summer and early fall; may be closed in waterfowl hunting season. In the Sioux language, Waubay means "a nesting place for birds." Breeding birds: blue-winged teal, mallard, gadwall, many others. The courtship water-dance of the western grebe can be seen on Windgate Arm of Waubay Lake in May and June.

Prairie hills; potholes. Precautions: stop at headquarters to register and learn about road conditions. Picnic area, observation tower, ice fishing on Waubay Lake during winter.

Checklist dated June, 1967. Also available: folder about refuge, with map.

WIND CAVE NATIONAL PARK, Hot Springs, South Dakota 57747. Twelve miles north of Hot Springs on U.S. 385.

200 species, including 58 which are rarely seen (a few times a year or less) in the park. Rare, uncommon, or endangered: golden and bald eagles, osprey, prairie and peregrine falcons, greater prairie chicken, sandhill crane, and Baird's sparrow. Common birds include kingbirds, black-billed magpie, warblers, woodpeckers, grouse, common nighthawk, cliff swallow, chickadee, house and rock wrens. Both the indigo and the lazuli bunting are present but rare.

28,059 acres, a grasslands, ponderosa pine forest, and riverbank park in the southeastern Black Hills. Eastern and western flora and fauna meet here. Wear rubber-soled walking shoes and take a sweater or jacket for the guided tours of the limestone cave. Cave is closed November through March. Ranger guided nature hikes in the summer. Nature trail of 1¼ miles to an observation tower. Camping May 15 to September 15, $2 per car per night.

Checklist dated January, 1973. Also, three mimeographed pages "Summer Birds of Wind Cave National Park," by J. Richard and Martha W. Gilliland (1969). This tells where in the park to look for specific birds, e.g., "Prairie Falcon. *Falco mexicanus*. Common; open short prairie; open areas in Beaver Creek Canyon."

TENNESSEE

CHEROKEE NATIONAL FOREST, P.O. Box 400, Cleveland, Tennessee, 37311. East of Cleveland on U.S. 64. South of Great Smoky Mountain National Park in the Appalachians. Rare, uncommon, or endangered: pileated woodpecker, turkey, others. Common: ruffed grouse, Louisiana waterthrush, others.

614,616 acres in two separate strips. Paint Creek flows through a gorge in this hemlock forest. Other streams, waterfalls. Elevation 1,980 feet to 4,332 feet. Camping, picnicking, swimming, boating. Hunting permitted under Tennessee game regulations.

No checklist. Three folders available: "Cherokee National Forest," "Protecting Endangered Wildlife on Your Southern National Forests," and a pamphlet on rare wildflowers.

GREAT SMOKY MOUNTAINS NATIONAL PARK, Gatlinburg, Tennessee 37738. Approaching from Tennessee, stop first at Sugarlands Visitor Center; from North Carolina on U.S. 441, stop at the Oconaluftee Visitor Center. A viewpoint on the trans-mountain road (U.S. 441) is Newfound Gap. From here a spur road leads to Clingman's Dome.

213 species, 71 of these rare or occasional. Rare or endangered: wood duck, turkey, Eastern bluebird, bald eagle. Best season: spring. Peak flights: spring warbler flights. 102 species of birds breed in the park.

Mountains, forested and rugged. Bring raingear. Don't disturb plant or animal life. The Appalachian Trail follows the mountain crest through the park; overnight trail shelters. Camping permits required. Other facilities: naturalist programs, LeConte Lodge (accessible by foot or horse only), campgrounds, finishing May to August (state license).

Checklist, dated 1968, compiled by Fred J. Alsop, III, seasonal ranger-naturalist. Also available: A. Stupka, *Notes on the Birds of Great Smoky Mountains National Park* (University of Tennessee Press, paper).

REELFOOT NATIONAL WILDLIFE REFUGE, P.O. Box 295, Samburg, Tennessee 38254. The refuge is the upper one-third of a great natural lake created by earthquakes in 1811 and 1812. In northwestern Tennessee, two miles east of Tiptonville on Route 21.

242 species in the refuge and neighboring areas. 29 of the species are noted as rare; plus 12 other accidental species. Rare, uncommon, or endangered: golden eagle, bald eagle (common in winter), osprey, turkey, black rail, Bewick's wren, worm-eating warbler, Le Conte's sparrow, others. Common: mallard, common egret, American widgeon, gadwall, dickcissel, barred owl, anhinga, common and purple gallinule, prothonotary and parula warblers, king rail, coot, others. Winter concentrations of grackles, red-winged blackbirds, cowbirds, and starlings.

A rugged wilderness refuge of 9,586 acres. (The lake is 12 miles long and four miles wide.) River flood plain, bottomlands, open water, swamps, upland bluffs. A cypress rookery of great blue herons and common egrets. Precaution: be wary of water moccasins. Regulations: campfires very restricted.

Note: Lake Isom National Wildlife Refuge, five miles south of Isom, is a 1,850-acre refuge used mainly to grow food for birds and administered from Reelfoot Refuge.

Checklist dated December, 1967. Also available: folder about refuge, with map.

ROAN MOUNTAIN STATE RESORT PARK, Box 37, Rt. 7, Roan Mountain, Tennessee 37687. 32 miles south of Elizabethton via U.S. 19E, State Rt. 143.

90 species. Among birds to be seen: winter wren, veery, soli-

tary vireo, nuthatches, several warblers, snow bunting. Best season: June.

600 acres. Spruce, fir, and a natural garden of gorgeous rhododendrons blooming in mid-June. The Appalachian Trail (hiking) crosses the mountain. Camping, fishing, picnicking.

No specific checklist available for the park; use the "Field List of Tennessee Birds" printed by the Tennessee Game and Fish Commission in cooperation with the Tennessee Ornithological Society.

TENNESSEE NATIONAL WILDLIFE REFUGE, Box 849, Paris, Tennessee 38242. In three units which attract hundreds of migrating waterfowl. On the Tennessee River at Kentucky Lake (a TVA lake), in central-western Tennessee. Kentucky Lake is 16 miles northeast of Paris on U.S. 79.

211 species, of which 11 are noted as rare. 93 species nest here. Rare, uncommon, or endangered: turkey, black vulture, bald eagle (common here in winter), osprey, yellow-throated vireo, several kinds of warblers, others. Common: Canada goose, great blue heron, red-shouldered hawk, greater yellow-legs, black-billed cuckoo, Carolina chickadee, Carolina wren, eastern meadowlark, American goldfinch.

51,000 acres of water, wooded areas, and land cultivated for bird food.

Checklist dated December, 1968. Birdwatchers visiting the refuge are asked to look for particular rare species (a list is given on the checklist) and, if they make positive observations, to notify the refuge manager.

Heard Museum seen from its wildlife sanctuary.

TEXAS

ARANSAS NATIONAL WILDLIFE REFUGE, P.O. Box 68, Austwell, Texas 77950. 512-286-3559. Seven miles southeast of Austwell, Texas, on Rt. 774.

328 species, of which 100 are rare or irregular. Besides the 328 species, there are 33 accidentals. Rare or endangered: Aransas is the main winter refuge for the whooping crane (might be seen from observation tower). Also rare: brown pelican, bald eagle, peregrine falcon, Attwater's prairie chicken, sandhill crane (commonly seen in spring). Best season: November to March, but something is coming through almost every month. "The first week of May is fantastic—warblers, orioles, grosbeaks, and buntings everywhere!" the refuge description says. Breeding birds: wading birds particularly. Whooping cranes migrate north at end of March.

Tidal marshes, wooded dunes, meadows and mottes (oak trees), ponds. Precautions: be alert against poisonous snakes. Don't feed or get too close to javelinas or raccoons. Bring insect repellent and sulfur powder. Facilities: walking trails only, lunch areas. No camping, but public camping at Goose Island State Park 30 miles south, or Port Lavaca State Pier Park 35 miles north.

Checklist dated March, 1973. Also available: map, two pamphlets on whooping cranes.

BENTSEN-RIO GRANDE VALLEY STATE PARK, Mission, Texas 78572. From Mission (which is a grapefruit-growing center), drive three miles west on U.S. 83, then three miles south on 2062.

221 species, of which 76 are rare or occasional here. Among birds with U.S. ranges confined largely or totally to South Texas: least grebe, white-tailed kite, gray hawk, black hawk, chachalaca, jacana, red-billed pigeon, white-fronted dove, groove-billed ani, buff-bellied hummingbird, ringed kingfisher, tropical kingbird, kiskadee flycatcher, green jay, long-billed thrasher, yellow-green vireo, olive-backed warbler, black-headed oriole, Lichtenstein's oriole.

588 acres of moist woodlands and dry chaparral brushlands. Nature trail and other trails, tent and trailer sites, picnicking, fishing on the Rio Grande.

Besides the bird checklist, there is available a list with funny little drawings (children will love it) of the park's "critters." Includes some birds such as the Lichtenstein's oriole, with helpful remarks on finding and identifying them.

BIG BEND NATIONAL PARK, Texas 79834. Three approaches: Marfa to Presidio on U.S. 67, then State Highway to west entrance; or State Highway 118 from Alpine to west entrance; or U.S. 385 from Alpine to north entrance.

380 species, 32 of these "hypothetical" and not well authenticated. Rare, uncommon, or endangered: Mississippi kite, osprey, caracara, golden and bald eagles, peregrine falcon, Baird's sandpiper, groove-billed ani, hummingbirds including the Lucifer, blue-throated, and white-eared, Sprague's pipit, Philadelphia vireo, warblers including worm-eating, colima (in Boot Canyon), hepatic tanager, pyrrhuloxia (common in park), Baird's sparrow. Common: green-winged teal, scaled quail, spotted sandpiper, lesser nighthawk, red-shafted flicker, ash-throated flycatcher, Say's phoebe, Mexican jay, black-crested titmouse, bushtit, cactus wren, mockingbird, black-tailed gnatcatcher, loggerhead shrike, Audubon's warbler, yellowthroat, brown-headed cowbird, house finch, brown towhee, rufous-crowned sparrow, black-throated sparrow, white-crowned sparrow.

Enormous (708,221 acres), beautiful park that has rivers and ponds, riparian areas, shrub desert, grasslands, mountain woodlands (the Chisos), and canyons. The sun shines here almost all through the year. Nature walks, evening programs, camping at Chisos Basin or Rio Grande Village, fishing in Rio Grande, lodge in Chisos Basin (reservations needed). Precautions and regulations: motorcycles may not be used on trails; road to Chisos Basin may be hard for large vehicles; do not climb steep rocks; no swimming; beware the cactus; be alert for rattlesnakes and do not molest them; drive slowly, especially at night, to avoid hitting animals; no hunting; no collecting or disturbing park features (rocks, plants, etc.); stay on trails—do not cut switchbacks.

Checklist revised 1971 by Roland H. Wauer. Also available: mimeographed sheet of information on park; folder, "Big Bend," with map. Write Big Bend Natural History Association, Big Bend National Park, Texas 79834 for further material, especially a book, *Birds of Big Bend and Vicinity* by Roland H. Wauer.

BUFFALO LAKE NATIONAL WILDLIFE REFUGE, P.O. Box 228, Umbarger, Texas 79091. 28 miles southwest of Amarillo on U.S. 60, then two miles south on Rt. 168.

275 species, 117 of which are considered rare or accidental on the refuge. 41 species nest on the refuge. Rare, uncommon, or endangered: Ross' goose, Mississippi kite, Cooper's hawk, golden and bald eagles, peregrine falcon, sandhill crane, white-rumped and Baird's sandpiper, Baird's sparrow. Birds that are very common here: six duck species, bobwhite, redwinged blackbird, others.

7,677 acres around Buffalo Lake. Winter visitor tour program which includes a banding demonstration. Prairie dog town; one area of lake open to fishing, boating, and waterskiing, one area open to fishing only, largest area of lake closed from November 1 to February 28 to all boating. Boat ramps; a recreational entrance permit is required, and boating regulations must be observed. Swimming permitted but lifeguards not provided, picnicking, camping. No property, natural feature, or animal or plant life may be disturbed, defaced, or destroyed. Pets must be confined to campsite. Firearms, weapons, or fireworks are prohibited.

Checklist dated July, 1974. Also available: flier about refuge.

HAGERMAN NATIONAL WILDLIFE REFUGE, Route 3, Box 123, Sherman, Texas 75090. 15 miles northwest of Sherman on U.S. 82.

265 species, 55 considered rare or accidental on the refuge. 62 species nest on the refuge. Rare, uncommon, or endangered: Mississippi kite, Cooper's hawk, golden and bald eagles, osprey, peregrine falcon, pigeon hawk, sandhill crane, black rail, white-rumped sandpiper (common here in spring), Baird's sandpiper, mourning warbler. Among the many birds that are very common here: great blue, green, and little blue herons, pintail, green-winged teal, American widgeon, red-tailed hawk, western sandpiper, mourning dove, roadrunner, great horned owl, barred owl, chimney swift, yellow-shafted flicker, red-bellied woodpecker, hairy and downy woodpeckers, blue jay, Carolina chickadee, tufted titmouse, Carolina wren, loggerhead shrike, eastern meadowlark, orchard oriole, brown-headed cowbird, cardinal.

11,320-acre area on Lake Texoma, on the Oklahoma border. Fishing from April to September.

Checklist dated November, 1969.

HEARD NATURAL SCIENCE MUSEUM AND WILDLIFE SANCTUARY, Route 7, Box 171, McKinney, Texas 75069. 214-542-5012. A privately supported institution, provided under the Bessie Heard Foundation. Four miles south of McKinney on Texas Rt. 5.

172 species. Among these, rare, uncommon, or endangered species are Philadelphia vireo and white-faced ibis. Especially interesting for birders from the north or west: Carolina wren, boat-tailed grackle, chuck-will's-widow.

The museum exhibits stress the natural history of north-central Texas, with some art exhibits also. A 265-acre sanctuary along Wilson Creek includes bottomland and upland, woodland and prairie. The aim is to preserve the land, with its native vegetation and wildlife, in as near-natural a condition as possible. To protect the trails, their use is restricted to guided tours, which may, by prearrangement, be especially angled for birdwatchers. Museum and sanctuary closed Monday.

Checklist revised July, 1971.

LAKE MEREDITH RECREATION AREA, P.O. Box 1438, Fritch, Texas 79036. Adjoins the Alibates National Monument, set up to protect ancient Indian flint quarries.

180 species. Rare, uncommon, or endangered: golden and bald eagles, ferruginous hawk, Mississippi kite (summer), Townsend's solitaire, sandhill crane, others. Common: hawks of several kinds (including Swainson's), ducks, geese, ladder-backed woodpecker, shrikes, scaled quail, others.

Lake Meredith is the Panhandle's largest lake, created by the Sanford Dam from the steep-walled Canadian River. Arid plains contrast with cottonwood-willow greenery in the creek beds. Picnic area, boat ramp. Waterskiing, hunting, fishing. An area, Rosita, is reserved for off-trail vehicles. Precautions: at Alibates, guided tours only and no collecting. At Lake Meredith, a visitor may collect and take home only a handful of rocks—no other natural objects. Observe boating regulations. Be wary of sudden windstorms.

Checklist dated March, 1974.

MC ASHAN ARBORETUM and BOTANICAL GARDEN, Memorial Park at 4500 Woodway, Houston, Texas 77024.

Typed list of 28 winter birds. Includes the red-bellied woodpecker, Carolina chickadee, Carolina wren, orange-crowned warbler, and others.

265 acres of trees, shrubs. Trails, exhibit rooms, laboratory, library, greenhouse.

MONAHANS SANDHILLS STATE PARK, Box 1738, Monahans, Texas 79756. 915-943-2092. West of Midland and six
miles northeast of Monahans off U.S. 80 on Park Road 41.

42 species, the most common of which are Harris' hawk,
sparrow hawk, great horned owl, pyrrhuloxia, scaled quail,
roadrunner, chipping and house sparrows, and cactus wren.
Rare or endangered: sandhill crane. Locally common and particularly interesting for eastern visitors: Lawrence's goldfinch,
Bullock's oriole, white-necked raven.

3,840 acres of sand dunes up to fifty feet high, some of which
are stabilized by shinoak and other plants. Some unstabilized
dunes keep changing shape with the winds. Freshwater ponds
lie between the dunes. Picnicking, tent and trailer sites, jeep
rides, self-guiding nature trail, summer campfire programs.
The Sandhills Museum at the park features natural history,
history, and geology, with some art exhibits. Feeding and
watering stations for birds and mammals, just outside the museum's plate glass windows, allow close looks at wildlife. The
Odessa Meteor Crater is 25 miles east of the park.

Bird checklist began September, 1973. Also available: the
Monahans Sandhills State Park folder, beautifully designed
with a good map of the park and concise information.

MULESHOE AND GRULLA NATIONAL WILDLIFE REF-
UGES, P.O. Box 549, Muleshoe, Texas 79347. Twenty miles
south of Muleshoe in the Texas Panhandle. Harbors the largest
population of lesser sandhill cranes in the United States.

Rare, uncommon, or endangered (besides the sandhills):
white-faced ibis, ferruginous hawk, bald eagle, osprey, prairie
and peregrine falcons, pigeon hawk, lesser prairie chicken,
snowy and mountain plovers, burrowing owl. Common: scaled
quail, ducks (including the ruddy duck), coot, avocet, great
horned owl, western kingbird, others. The population of Canada geese has been increasing each year since 1965. Best season: winter (50,000 to 100,000 sandhill cranes present from
mid-September for several months).

5,809 acres: three lakes, marshes, short-grass plains, rimrock
and draws leading into the lakes. Five miles of tour roads.

Camping, picnicking. Regulations: no boating, hunting, or collecting. Permission required for photography blinds.

Checklist dated July, 1973. Eight more species seen since list was issued.

PADRE ISLAND NATIONAL SEASHORE, 10235 So. Padre Island Drive, Corpus Christi, Texas 78418. Reachable by causeways from Corpus Christi or Port Isabel.

363 species, of which 104 are rare, accidental, or hypothetical (meaning possibly on the island because occurring nearby). Among the species which are commonly-to-irregularly seen are the following rare, generally uncommon, or endangered: least grebe, reddish egret, Mississippi and white-tailed kites, Cooper's hawk, osprey, caracara, peregrine falcon, American merlin, sandhill crane, Baird's and buff-breasted sandpipers, Hudsonian godwit, Sandwich tern, groove-billed ani, Sprague's pipit, Philadelphia vireo, golden-winged warbler, mourning warbler. Other birds to be seen here that will be unusual sights for birdwatchers from other parts of the country: magnificent frigatebird, reddish egret, roseate spoonbill, purple gallinule, royal tern, tropical kingbird, great-tailed (boat-tailed) grackle. The Audubon's shearwater is sometimes seen in summer. This is near the limit of its range.

The National Seashore is 81 miles of this long narrow barrier reef, Padre Island. Observation tower overlooks the uncluttered beach, dunes.

Checklist dated 1974, compiled by Richard E. McCamant and Robert G. Whistler.

PALO DURO CANYON STATE PARK, Route 2, Box 114, Canyon, Texas 79015. Fifteen miles east of Canyon on Texas Rt. 217.

186 species, 37 of which nest in the canyon. Rare, uncommon, or endangered: Mississippi kite, golden and bald eagles, sandhill crane, pigeon hawk or merlin, black swift, Williamson's sapsucker, Baird's sparrow. Species that are very common: turkey vulture, bobwhite, scaled quail, common flicker,

golden-fronted woodpecker, ladder-backed woodpecker, cliff swallow, blue jay, black-crested titmouse, bushtit, Bewick's wren, cañon wren, rock wren, mockingbird, American robin, mountain bluebird, house sparrow, western meadowlark, cardinal. All seasons good for birdwatching. Winter birdwatching is a real pleasure in this wind-shielded spot.

A canyon on the eastern edge of the Texas High Plains (Llano Estacado). Includes river woodlands, grasslands, and brushlands, ponds, and wooded scarps of the canyon. 16,046 acres. Trails, riding, picnicking, camping. In the amphitheater, nightly except Sunday from mid-June to late August, the musical drama, "Texas," by Paul Green, about Texas life in the 1880's, is presented.

Checklist dated August, 1975, compiled and reviewed by Kenneth D. Seyffert of Amarillo, Charles Smith of West Texas State University, and Peggy Acord of the Panhandle Audubon Society (Amarillo).

SAN JACINTO STATE PARK, San Jacinto Battleground, Houston, Texas. Six and a half miles southeast of Houston on State Rt. 225, then four miles north on Texas 134. Next to the Houston Ship Channel.

43 species (actual park sightings). Many gulls. Among other birds: red-headed woodpecker and ground dove.

An oak wood, marshes, bays. A pool that birds appreciate is in front of the monument to the Battle of San Jacinto, 1836.

Undated checklist.

SANTA ANA NATIONAL WILDLIFE REFUGE, Route 1, Box 202A, Alamo, Texas 78516. 7.5 miles south from U.S. 83 at Alamo to US 281; then east for one-half mile.

320 species, of which 72 are rare or accidental. Common: various doves, indigo and painted buntings. Many birds and mammals native to Mexico may be seen. Rare or endangered: chachalaca, peregrine falcon, rose-throated becard, groove-billed ani, buff-bellied hummingbird, jacana. Peak flights: spring flights of up to 20,000 broad-winged hawks. Breeding

birds: least grebe, black-bellied tree duck, 72 other species. Birds considered unique to South Texas: least grebe, black-bellied tree duck, masked duck, hook-billed kite, red-billed pigeon, ruddy ground dove, white-fronted dove, green parakeet, yellow-headed ani, pauraque, green violet-eared hummingbird, green and ringed kingfishers, tropical kingbird, kiskadee flycatcher, green jay, Mexican crow, long-billed thrasher, clay-colored robin, rufous-backed robin, yellow-green vireo, Brewster's and olive-backed warblers, black-headed and Lichtenstein's oriole, white-collared seedeater, olive sparrow.

2,000 acres of subtropical woodland including ebony trees, with patches of mesquite and cactus, on the banks of the Rio Grande. Many butterflies. Precautions: spray cuffs for chiggers. Facilities: one-way 6.7-mile auto tour, foot trails, three photo blinds at various places, lunch area.

Sixty miles to the east lies another interesting National Wildlife Refuge, Laguna Atascosa, another place with very rich and varied birdlife.

Checklist dated July, 1973. Also available: map and description of Chachalaca Trail; folded map of refuge.

Bear River Migratory Bird Refuge. (*Photo courtesy of U.S. Fish and Wildlife Service.*)

UTAH

BEAR RIVER MIGRATORY BIRD REFUGE, P.O. Box 459, Brigham City, Utah 84302. Fifteen miles west of Brigham City.
222 species, of which 82 are rare or accidental. Rare or endangered: bald eagle, prairie falcon, peregrine falcon, sandhill crane, snowy plover, long-billed curlew, burrowing owl. Best season: February to June for migration and breeding. A million ducks in the fall (August to November). Peak flight: mid-October concentration of whistling swans. Breeding birds: 60 species nest—marsh birds, shore birds, 5,000 breeding pairs of avocets. Birds that are also common: bitterns, rails, gulls, grebes, short-eared owls. In summer, white pelicans.

North of Great Salt Lake, framed by Promontory Mountains and Wasatch Range. Marsh, open water, mud flats. No trees (birds nest on ground). Precaution: don't disturb birds. Facilities: 12-mile loop road. 100-foot observation tower. Controlled hunting program, fall and winter. Fishing allowed near headquarters. Rest rooms, drinking water, camping and picnic areas.

Checklist dated July, 1973. Also available: nicely printed tour guide in color and black and white, seasonal abundance diagrams of 83 species, map with other information, sheets of information on single species.

BRYCE CANYON NATIONAL PARK, Bryce Canyon, Utah 84717. 26 miles southeast of Panguitch on U.S. 89, Utah 12.
164 species, of which 53 are rare in the park. Outside of the 164, 17 species have been recorded very infrequently. Rare, uncommon, or endangered: golden eagle (a permanent resident), turkey, flammulated owl, black rosy finch, and others.

Southwestern birds to be seen frequently: Say's phoebe, canyon and rock wrens, gray vireo, black-headed grosbeak, others. The glowing Pink Cliffs and other rock formations. Two rivers, a reservoir, springs, and ponds. Visitor center has orientation shows, geologic displays. Park open all year, but in winter park road open only to Paria View. Ranger naturalist talks in summer, guided hikes, riding, bus tour of rim drive. Camping from May to October.

Checklist compiled by R. H. Gerstenberg and R. W. Russell. For other material on the park, write the Bryce Canyon Natural History Association, Bryce Canyon, Utah 84717.

CAPITOL REEF NATIONAL PARK, Torrey, Utah 84775. 76 miles southeast of Richfield on Utah 24. Part of the Waterpocket Fold, a geologic fold so called because pockets, or tanks, of water exist beside it.

"Interim Checklist" (undated) shows 140 species, which are particularly numerous in finches, grosbeaks, and warblers.

36,393 acres of interesting rock formations and archaeological ruins. A red sandstone cliff topped by white sandstone domes resembling capitol domes (hence the park's name). Green vegetation along the Fremont River. Scenic drive, slide program, guided walks in summer, campground, picnicking. Regulations: no hunting or trapping. No firearms. Backcountry camping permits needed for overnight camping trips. Do not gather or cut native wood for a fire. Pets must be leashed; not allowed more than 100 yards from roads. Do not disturb Indian artifacts. Do not collect rocks.

Besides the checklist, there is a flier about Capitol Reef.

FISH SPRINGS NATIONAL WILDLIFE REFUGE, Dugway, Utah 84022. An isolated marshy refuge on the south edge of the Great Salt Desert 78 miles northwest of Delta, Utah on a road that runs through the Drum Mountains and the Black Rock Hills or (recommended, though longer, route) from Tooele via Rt. 36 south, then west on gravel roads. Check on road conditions before driving to refuge.

166 species, 54 of which are rare on the refuge. Rare, uncommon, or endangered: white-faced ibis, hooded merganser, ferruginous hawk, golden eagle, osprey, Baird's sandpiper, Lapland longspur (rare for this latitude). Warm water from the springs encourages year-round residence of a variety of marsh birds. Common: swans, Canada goose, mallard, green-winged and cinnamon teal, pintail, widgeon, gadwall, canvasback, bufflehead, goldeneye, ruddy duck, mergansers, and many others. The greater sandhill crane nests here. Best seasons for birdwatching: late fall and early spring.

Precautions and regulations: auto touring only on gravel roads. All plants and animals are protected. No camping on refuge (there is a Bureau of Land Management campground outside the refuge). No swimming—dangerous because of deep mud and quicksand. Hunting in season.

Checklist dated April, 1968. Also available: folder about refuge.

FLAMING GORGE NATIONAL RECREATION AREA, Vernal, Utah 84078. Forty miles north of Vernal on Utah 44, 260. In Ashley National Forest.

153 species, 124 of them land birds, and 29 water or shore birds. 57 are permanent residents, 77 are summer residents, seven are winter residents, nine are migrants, and three are casual. Rare, uncommon, or endangered: hooded merganser, goshawk, golden and bald eagles (permanent residents), osprey, pigeon hawk, Baird's sandpiper, white-throated swift, Williamson's sapsucker. The bird population is strong on hawks and falcons, crows and swallows.

Visitor centers at Flaming Gorge Dam and Red Canyon (the latter on secondary road off Utah 44, west of junction with Utah 260). Fishing (all year), picnicking, boat ramps, water-skiing, campgrounds.

The checklist is based upon "Birds of Flaming Gorge Reservoir Basin," White and Behle, in *Ecological Studies of the Flora and Fauna of Flaming Gorge Reservoir Basin, Utah and Wyoming* (University of Utah Anthropological Papers, No. 48, 1960).

OURAY NATIONAL WILDLIFE REFUGE, Box 191, Vernal, Utah 84078. Via Utah 88, 30 miles south of Vernal on the Green River. A prime resting place for thousands of waterfowl in spring and fall migration.

136 species, of which 33 are rare here. Rare, uncommon, or endangered: sandhill crane, white-faced ibis, Cooper's hawk, golden and bald eagles (both common here in spring and winter), peregrine falcon. Both the eastern and the western kingbird nest here; so do three kinds of grebe, the long-billed curlew, the black-billed magpie, and others. Birds to expect to see: whistling swans, a variety of gulls and terns, great horned owls, red-tailed hawks, flickers, evening grosbeaks. Concentrations of waterfowl in October and November.

10,466 acres of open water, marshes, and fields. A belt of woodlands along the river. The road along the top of the dikes is open to visitors, except in winter.

Checklist dated April, 1968.

ZION NATIONAL PARK, Springdale, Utah 84767. The spectacular access to this park, through a tunnel, then down over switchbacks, is from Route 89 and the East Gate along the Zion-Mt. Carmel Highway.

248 species, of which 57 are casual or accidental. Rare, uncommon, or endangered: golden eagle, goshawk, ferruginous hawk, flammulated owl, others. Common: turkey vulture, scrub jay, western kingbird, dipper, yellow-breasted chat, others. Best month: May, for both birds and wildflowers. September and October are good for clear pleasant weather.

147,094 acres. A land of colorful rocks, cut by the Virgin River. Desert vegetation, low on the river banks; pine and fir on the upper reaches of the canyons. Water seeps down from the cliffs and streams over rock faces in wet seasons, making hanging gardens. Visitor center, interpretive program, scenic drive, two self-guiding nature foot-trails, other trails. Riding, lodge, cabins. Park is open all year, but accommodations only from May 15 to October 1. Precautions: check vehicle lights beforehand, for driving through tunnel. Rule: pets must be leashed.

Checklist dated February, 1975.

VERMONT

MISSISQUOI NATIONAL WILDLIFE REFUGE, RD 2, Swanton, Vermont 05488. Near the Canadian border, 40 miles north of Burlington on the Missisquoi River delta. Headquarters on Route 78, 2½ miles northwest of Swanton.

185 species recorded since 1943. Of these, 18 are rarely seen. Rare, uncommon, or endangered: red-necked grebe, bald eagle, osprey, pigeon hawk, hawk owl, yellow-throated and Philadelphia vireos. Common: black duck, wood duck, Canada goose, woodcock, common tern, pileated woodpecker, black-capped chickadee, red-winged blackbird.

4,794 acres of meadow, freshwater marsh, bog, brush, forest, and open bays on Lake Champlain. Boat ramp, nature trail. Fishing. Waterfowl hunting under special regulations.

Checklist dated August, 1971.

VIRGINIA

BACK BAY NATIONAL WILDLIFE REFUGE, Pembroke #2 Bldg., Suite 218, 287 Pembroke Office Park, Virginia Beach, Virginia 23462. 804-490-0505. 25 miles southeast of Norfolk.

257 species, of which 35 are noted as rare. 58 species breed here. Rare, uncommon, or endangered: Ipswich subspecies of Savannah sparrow (in winter), sooty shearwater, glossy ibis, black scoter, osprey (common here), black rail, and others. Common (besides those listed below): American bittern, pintail, American widgeon, semipalmated sandpiper, gulls, barn swallow, purple martin, both common crow and fish crow, yellow-rumped warbler, yellowthroat. Best season: winter. Very large populations of whistling swans, snow geese, Canada geese, and many ducks.

4,600 acres. Both fresh and brackish marshes, open water, dunes, and small woods.

Checklist dated June, 1974.

BLUE RIDGE PARKWAY, P.O. Box 1710, Roanoke, Virginia 24008. 469 miles of a scenic parkway between Shenandoah and Great Smoky Mountain National Parks.

Checklist for the Peaks of Otter (86 miles south of Waynesboro) shows 128 species. Rare, uncommon, or endangered: yellow-throated vireo, turkey, a few others, mostly represented by less than five records. Twenty-two species of warblers present in what the list defines as "summer"; six kinds of woodpeckers; nine raptors (red-tailed and sparrow hawks are present summer and winter). The screech owl, barred owl, and great horned owl are permanent residents.

View points, picnic areas, nature trails. Open all year, but best traversed in the May to October period (at other times, there may be ice and snow). Lodging (from north to south) at the Peaks of Otter, Rocky Knob Cabins, Doughton Park, and Pisgah Inn. Fishing. Precaution: this is a leisure travel road meant for low speed.

"Preliminary Checklist of Birds, Virginia Peaks of Otter Area, Blue Ridge Parkway" compiled largely by the Roanoke Valley Bird Club.

CHINCOTEAGUE NATIONAL WILDLIFE REFUGE, P.O. Box 62, Chincoteague, Virginia 23336. 703-336-6122. The southern one-third of Assateague Island which is a barrier beach, Chincoteague, is the home of the famous ponies. The annual pony penning, roundup, swim, and sale is the last week of July. Chincoteague is within the boundaries of Assateague Island National Seashore. Refuge headquarters are three miles east of Chincoteague town.

254 species, of which 33 are described as rare. Rare, uncommon, or endangered: red-necked grebe, bald eagle, osprey, black rail, and others. Common: sandpipers, plovers, curlews, turnstones, willets, yellowlegs, snowy egret, brant, laughing gull, others. Best season: April and May for shorebirds.

9,439 acres of sandy beaches, sand dunes, saltwater marshes, and pines and oaks, 13 miles long. Most acreage is in Virginia; some is in Maryland. A coastal public use area offers swimming, picnicking, surf fishing, and nature study. Only foot traffic permitted, cruises (fees), guided walks. Deer hunting in season.

Checklist dated April, 1966. Also available: map with list of services, folder about refuge, flier on greater snow geese, list of mammals, summer activities list, folder of common summer birds and one of winter birds, birdlist with silhouettes.

MACKAY ISLAND NATIONAL WILDLIFE REFUGE, Box 6128, Virginia Beach, Virginia 23456. South on Virginia State Highway 615 to the community of Knott's Island. The refuge is mostly in northeastern North Carolina, but some of it is in

Virginia. It is administered by the Back Bay National Wildlife Refuge.

134 species, eight of them described as rare. Rare, uncommon, or endangered: hooded merganser, black vulture (common here), osprey (common here), white-rumped sandpiper, others. Common: American widgeon, tree swallow, barn swallow, yellowthroat, rufous-sided towhee, others. Best season: winter. 20,000 greater snow geese winter over.

6,995 acres, only 842 of them in Virginia, the rest in North Carolina. A refuge on a peninsula; embracing several kinds of habitat, peninsulas attract many varied birds.

Preliminary checklist dated January, 1971.

PRESQUILE NATIONAL WILDLIFE REFUGE, P.O. Box 620, Hopewell, Virginia 23860. Headquarters are in Room 202, Tarton Building, Hopewell. The refuge, a man-made island in the James River, can only be reached by private boat or by refuge-operated ferry, so the refuge manager must be notified of visits in advance.

199 species, plus eight which are very rare or accidental. Rare, uncommon, or endangered: osprey (common in spring and summer), red-headed woodpecker, others. A colony of bank swallows has dug into the steep clay banks. It is the only such colony known for a radius of 100 miles. Best season: winter. Concentrations of Canada geese (sometimes over 10,000), snow geese, and ducks. Also common in winter: water pipit, turkey, pied-billed grebe, gulls, ruddy duck, others.

1,329 acres of tidal swamp, tidal marsh, and upland agricultural land. Deer hunting in season. The water around the refuge is closed to the hunting of waterfowl.

Checklist dated March, 1971.

SHENANDOAH NATIONAL PARK, Luray, Virginia 22835. A great national park, 80 miles long and very close to several big eastern centers of population. Entrances at Front Royal, Thornton Gap, Swift Run Gap, and Rockfish Gap (the latter the link with the Blue Ridge Parkway). Park headquarters is five miles east of Luray on U.S. 211.

188 species. Rare, uncommon, or endangered: upland plover, yellow-throated and Philadelphia vireos, others. The stellar part of the park birdlist is the warblers—34, including almost all of the rarest eastern species. Common or transient: several kinds of owls, several kinds of flycatchers, many others.

212,304 acres of forests, fields, streams, waterfalls, flowers, and 60 mountain peaks. The Skyline Drive is a 105-mile-long roadway along the crest of the park. The Appalachian Trail, a foot trail, follows the crest for 94 miles, with spur trails; open shelters for camping on this trail. Visitor centers (Dickey Ridge at Mile 46 and Byrd Visitor Center near Mile 51), interpretive programs, short nature trails, riding, fishing (Virginia license). Picnicking, camping, lodges (open April to October). The park is open all year. Regulations: pets must be leashed. No collecting. Stay on trails. No hunting. Speed limit: 35 MPH.

Checklist dated June, 1966, compiled by Dr. E. J. Wilhelm, Jr. Also available: folder about park. For further publications, write to the Shenandoah Natural History Association, Luray, Virginia 22835, for a list of titles.

WASHINGTON

COLUMBIA NATIONAL WILDLIFE REFUGE, Othello, Washington 99344. In southeastern Washington, north of Pasco and ten miles north and west of Othello.

197 species, 32 described as rare. Rare, uncommon, or endangered: prairie and peregrine falcons, sandhill crane, hooded merganser, ferruginous hawk, golden eagle, pectoral and Baird's sandpiper, others. Common: several kinds of ducks, including the ruddy duck; California quail, black-billed magpie, several kinds of blackbirds, vesper sparrow. Best seasons: December and January for waterfowl concentrations, May for songbirds, summer for waterfowl broods.

28,800 acres of ponds, lakes, sloughs, streams, wet meadows, marshes, and sagebrush hills. Fishing and waterfowl hunting.

Undated checklist.

MC NARY NATIONAL WILDLIFE REFUGE, P.O. Box 308, Burbank, Washington 99323. In southeastern Washington, three miles east of Burbank, six miles south of Pasco. The area is known locally as Burbank Slough.

159 species, 23 described as rare. Another 16 species are listed as accidentals. Rare, uncommon, or endangered: Wilson's phalarope (though this is common here), Ross' goose, golden eagle, merlin, sandhill crane, burrowing owl, Townsend's solitaire, others. Common: mallard, American widgeon, pintail, green-winged teal, other ducks, Canada goose, whistling swan, avocet, long-billed curlew, killdeer, long-billed dowitcher (not as common as the other birds mentioned here), redwinged and yellow-headed blackbirds, ring-necked pheasants, California quail. Best month: November—40,000 or more

ducks and geese. Also, spring for migrating ducks, and June and July for nesting activity.

3,366 acres of impoundments and croplands. Part of the refuge is Strawberry Island in the Snake River and the six Hanford Islands in the Columbia River.

Checklist dated March, 1974.

MOUNT RAINIER NATIONAL PARK, Longmire, Washington 98397. A study in glaciers and in the high-and-low altitude habitats of birds. Main entrance: Nisqually, on the southwest.

157 species. Rare, uncommon, or endangered: harlequin duck, golden and bald eagles, osprey, peregrine falcon, merlin, black-backed three-toed woodpecker, chestnut-backed chickadee, others. Common (depending on altitude): white-tailed ptarmigan, pygmy owl, Vaux's swift, violet-green swallow, gray-crowned rosy finch, others. Best season: summer.

241,983 acres. The peak of Rainier is 14,410 feet high. The valleys are filled with spruce, fir, hemlock, and red cedar. Rainier is a volcanic mountain not entirely dead—steam vents at one place—although the last great eruption was 2,000 years ago. Interpretive services. Four visitor centers: Paradise, Longmire, Sunrise, Ohanapecosh. Exhibits, guided walks, very beautiful wildflowers, hiking trail, with spur trails, around the mountain. Mountain climbing (all climbers must register), scenic drives. In winter, skiing. Hotels, campgrounds (campfire permits needed), fishing, boats (no motors). Most roads closed by snow in winter.

Preliminary checklist, dated June, 1975, compiled by Michael A. Spindler.

OLYMPIC NATIONAL PARK, 600 East Park Ave., Port Angeles, Washington 98362. A northern rain-forest park in the far northwest corner of the United States. On a major flyway, and with many kinds of birds, at various altitudes. Access by rail, bus, or automobile, 90 miles northwest of Olympia on U.S. 101.

249 species, 33 described as rare. Rare, uncommon, or en-

dangered: oystercatcher, bald eagle, pectoral sandpiper, sooty shearwater, osprey, glaucous-winged gull, black-backed woodpecker, gray-crowned rosy finch, others. Common: several kinds of cormorants, ducks, gulls, and mergansers; pigeon guillemot, several kinds of woodpeckers, violet-green swallow, chickadees, mountain bluebird, kinglets, western tanager, others.

896,599 acres. Glaciers, alpine meadows, valleys, lakes, and green and dripping forests of great trees. On the Pacific coast, miles of beaches and islands of seabirds. Pioneer Memorial Museum at Port Angeles, and two other visitor centers. A scenic mountain road, nature trails, guided nature walks, 600 miles of hiking trails, mountain climbing (climbing parties must register), campgrounds, lodges. Three Indian villages on the coast.

Undated checklist.

TURNBULL NATIONAL WILDLIFE REFUGE, Route 3, Box 385, Cheney, Washington 99004. 509-235-4723. Six miles south of Cheney on Cheney-Plaza Highway, then two miles east.

200 species, 26 described as rare. 115 birds nest on the refuge. Rare, uncommon, or endangered: red-necked grebe, peregrine falcon, merlin, osprey, turkey, and others. Common: trumpeter swan (a colony was established here in 1967), Canada goose, several kinds of ducks, ruffed grouse, California quail, coot, black tern, tree swallow, pygmy nuthatch, dark-eyed junco, and others. As many as 50,000 waterfowl to be seen during the fall.

17,200 acres. Lakes and marshes, pine, aspen, and grassland. Display pool near headquarters, hiking, picnic area, five-mile auto tour. No food sold on refuge. No camping.

Undated checklist. Also available: folder about refuge.

WILLAPA NATIONAL WILDLIFE REFUGE, Ilwaco, Washington 98624. In southwestern Washington, off Rt. 101.

256 species, of which 29 are rare (seen at intervals of two to

five years). An additional 18 accidentals have been seen. Rare or endangered: brown pelican, Aleutian Canada goose. Best season: winter, since the refuge is a wintering area for canvasbacks, black brant, Canada geese, other wildfowl. Breeding birds: great blue heron, Canada goose, bald eagle, sora, others.

Terrain and vegetation: Willapa Bay, tidal marsh and uplands, spruce-pine. Facilities: photo blinds.

No date given on checklist.

WEST VIRGINIA

HARPERS FERRY NATIONAL HISTORIC PARK, Harpers Ferry, West Virginia 25425. At the point of land reaching out into the junction of the Potomac and Shenandoah Rivers.

136 species. Rare, uncommon, or endangered: osprey, bald eagle. Common: several kinds of herons, many kinds of wood warblers, several kinds of ducks (both surface-feeding and diving), bobwhite, belted kingfisher, several kinds of woodpeckers, robins. Best season: May and June, for both warblers and flowering trees.

No picnic areas or campgrounds in the park, but some are nearby.

Undated, duplicated checklist compiled by Frank Anderson, former Superintendent, Harpers Ferry National Monument. Also available: folder about the park, shop guide to the area, folders on historic houses, folder about trail overlooking the rivers.

MONONGAHELA NATIONAL FOREST, P.O. Box 1231, Elkins, West Virginia 26241. East of Elkins on U.S. 33. A very large isolated forest in the heart of the Alleghenies, with a fabulous count of warblers.

183 species. Rare, uncommon, or endangered: the list of warblers numbers 35 and includes these rarities—golden-winged, blue-winged, Cape May, Connecticut, mourning warblers. Common: mallard, wood duck, turkey vulture, red-shouldered hawk, ruffed grouse, yellow-bellied sapsucker, whippoorwill, and others.

819,600 acres. High mountains (Spruce Knob is 4,862 feet

high). Forests of red spruce, red pine, and other trees. Swimming, fishing, boating, camping, hunting.

A checklist is now being compiled. In existence is a list of West Virginia birds compiled by Charles O. Handley, Sr., checked for birds seen in the forest, and now being reviewed by bird enthusiasts.

Green Bay Wildlife Sanctuary. (*Photo by Ty Baumann.*)

WISCONSIN

GREEN BAY WILDLIFE SANCTUARY, Sanctuary Road, Green Bay, Wisconsin 54302.

22 species. Rare, uncommon, or endangered: golden and bald eagles, hoary redpoll, yellow-throated vireo, others. Common: Canada goose, mallard, black duck, ruffed grouse, ring-necked pheasant, herring gull, downy and hairy woodpeckers, cardinal, others.

The sanctuary manager notes that donations (for feed, equipment, medicine) are always appreciated since they feed 2,000 waterfowl through the winter. The birds consume over 70 tons of feed annually.

Checklist ("Birds of Wisconsin," c/o Harold Kruse, Loganville, Wisconsin) marked for sanctuary birds.

HORICON NATIONAL WILDLIFE REFUGE, Route 2, Mayville, Wisconsin 53050. In southeastern Wisconsin: from Waupon, six and a half miles east on WIS 49 and four miles south on County Z.

198 species, plus another 41 reported but "not normally expected to be present." Rare, uncommon, or endangered: hooded merganser, Cooper's hawk, sandhill crane, Wilson's phalarope, eastern bluebird, red-headed woodpecker, yellow-throated and Philadelphia vireos, several kinds of warblers, Henslow's sparrow. Birds common here: Canada goose, tree swallow (in summer), short-billed marsh wren, redwinged blackbird, common gallinule.

21,000 acres in the northern two-thirds of the Horicon Marsh. The marsh's southern two-thirds are managed by the Wisconsin Department of Natural Resources as a public use area. The Rock River runs through the marsh. Horicon is largely cattail marsh, open shallow water, corn and alfalfa fields, brushy marsh borders, and small woodlots. Several tree-covered islands (one has a heron and egret rookery). Permits required for use of refuge roads.

Checklist dated September, 1972.

MACKENZIE ENVIRONMENTAL CENTER, Poynette, Wisconsin 53955. One and a half miles east of Poynette on County Q.

131 species seen at various times during year. Rare or endangered: sandhill crane; Iceland gull seen 1966, 1970.

Model nursery, arboretum, nature trails, fire tower, picnic ground.

Checklist: "Birds of Wisconsin," issued by Wisconsin Society for Ornithology, Supply Dept., c/o Harold Kruse, Loganville, Wisconsin. 10 for 25¢. Filled out by two Center volunteers, 1974.

NECEDAH NATIONAL WILDLIFE REFUGE, Necedah, Wisconsin 54646. West-central Wisconsin. Four miles west of Necedah; east of Tomah.

227 species, including 44 that are rare. Rare, uncommon, or endangered: turkey, sandhill crane, hooded merganser, golden and bald eagles, osprey, white-rumped and Baird's sandpipers, redheaded woodpecker, eastern bluebird, northern shrike, many kinds of warblers, Henslow's sparrow. Birds common here: ruffed grouse, sharp-tailed grouse, rose-breasted grosbeak, blue-winged teal. A small breeding flock of Canada geese was established by introducing captive geese in 1939. The original flock is gone, but their descendants return every spring. Best seasons for waterfowl migrations: late April and mid-October (several thousand Canada geese and snow geese).

40,000 acres with many ponds and marshy areas separated by sandy ridges and islands. Man-made impoundments. Jack pine and scrub oak on the uplands and scrub willow in the lowlands. Fishing, boating (no motors), deer hunting.

Checklist dated January, 1975.

WYOMING

GRAND TETON NATIONAL PARK, Moose, Wyoming 83012. Reachable by air from Denver or Salt Lake City; by road south from Yellowstone or north through Jackson on routes 26, 89, or 187.

219 species, of which 77 are rare or accidental. Rare or endangered: goshawk, osprey, blue grouse, northern three-toed woodpecker (rarely seen here), trumpeter swan, others. Best seasons: spring and summer. The canyons are ideal places to watch the violet-green swallow; perch on a hillside to catch its iridescent flashes.

310,358 acres of mountains, glaciers, meadows, forests, lakes and the banks of the Snake River. Precautions: register long hikes with rangers, stay on trails. Facilities: picnic areas; on Jackson Lake, campgrounds, a swimming beach, marinas; mountaineering instruction, fishing (state license), horseback riding, float trips (see a bald eagle's nest on the banks of the Snake River), lodges.

Checklist dated 1973. Includes mammals. Also available: large foldout map of Grand Teton National Park on one side, Yellowstone National Park on the other, list of publications of Grand Teton Natural History Association.

NATIONAL ELK REFUGE, P.O. Box C, Jackson, Wyoming 83001. 307-733-2627. Just south of Grand Teton National Park, on the east edge of Jackson. Trumpeter swans nest on marsh areas near refuge headquarters.

145 species plus 28 accidental species. 46 species nest on the refuge. Rare, uncommon, or endangered: golden and bald eagles, sandhill crane, others. Common: mallard, pintail, gad-

Tetons seen from Snake River. (*Photo by Emily Jones.*)

wall, green-winged and cinnamon teal, Barrow's goldeneye, bufflehead, magpie, raven, Brewer's blackbird, mountain bluebird, vesper sparrow, and others.

23,754 acres on the flat valley land just east of the Grand Teton. The Gros Ventre River borders the refuge for nine miles on the northwest. Cottonwood, aspen, spruce. Grass-and-sagebrush-covered foothills.

Checklist dated July, 1971.

YELLOWSTONE NATIONAL PARK, P.O. Box 168, Yellowstone National Park, Wyoming 82190. Known for bears and geysers, but good for birds, too. North entrance, on U.S. 89, is nearest park headquarters. Entrances also on west, south, east, and northeast.

Rare, uncommon, or endangered: trumpeter swan, osprey, bald eagle, sandhill crane, others. Common: blue grouse, California gull, great horned owl, cliff swallow, gray jay, black-billed magpie, mountain chickadee, others. Seasons: Summer is best, though the northern part of the park is open to cars all year.

Immense: 2,250,000 acres of the world's largest collection of geysers and hot springs. Yellowstone Lake, a Grand Canyon, waterfalls, great fields of grazing elk and buffalo. Several visitors' centers, self-guiding nature walks (can be slippery—don't fall into pools), camping, lodges, trails, scenic drives. Fishing. Riding. Rules: do not approach or feed bears or any other animals. No collecting. Park season is May 1 to October 1.

Checklist compiled by Richard F. Follett, 1972.

The eastern end of the Virgin Islands National Park. (*Photo courtesy of National Park Service.*)

VIRGIN ISLANDS

VIRGIN ISLANDS NATIONAL PARK, Box 806, Charlotte Amalie, St. Thomas, Virgin Islands 00881. Nearly two-thirds of the island of St. John and most of the offshore waters that gleam with colorful fish make up the only United States National Park in the West Indies. Accessible by air or ship to St. Thomas. Package jeep tours or scenic boat tours can be privately arranged in St. Thomas.

65 species, mostly exotic and colorful, among which a first time visitor from the north will be particularly struck with the banana-quit (common), white-tailed tropic bird, magnificent frigatebird, mangrove cuckoo, smooth-billed ani, Antillean crested hummer, and many others.

15,150 acres of mountains and beaches, surrounded by a world of waters. Cruz Bay Visitor Center. Taxis for tours may be hired at Cruz Bay. You-drive-it vehicles require temporary Virgin Islands license. Drive slowly. The one park where hikes can be on land or underwater. Snorkel and scuba equipment can be rented. Petroglyphs. Fishing, snorkeling, camping, cottages. No backcountry camping. Rules: don't swim alone or in heavy surf. Pets must be leashed. Spearfishing and waterskiing prohibited. No collecting. Bring insect repellent and suntan lotion. Warning: do not eat strange wild fruits—they may be poisonous. Climate is mildly tropical and pleasantly breezy.

Undated checklist. Also available: folder about park, trail guide for safe hiking. For *Birds of the Virgin Islands* by Dea Murray ($3.95), write Eastern National Parks and Monuments Association, Virgin Islands Agency, c/o Virgin Islands National Park.

CANADA—EAST

New Brunswick

FUNDY NATIONAL PARK, Alma, New Brunswick EOA 1BO. 506-887-2000. Eight miles of the park are on the Bay of Fundy, the place of the famous high tides. Between St. John and Moncton. Headquarters on Highway 114 at the mouth of the Upper Salmon River, a mile south of Alma.

Rare, uncommon (here), or endangered: Barrow's golden-eye, common eider, common scoter, hooded merganser, goshawk, bald eagle, osprey, glaucous and Iceland gulls, black-backed three-toed woodpecker.

Sandstone cliffs along the shore. Forests inland. Nature trails, tent-trailer campground, other campgrounds, lodge, golf, tennis, bowling green, heated saltwater swimming pool. Park is open all year; most services available from late May to mid-September. The Bay of Fundy may be crossed by ferryboat.

Checklist dated 1973, in French and English. Does not state how abundant any of the species are.

KOUCHIBOUGUAC NATIONAL PARK, Kouchibouguac, Kent County, New Brunswick EOA 2AO. 506-876-3973. A new park. Take Highway 11 southeast from Chatham, turn east on 117.

116 species in spring, of which 11 are abundant, 18 rare. Rare or endangered: osprey. Breeding birds: 87 species. Common birds characteristic of this area: double-crested cormorant (spring), common golden-eye, blue-winged teal, common and

red-breasted mergansers, black duck, sanderling and dowitcher
(both in fall), ruffed grouse (spring), American woodcock
(spring and summer), common flicker, yellow-bellied sapsucker, yellow and palm warblers, other warblers, many other
species.

Beaches, sandbars (15½ miles of off-shore sandbars), tidal
lagoons, forests, marshes, peat bogs. Tamarack dominant. Facilities: information exhibit center, campground, picnic area,
canoeing, supervised swimming, fishing.

Checklist just published, 1975, in French and English. Indicates habitat as well as frequency of sighting, and is the result
of a survey by Eric Tull, 1973-1974. Also available: bilingual
folder including map of park.

Newfoundland

TERRA-NOVA NATIONAL PARK, Glovertown, Newfoundland AOG 2LO. 709-533-2291. The Trans-Canada Highway
(Rt. 1) cuts through this park, which is on Newman Sound, 35
miles south of Gander. Headquarters on the Trans-Canada,
midway between park boundaries. This is a place to see Arctic
birds, along with temperate-climate birds.

109 species in all in the park, of which eight are of occasional or casual occurrence. Rare northern birds here: Arctic
tern, dovekie (common in winter), snowy owl, snow bunting,
common eider, willow ptarmigan, Iceland gull. Nesting birds:
great black-backed gull, common tern, belted kingfisher, flicker,
downy woodpecker, Canada jay, raven, crow, black-capped
and boreal chickadees, robin, hermit and Swainson's thrushes,
ruby-crowned kinglet, black-throated green warbler, yellowthroat, pine grosbeak, red crossbill, white-winged crossbill,
slate-colored junco, white-throated and fox sparrows.

A beautiful wild fjord coastline. Icebergs may come sailing
by; pilot whales have been sighted. There is a northern forest

inland. Campground. Bungalow accommodations open May 1 to October 31. Nature trails.

Bilingual temporary checklist reflecting ongoing research, dated September, 1971.

Nova Scotia

CAPE BRETON HIGHLANDS NATIONAL PARK, Ingonish Beach, Nova Scotia BOC 1LO. Telephone: Ingonish 31. On the north end of Cape Breton Island. Three miles north of Cheticamp on the Cabot Trail, a highway.

181 species seen in the park, plus, separately listed, 23 species sighted near its boundaries. Rare, uncommon, or endangered: Barrow's goldeneye, harlequin duck, common eider, hooded merganser, goshawk, golden and bald eagles, osprey, merlin or pigeon hawk, white-rumped sandpiper, glaucous and Iceland gulls, Arctic tern, dovekie, pileated and black-backed three-toed woodpeckers, Cape May and mourning warblers.

367 square miles. Mountains, valleys, rocky cliffs. Hiking trails, swimming at Ingonish Beach and at freshwater lakes, bungalows available at Ingonish Beach in summer.

Undated checklist.

KEJIMKUJIK NATIONAL PARK, Box 36, Maitland Bridge, Anna. Co., Nova Scotia BOT 1NO. One of Canada's newest national parks. Access via Highway 8.

155 species, including 20 of hypothetical status. 60 species breed here. Rare, uncommon, or endangered: goshawk, osprey, bald eagle, pileated woodpecker, others. Common: ruffed grouse, barred owl, common nighthawk, common flicker, American redstart, palm warbler, others.

Miles of forests, lakes, islands. At Merrymakedge Beach: swimming, boating, fishing, hiking, naturalist programs. Campgrounds in preparation. Two wilderness canoe trails. Pictographs of battle scenes drawn by the Micmac Indians who once occupied this land. In winter: cross-country skiing, snowmobiling, snowshoeing.

Preliminary checklist of bird status based mostly upon summer distribution. Bilingual checklist is now being printed.

Ontario

GEORGIAN BAY ISLANDS NATIONAL PARK, Box 28, Honey Harbour, Ontario POE IEO. 705-756-2415. Access by water taxi or private boat from Midland, Honey Harbour (the best access: reach it on Highway 501), Penetanguishene, or Tobermory (for Flowerpot Island). Administration building on the mainland at Honey Harbour. The park is open year-round unless ice on the bay prevents this. The largest campground, on Beausoleil, is open from approximately May 15 to September 15.

259 species, of which 84 are rare visitors. Rare, uncommon, or endangered: hooded merganser, goshawk, Cooper's hawk, bald eagle, osprey, hawk owl, pileated woodpecker, eastern bluebird, Philadelphia vireo, Cape May warbler, snow bunting. Woodcocks, winter wrens, orioles, swallows, and downy woodpeckers nest on Flowerpot Island.

Five and a half square miles of recreational and camping areas. 50 islands scattered along 40 miles of Georgian Bay. Glaciated rock-weathered pine, and maple-beech-oak woods. Unusual geologic formations and caves on Flowerpot Island. Campgrounds on Beausoleil Island (docks, pumps for water, nature trails there), picnic areas. No food provided on islands —bring your own. Fishing (Ontario license). Precautions: observe boating regulations. On Beausoleil, be wary of Massauga rattlesnake, which is timid and tries to avoid people.

Stay away from it. Do not kill it—it's an endangered species. Leave all wildlife, including plants, undisturbed.

Undated bilingual checklist. Also available: folder on park, "Interpretive Program" folder, "Flowerpot Island" folder.

POINT PELEE NATIONAL PARK, RR #1, Leamington, Ontario N8H 3V4. Thirty miles southeast of Windsor, on Rt. 3. One of the finest bird-watching sites in North America. At the southernmost point in Canada, a latitude that, farther west, borders northern California. Two major bird migration flyways overlap at Point Pelee. The park dips into Lake Erie.

336 species and two hybrids. Over 250 species use Pelee as an important migratory stopover. Some 90 birds nest in the park. Among the birds common here: horned grebe, great blue heron, black-crowned night heron, blue-winged teal, greater scaup, red-breasted merganser, ring-necked pheasant, American coot, American woodcock, ring-billed gull, downy woodpecker, eastern wood pewee, purple martin, black-capped chickadee, long-billed marsh wren, gray catbird, cedar waxwing, red-eyed vireo, Cape May warbler (very rare in most refuges), northern oriole, cardinal, indigo bunting, rufous-sided towhee, swamp sparrow. The extremely rare Kirtland's warbler has been seen here, but not every year. Spring migration peaks in mid-May, but birding is good year-round.

The park covers a little less than ten square miles. Freshwater marshes, sand beaches on Lake Erie. Interpretive programs, boardwalk trail over the marsh, twenty-foot observation tower, other hiking trails. Fishing (in park waters without permit; Ontario permit required for Lake Erie fishing). Camping only in organized groups and by special arrangement. Curtailed vehicular traffic south of the Interpretive Centre in the summer—a free tramway is substituted. Do not disturb wildlife. Park is open year-round, but some of the visitor services only operate in the summer.

Bilingual checklist dated January, 1975. (Park birding records reach back to 1877.) Also available: folder about park, with map.

QUETICO PROVINCIAL PARK, Atikokan, Ontario POT 1CO. On the United States-Canadian border, 40 miles west of Thunder Bay. Canadian entrance to the park is at Dawson Trail Campgrounds, 29 miles east of Atikokan on Highway 17. U.S. entrance from Ely or Grand Marais, Minnesota.

190 species, among which, notably, are two endangered species that nest in the park, bald eagle and osprey. Common: raven, gray jay, black-backed three-toed woodpecker, boreal chickadee, great gray owl, spruce grouse, and many kinds of warblers, among them the Nashville, magnolia, and mourning. In the non-coniferous stands of aspen, birch, maple, or elm: black-billed cuckoo and scarlet tanager. In spring and fall: dunlin, sandhill crane, clay-colored sparrow, northern phalarope.

1750 miles of lake-studded wilderness. Bare bedrock, expanses of berry bushes, largely coniferous forests of jack pine and black spruce. No roads. Campgrounds at Dawson Trail. Great canoeing country. Precaution: bring insect repellent.

Checklist compiled by D. J. Haddow, 1972; revised December, 1973.

ROYAL BOTANICAL GARDENS, Box 399, Hamilton, Ontario L8N 3H8. This is the famous Hendrie Valley Sanctuary, off Highway 6 at Snake Road in Western Hamilton.

Common: common crow, ring-billed gull, black-capped chickadee, robin, cardinal, belted kingfisher, common merganser, red-tailed hawk, great blue heron, rose-breasted grosbeak, Philadelphia vireo, many kinds of swallows, ovenbird. A wealth of warblers: yellow, black-throated green, magnolia, Blackburnian, Cape May, and others. Late May is the perfect time for these gardens.

A rock garden, a teahouse, a Spring Garden (a sight to see in May and June), a Children's Garden, formal sunken gardens, and Coote's Paradise, a natural marsh and game preserve.

No checklist, but an interpretive leaflet and walking guide by Dr. James Pringle, dated 1975.

ST. LAWRENCE ISLANDS NATIONAL PARK, Box 469, RR #3, Mallorytown, Ontario KOE 1R9. 613-923-5241. Seventeen islands and 80 rocky islets of the Thousand Islands in the St. Lawrence River between Kingston and Brockville. Southwest of Brockville along Highway 401. The islands can be reached by water taxi.

303 species, of which 46 are hypothetical (identified by only one observer), accidental, or now extinct (the passenger pigeon—bird records around Kingston have been kept for many years). 129 birds nest in the islands, among these: green heron, sora, Caspian tern, several kinds of owls, five kinds of swallows, eastern bluebird, scarlet tanager, many others. Rare, uncommon, or endangered: bald eagle, osprey, peregrine falcon, merlin, turkey, white-rumped and Baird's sandpipers, glaucous and Iceland gulls, blue-winged warblers, others.

Part of the park is on the mainland; has a good beach. The islands are accessible by boat only. Camping (permit required), picnic areas, boat ramp and dock at Mallorytown. All the islands have docks, campsites, and wells for water. Precaution: river water should be boiled before drinking.

The park does not have a checklist of birds, though they do for mammals, fish, and reptiles and amphibians. They maintain an observation file of all flora and fauna. For birds, they use the 1973 bird checklist (covering most of the park area) prepared by the Kingston Field Naturalists, P.O. Box 831, Kingston, Ontario.

WASAGA BEACH PROVINCIAL PARK, Wasaga Beach, Ontario on Route 92, northeast of Stayner.

116 species, of which 55 are marked "occasional" on the checklist. Rare, uncommon, or endangered: osprey, mourning warbler. Among birds easily seen here: brant, sparrow hawk, ruffed grouse, Virginia rail, screech owl, Traill's flycatcher, several kinds of swallows, catbird, Blackburnian warbler, northern oriole, song sparrow, others.

South shore of Georgian Bay. Naturalist services, campgrounds.

Undated checklist.

WYE MARSH WILDLIFE CENTRE, Box 100, Midland, Ontario L4R 4K6. Reachable from Midland, Ontario. Headquarters are in Midland.

180 species. Species that are abundant here: black duck, horned lark, tree and bank swallows, starling, yellow warbler, myrtle warbler, chestnut-sided warbler, yellowthroat, American redstart, grackle, brown-headed cowbird, American goldfinch, slate-colored junco, swamp and song sparrows. Rare, uncommon, or endangered: hooded merganser, goshawk, pileated woodpecker.

The wildlife management area is around Wye Lake, near Georgian Bay.

1972 checklist now being revised, to be ready in spring, 1976.

Prince Edward Island

PRINCE EDWARD ISLAND NATIONAL PARK, P.O. Box 487, Charlottetown, Prince Edward Island, C1A 7L1. 902-672-2211. Reachable from Charlottetown airport, or car ferry from Caribou, Nova Scotia; or car, bus, and train via ferry from Cape Tormentine, New Brunswick.

In Prince Edward Island as a whole, 262 species, of which 31 are very common, 24 rare (1 to 5 birds seen per season). Rare or endangered: bald eagle, osprey, peregrine falcon, boreal owl. Best season: late July to early autumn. Park open through year; full facilities May to October. Breeding birds: great blue heron, bald eagle, 108 others in the island as a whole.

Woodland, marsh, 25 miles of beach, high cliffs, ponds. Precautions: no picking or collecting, no feeding or molesting wild animals, dogs must be leashed. Interpretive nature program, supervised swimming (fairly warm water, because the Gulf Stream is perceptible here), canteens, toilets, cabins, boating (no motorboats on fresh water in park), fishing by permit, tent and trailer camping, tennis, golf, lawn bowling, riding.

Checklist for park now being revised and translated to make it bilingual. Checklist, dated 1974, available for Prince Edward Island as a whole. Write: Dept. of the Environment and Tourism, P.O. Box 2000, Charlottetown, P.E.I., Canada C1A 7N8. Also available from park: printed folder about the park with map showing roads, trails, ferry access, etc.

Québec

FORILLON NATIONAL PARK, P.O. Box 1220, Gaspé, Province of Québec, GOC 1RO. 418-368-5505. On the tip of the Forillon Peninsula, which juts off the end of the Gaspé Peninsula into the Gulf of St. Lawrence. Park is on Highway 6, at outer end of the peninsula. Park headquarters in Gaspé.

The outstanding bird feature of this seacoast park is the more than 300 nests of the double-crested cormorant on the cliffs of the Forillon Peninsula. Also nesting here: blue-winged teal, common goldeneye, rough-legged hawk, ruffed grouse, American woodcock, common snipe, spotted sandpiper, great black-backed and herring gulls, black-legged kittiwake, razor-bill, black guillemot, chimney swift, ruby-throated humming-bird, yellow-bellied sapsucker, swallows, red-breasted nuthatch, hermit and gray-cheeked thrushes, kinglets, several warblers, redwinged blackbird, several sparrows, slate-colored junco. Rare, uncommon, or endangered: Leach's petrel (one observation), Barrow's goldeneye, harlequin duck, common eider, hooded merganser, goshawk, Cooper's hawk, golden and bald eagles, osprey, gyrfalcon, peregrine falcon (all seasons), pigeon hawk, Hudsonian godwit, glaucous and Iceland gulls (fall and winter), dovekie, hawk-owl, black-backed three-toed wood-pecker, Cape May warbler, hoary redpoll (rare here), snow bunting.

92 square miles, featuring bird cliffs. Interpretive program, nature trails, campgrounds (some for tent-trailer), picnic areas.

Bilingual checklist dated 1974 (still in process when seen).

LA MAURICIE NATIONAL PARK, P.O. Box 758, Shawinigan, Province of Québec G9N 6V9. 819-536-2638. A new park in the Laurentians. Sixty miles north of Trois Rivières on Highway 19, about halfway between Québec City and Montreal.

Incomplete undated checklist, in French, shows a wealth of water birds, hawks, woodpeckers, and swallows, though not indicating frequency of any species' occurrence. Among rare or endangered species listed: goshawk, bald eagle, osprey (mainly in spring), peregrine falcon, snowy owl, pileated and black-backed three-toed woodpeckers. The common loon, common merganser, and black duck nest in the park. In winter, there are flocks of evening- and pine-grosbeaks.

210 heavily wooded square miles. A transition zone between boreal coniferous forest and deciduous forest. Rounded glacial features. More than 60 lakes. Many streams and rivers. In May and June, a wide range of lovely wildflowers. Small bogs harbor carnivorous plants. Park interpretive program, nature trail, campgrounds (tent-trailer), picnic areas, canoeing. In winter snowshoeing and cross-country skiing south of Lake Wapizagonke. Fishing (permit required). Regulations: visitors wishing to enter the park by boat or seaplane must first obtain the superintendent's permission. Dogs must be leashed. Wildlife—plants, animals, etc.—must not be disturbed. Extreme care must be used with fires.

Besides checklist, an excellent folder about the park is available.

PARC DES LAURENTIDES (Laurentides Provincial Park), Stoneham, Québec, Canada. Highways 54 and 54A run between Alma and Chicoutimi on the north and Québec City on the south through this enormous wilderness park.

45 species in 1975. Rare, uncommon, or endangered: osprey. Among other birds mentioned (the checklist of birds observed in 1975 does not indicate how common each species is): tree, barn, bank, and cliff swallows, common loon, both the black-capped and the boreal chickadee, saw-whet owl.

4,000 square miles of wilderness, boasting high mountains

and more than 1500 lakes. Three camping areas: Kiskissink, Stoneham, and St. Urbain. A guide is necessary for hikers in the more remote parts of the park. Moose and bears may be seen.

Checklist of birds observed in 1975.

CANADA—CENTRAL AND WEST

Alberta

BANFF NATIONAL PARK, Banff, Alberta TOL OCO. 403-762-3324. Canada's oldest national park. On the east slope of the Rockies, 81 miles west of Calgary. On the Trans-Canada Highway. Also accessible by rail.

224 species, of which 82 are rare or hypothetical. Rare, uncommon, or endangered: trumpeter swan (rare migrant here), harlequin duck, goshawk, golden and bald eagles, osprey, gyrfalcon (in winter), pileated and black-backed three-toed woodpeckers, hoary redpoll. Nesting birds: water ouzel (dipper), evening grosbeak, gray-crowned rosy finch, white-winged and red crossbills, Brewer's and white-crowned sparrows, golden-crowned kinglet, red-breasted nuthatch, three kinds of chickadees, gray (Canada) jay, several kinds of woodpeckers, others. April and May waterfowl migration is heavy. Good place to see this: Vermilion Lake.

2,564 square miles. Ice-capped peaks, deep valleys, glaciers, waterfalls, and lakes (especially Lake Louise). Mineral hot springs. Park museum, interpretive program, conducted hikes, nature walks, many accommodations, campgrounds, picnic areas. Canoeing, rowing (motors not permitted), riding, skiing. Sky lifts to the tops of some mountains. Cruise available on Lake Minnewanks.

Bilingual checklist dated 1973.

JASPER NATIONAL PARK, Jasper, Alberta TOE 1EO. 403-852-4401. One of the largest parks in North America. On east slope of Rockies, 235 miles west of Edmonton. On Highways 16 and 93. Can also be reached by rail.

Birdlist (218 species) is very similar to that of Banff National Park, except that Jasper has more of the far-northern species (the Arctic loon, common scoter, willow ptarmigan, wandering tattler, mew gull) and Banff has more of the temperate species.

4,200 square miles of ice-capped mountains, great valleys, icefields, lakes. Mineral hot springs, with swimming pool. Interpretive program, self-guided or conducted hikes, many accommodations, campgrounds. Fishing (national park permit), boating, golf, tennis, sky tram to top of Whistler Mountain, hiking (more than 400 miles of trails), riding, outdoor heated pool. Cruises on Maligne Lake (motors are allowed on Pyramid, Medicine, and Maligne Lakes). In winter, skiing, tobogganing, curling, hockey, skating. Ski-tourers must register with park warden. Snow vehicles on designated trails only. Do not feed or molest any wildlife.

Bilingual checklist dated 1973. Also available: bilingual folder about park, with map.

WATERTON LAKES NATIONAL PARK, Waterton Park, Alberta TOK 2MO. 403-859-2262. The Canadian section of Waterton-Glacier International Peace Park. Routes 5 or 6 lead into the park.

239 species, of which 51 are hypothetical or infrequently seen. Rare, uncommon, or endangered: harlequin duck, golden and bald eagles (breed here), osprey (also breeds here), whooping crane (migrant), Brewer's (timberline) sparrow (breeds here), others. Breeding birds: pied-billed grebe, Barrow's goldeneye, hooded and common mergansers, grouse, white-tailed ptarmigan, Wilson's phalarope, great horned owl, calliope hummingbird, several kinds of woodpeckers, black-billed magpie, dipper (water ouzel), mountain bluebird, bobolink, western tanager, others. The checklist very helpfully suggests specific, varied regions of the park where birding is good.

203 square miles. Timberline is at 7,000 feet. Park center is around Waterton Lake. A 2½-hour cruise is available on the

lake. This is a mountain park with many lakes and splendid views. From the east, the Rockies rise spectacularly from the flat prairie. More than 110 miles of foot trails, fishing (National Parks permit), riding, canoeing, rowing (motorboats allowed on Waterton Lake), interpretive program, hotels, motels, chalets, campgrounds (tent-trailer). Precaution: overnight hikers, climbers, and anyone traveling off established trails must register in and out with a park warden. Park is open year-round, but most visitor facilities are only open in summer.

Checklist dated 1974. Also available: folder about park, with map.

British Columbia

KOOTENAY NATIONAL PARK, P.O. Box 220, Radium Hot Springs, British Columbia VOA 1MO. 604-347-9615. Southeastern British Columbia on west slope of Rockies. 65 miles of the Banff-Windermere Highway run through this long narrow park. Eastern entrance through Castle Mountain in Banff National Park on Highway 93. Western entrance at Radium Hot Springs. Just north of Kootenay is Yoho National Park. Daily bus service from the west (Golden or Cranbrook) to Radium Hot Springs. Landing strip for light aircraft at Radium Hot Springs.

152 species, 60 of which are rare or accidental. Rare, uncommon, or endangered: harlequin duck, goshawk, golden and bald eagles, osprey, Baird's sandpiper, hawk owl. Abundant birds: in the Douglas fir, pine siskin and Audubon's warbler; in the Engelmann's spruce forest, northern three-toed woodpecker, olive-sided flycatcher, Canada jay, red-breasted nuthatch, olive-backed thrush, and evening grosbeak.

A park of very varied elevations, producing contrasting vegetation and supporting a variety of wild creatures. 543 square miles. Broad valleys, high glaciers, deep canyons, mineral hot springs, alpine lakes. Near the hot springs, Indian pictographs.

Hiking, self-guided walks, hotel and cabin accommodations, campgrounds, picnic areas. Fishing. No boats, canoes, rafts, or floats are permitted on the lakes. Permission is required for boating on the Kootenay River. Off-trail hikers and climbers must register with the park warden. All wildlife must be left undisturbed. The park is open all year, but most tourist services are only available from May to September.

Bilingual checklist, dated 1974. Also available: folder about park, with map; bilingual folder about Radium Hot Springs trail; bilingual folder, "Fireweed Trail," about a big fire in the Kootenay in 1968, and the burned area's regeneration.

MANNING PROVINCIAL PARK, c/o Provincial Parks Branch, Dept. of Recreation and Conservation, Parliament Buildings, Victoria, British Columbia V8W 2Y9. Park is on Highway 3 between Hope and Princeton, on the State of Washington border.

173 species, 50 rare in the park. Rare, uncommon, or endangered: red-necked grebe, pileated woodpecker, harlequin duck, others. Common: Clark's nutcracker, dipper, common loon, red crossbill, others.

179,000 acres of mountains and alpine meadows. Nature House (exhibits of plants, wildlife, and history), guided nature walks, four campgrounds.

Checklist, revised by K. R. Beckett, 1969.

MOUNT REVELSTOKE AND GLACIER NATIONAL PARKS, P.O. Box 350, Revelstoke, British Columbia V0E 2S0. 604-837-5155. Glacier National Park, a very mountainous park with miles of hiking trails, is 29 miles east of Revelstoke, accessible, as is Revelstoke, via the Rogers Pass section of the Trans-Canada Highway.

185 species, of which 29 are occasional or casual. Rare, uncommon, or endangered: harlequin duck, hooded merganser, golden eagle, and osprey. Common: Clark's nutcracker, eastern kingbird, black-capped chickadee, red-breasted nuthatch, varied thrush, cedar waxwing, yellow, Audubon's and

MacGillivray's warblers, American redstart, lazuli bunting, evening grosbeak, and several kinds of sparrows. The checklist suggests the Beaver River marsh in Glacier Park, the marshes along Silver Creek and the Illecillewaet River in Mount Revelstoke Park, and some burned-over areas in Revelstoke, as producing a variety of birds.

Revelstoke is a mountaintop plateau, with a nine-mile summit trail that has awesome views. In the winter (November through March), Revelstoke is a ski-jumping center. Campgrounds at Revelstoke; campgrounds and motor hotel, open in summer, at Glacier. Precaution: register climbs and overnight hikes with the wardens.

Preliminary undated checklist.

PACIFIC RIM NATIONAL PARK, P.O. Box 280, Ucluelet, British Columbia VOR 3AO. 604-726-7721. A new park on the western coast of Vancouver Island. Take Highway 4 west from Parksville through Port Alberni to the park.

238 species, of which 67 are very rare, casual, or accidental. Rare, uncommon, or endangered: yellow-billed loon, several kinds of shearwater, trumpeter swan, harlequin duck, goshawk, ancient murrelet, tufted puffin, northern shrike (common here), others. Among birds common in the park: common loon, Brandt's cormorant, bald eagle, surfbird (a Pacific Coast specialty), glaucous-winged gull, marbled murrelet, rufous hummingbird, western flycatcher, Townsend's and Wilson's warbler, American goldfinch.

150 square miles of coast and rain forest (primarily Sitka spruce and western red cedar). Sandy beaches, many islands, lakes, and bogs. The coast is a good place to observe sea lions. Swimming, fishing, surfing. Campgrounds.

Preliminary bilingual checklist.

WELLS GRAY PROVINCIAL PARK, Box 297, Clearwater, British Columbia VOE 1NO. Access from Highway 5 at Clearwater Station or from Mahood Falls. Park headquarters is near

Dawson Falls, Wells Gray Park. (*British Columbia Government photograph.*)

Clearwater. Wells Gray gets birds from both eastern and western North America, which makes for interesting birding.

88 species. Rare, uncommon, or endangered: osprey, white-winged crossbill, others. Common: greater yellowlegs, Barrow's goldeneye, Canada goose, white-tailed ptarmigan, golden-crowned and savannah sparrows, sparrow hawk, saw-whet owl, redstart, veery, others.

More than 1,300,000 acres of primitive wilderness, alpine meadows, and lower-altitude forests in the Cariboo and Columbia Mountains, including the Clearwater River watershed. Beautiful waterfalls. To the north, there are unnamed and unclimbed peaks and glaciers. Mineral springs. Campgrounds, lodge. Bring in all supplies needed—no stores here. Careful with fire. Don't litter. Pets must be leashed. No vehicles on trails.

Birdlist is "The Birds of Wells Gray Park, British Columbia; an Annotated List" by R. Y. Edwards and R. W. Ritcey (British Columbia Dept. of Recreation and Conservation, 1967).

YOHO NATIONAL PARK, Field, British Columbia VOA 1GO. 604-343-6324. In eastern British Columbia on the west slope of the Rockies. The Trans-Canada Highway crosses Yoho. The park is also accessible by rail.

140 species. There is very little difference between this list and Kootenay's to the south, except that the Yoho observers have spotted the whistling swan, surf scoter, sparrow hawk, sharp-tailed grouse, three owls, and Brewer's sparrow.

Yoho is Indian for "Wow!," a good word to apply to these 507 square miles of lofty peaks, magnificent waterfalls, and beautiful lakes. More than 250 miles of hiking trails. Lodges (some open all year), campgrounds.

Bilingual checklist dated 1974.

Manitoba

RIDING MOUNTAIN NATIONAL PARK, Wasagaming, Manitoba ROJ 2HO. 204-848-2811. In southwestern Manitoba, west of Lake Manitoba. Take Highway 10 for 70 miles north from Brandon.

233 species, of which 35 are rare or very rare. Among the species commonly seen: American bittern, blue-winged teal, red-tailed hawk, sora, common snipe, Franklin's and ring-billed gulls, Philadelphia vireo (this is the region of greatest abundance for this bird, which is ordinarily rarely seen), great horned owl, Tennessee and mourning warblers, others. Rare, uncommon, or endangered: black scoter (known as the common scoter, but is not common), gray partridge, golden and bald eagles, sandhill crane, parasitic jaeger, pileated and black-backed three-toed woodpeckers, others. Best season: summer.

1,149 square miles. A high-elevation sanctuary—about 2,500 feet in altitude. Forests of both northern and eastern types, and western grassland. Interpretive center and program. Nature walks and naturalist-led car caravans. Boating, fishing, golf, tennis, lawn bowling, riding, sailing, swimming. Skiing in winter. Hotel and cabin accommodations, campgrounds.

Checklist dated September, 1973.

TURTLE MOUNTAIN PROVINCIAL PARK, Box 820, Boissevain, Manitoba ROK OEO. A relatively new park, which holds the International Peace Garden on the Manitoba-North Dakota border. The park is on Highway 10.

More than 100 species. Rare, uncommon, or endangered: Connecticut warbler, pileated woodpecker. Common: mallard, wood duck, common nighthawk, belted kingfisher, others.

47,000 acres of hills, woods, and valleys. 29 lakes. Fishing, camping.

No checklist available. The park uses the 1974 interim checklist of Spruce Woods Provincial Park, 50 miles northwest of Turtle Mountain and 35 miles west of Austin.

Northwest Territories

WOOD BUFFALO NATIONAL PARK, P.O. Box 750, Fort Smith, Northwest Territories XOE OPO. 403-872-2349. The whooping crane was found to be breeding in this park, the largest and the farthest north of the Canadian national parks. Reachable via the Mackenzie Highway to Hay River and Highway 5 to Fort Smith. Fort Smith is approximately 850 road miles from Edmonton, the last 480 miles of the way on gravel roads. There are daily flights by Pacific Western Airlines from Edmonton and Yellowknife to Fort Smith. Main park roads are open through the year, but in the spring or after rains they may be soft in places.

To protect the whooping crane nesting grounds, there is a height restriction for aircraft over the part of the park north of Highway 5. Also, when the great birds are nesting their area is closed from the ground. 195 species, plus 31 hypothetical or accidental species. Rare, uncommon, or endangered, besides the whooping crane: Ross' goose, golden and bald eagles, goshawk, osprey, gyrfalcon, peregrine falcon, merlin, sandhill crane, white-rumped and Baird's sandpiper, Hudsonian godwit, black-backed three-toed woodpecker, Philadelphia vireo, Cape May warbler, hoary redpoll, others. The fall waterfowl concentration is a great spectacle. The park holds the northernmost colony of pelicans (white) in North America.

17,300 square miles of forests and open plains straddling the Alberta-Northwest Territories border between Athabasca and Great Slave Lakes. The park is the home of the largest remaining herd of bison on the continent. Salt plains, sink holes (Karst topography), plateau forests, lakes, and a 200-foot high escarpment that can be seen from Highway 5. Summer interpretive program. Campground (no water or electricity) at

Pine Lake about 40 miles southwest of Fort Smith. For camping elsewhere, a permit is needed. Picnic areas. Motor boats may be used with permission on the Peace, Slave, and Athabasca Rivers. Fishing (National Park permit). Regulations: all wildlife and all plants, trees, rocks, and fossils are to be left undisturbed. Dogs must be leashed. Extreme care with fires. Drive slowly: watch for animals crossing the road.

Bilingual checklist dated 1974. Also available: folder on park and "Information Supplement 1975."

Saskatchewan

CYPRESS HILLS PROVINCIAL PARK, Box 850, Maple Creek, Saskatchewan, SON 1NO. In western Saskatchewan. South on Rt. 21 from Rt. 1.

207 species in the Cypress Hills region as a whole. Over half of these breed in the hills. Rare, uncommon, or endangered: trumpeter swan (breeds here), hooded merganser, golden and bald eagles, osprey, ferruginous hawk, pigeon hawk, sandhill crane, Baird's sandpiper, Sprague's pipit, McCown's longspur, others. Among breeding birds: Audubon's and MacGillivray's warblers, Oregon junco, yellow-shafted and red-shafted flickers, white-crowned sparrow, double-crested cormorant, Canada goose, roughwinged swallow, and others. There is an interesting correlation between golf and birding in this park. In May and early June, early each morning, sharp-tailed grouse perform their mating dances on the golf fairway near the road at the southern edge of the park.

The park is in two separate blocks of land, center (east) and west. Forest of lodgepole pine, white spruce, and aspen, interlaced with streams and brooks. An area rich in fossils. Interesting "knob and kettle" glacial topography. Auto tours, two self-guiding nature trails, golf, fishing, cabins. Precaution: obey the forest fire prevention rules.

Bird checklist included in a 28-page pamphlet: "The Cypress

Hills; A Natural History" (Saskatchewan Museum of Natural History, 1973). Also available: two circulars "West Block Auto Tour" and "Center Block Circle Auto Tour."

NIPAWIN PROVINCIAL PARK, Nipawin, Saskatchewan. In northern Saskatchewan, on Highway 106 north of Smeaton. Address inquiries to Province of Saskatchewan, Dept. of Northern Saskatchewan, Resource Development, Box 130, Smeaton, Saskatchewan.

31 species commonly observed, including rarities: bald eagle, red-necked (Holboell's) grebe, and Connecticut warbler. Particularly interesting northern birds: common goldeneye, black tern, northern (common) raven (*Corvus corax*), boreal chickadee.

A wilderness park. Campgrounds—access by gravel roads. No formal checklist but a typewritten list from the Conservation Officer.

PRINCE ALBERT NATIONAL PARK, Box 100, Waskesiu Lake, Saskatchewan S0J 2Y0. 306-663-3511. Central Saskatchewan. Off Highway 2, then west at Rt. 264, 60 miles north of the city of Prince Albert. A great place for canoe-tripping.

196 species plus 21 "hypotheticals" (not actually seen). Rare, uncommon, or endangered: goshawk, golden and bald eagles, osprey, merlin, sandhill crane, Baird's sandpiper, hawk owl, black-backed three-toed woodpecker, northern shrike, Philadelphia vireo, Cape May warbler. The checklist notes that the greater prairie chicken has been "extirpated." Some of the species most commonly seen: common loon, tree and barn swallows, gray jay, common raven, common crow, American robin, snow bunting, and others.

1,496 square miles of forest dotted with lakes and interlaced with streams. Transition between northern forests and prairie grassland. Interpretive Centre and program. Fishing (National Park permit). Motels, bungalows, campgrounds.

Checklist in process; early version dated August, 1975.

INDEX

(Note: N.W.R. means National Wildlife Refuge.)

Acadia National Park, 86
Agassiz N.W.R., 100
Ager (Chet) Nature Center, 114
Alabama (Univ. of) Arboretum, 7
Albatross, Laysan, 8
Aleutian Islands N.W.R., 8
Alibates National Monument, 169
Amakihi, 68
Anaho Island N.W.R., 117
Anhinga, 60, 62, 63, 65, 85, 105, 162
Ani
    Groove-billed, 23, 84, 166, 171, 172
    Smooth-billed, 197
Apapane, 68
Aransas N.W.R., 3, 165
Arbuckle Recreation Area, 145
Arizona-Sonora Desert Museum, 3, 13
Arnold Arboretum, 89
Arrowwood N.W.R., 137
Assateague Island National Seashore, 181
Audubon Canyon Ranch, 29
Audubon Center, Greenwich, 54
Audubon Fairchild Garden, 54
Audubon N.W.R., 137
Austin Ornithological Research Station, 95
Auklet, Parakeet, 8
Avocet, 33, 35, 51, 70, 71, 115, 116, 126, 138, 145, 148, 159, 170, 184

Back Bay N.W.R., 180
Badlands National Monument, 158
Banana-quit, 197
Bandelier National Monument, 3, 125

Banff National Park, 209, 211
Bartholomew's Cobble, 3, 89
Batsto Nature Center, 119
Bear River Migratory Bird Refuge, 175
Becard, Rose-throated, 172
Bennett Springs State Park, 107
Benton Lake N.W.R., 111
Bentsen-Rio Grande Valley State Park, 165
Big Basin Redwoods State Park, 29
Big Bend National Park, 3, 166
Big Lake N.W.R., 25
Bitter Lake N.W.R., 126
Bittern
    American, 60, 80, 100, 216
    Least, 19, 60, 81
Blackbeard Island, 157
Blackbird
    Brewer's, 35, 49, 195
    Red-winged, 49, 93, 129, 138 150, 162, 179, 191
    Rusty, 96
    Yellow-headed, 33, 100, 159, 184
Blackwater N.W.R., 88
Block Island N.W.R., 153
Blue Ridge Parkway, 180
Bluebird
    Eastern, 54, 60, 66, 73, 83, 93, 121, 133, 150, 161, 191, 192, 201, 204
    Mountain, 18, 47, 49, 50, 52, 147, 148, 158, 172, 186, 195, 210
    Western, 18, 38, 39, 47, 101, 148
Bobolink, 98, 210
Bobwhite, 3, 26, 63, 74, 81, 99, 131, 145, 167
Bombay Hook N.W.R., 56
Boone (Daniel) National Forest, 81

Bosque del Apache N.W.R., 126
Boundary Waters Canoe Area, 102
Bowman's Hill State Wildflower Preserve, 149
Boyd Hill Nature Park, 59
Brandywine Creek State Park, 56
Brant, 121, 181, 204
    Black, 41, 187
Brigantine N.W.R., 119
Bryce Canyon National Park, 175
Buckley (Clyde E.) Wildlife Sanctuary, 81
Buffalo Lake N.W.R., 167
Bufflehead, 133, 177, 195
Bunting
    Indigo, 60, 63, 76, 77, 83, 106, 110, 151, 172, 202
    Lark, 52, 111, 158
    Lazuli, 21, 49, 213
    Painted, 60, 106, 146, 157, 172
    Snow, 99, 133, 163, 199, 201, 206, 219
    Varied, 34
Bushtit
    Black-eared, 15
    Common, 15, 39, 45
Butler (Arthur W.) Memorial Sanctuary, 128

Cabeza Prieta Game Range, 13
California Woods Outdoor Education Center, 143
Camas N.W.R., 70
Cannon (Clarence) N.W.R., 73
Canvasback, 31, 116, 117, 133, 137, 159, 177, 187
Cape Breton Highlands National Park, 200
Cape Cod National Seashore, 91
Cape Hatteras National Seashore, 135
Cape Romain N.W.R., 3, 155
Capitol Reef National Park, 176
Cardinal, 25, 55, 63, 66, 76, 133, 168, 191, 203
Carolina Sandhills N.W.R., 155
Catbird, 55, 66, 159, 204
Catoctin Mountain Park, 88
Cedar Point N.W.R., 144
Chachalaca, 157, 166, 172
Channel Islands National Monument, 30

Chassahowitzka N.W.R., 59
Chat, Yellow-breasted, 33, 178
Chautauqua N.W.R., 72
Cherokee National Forest, 161
Chickadee
    Black-capped, 52, 89, 95, 133, 179, 199, 202, 203, 207, 212
    Boreal, 87, 96, 98, 199, 203, 207, 219
    Carolina, 7, 26, 53, 106, 109, 168
    Chestnut-backed, 39, 41, 45, 46, 147, 185
    Gray-headed, 11
    Mountain, 49, 50, 52, 115, 195
Chincoteague N.W.R., 181
Chiricahua National Monument, 15
Chuck-will's-widow, 26, 63, 67, 105, 146, 168
Colorado National Monument, 48
Columbia N.W.R., 184
Connecticut Arboretum, 54
Constitution Island Audubon Sanctuary, 128
Coot, American, 27, 45, 105, 146, 162, 186
Corkscrew Swamp Sanctuary, 60
Cormorant
    Brandt's, 41, 213
    Double-crested, 30, 139, 206
    Great, 133
    Olivaceous, 84
    Pelagic, 8
Cornell Laboratory of Ornithology, 129
Coronado National Forest, 21
Cowbird, Brown-headed, 30, 92, 166, 168, 205
Crab Orchard N.W.R., 72
Crane
    Sandhill, 138, 139, 142, 165
    Florida Sandhill, 59, 63
    Greater Sandhill, 116, 127, 177
    Lesser Sandhill, 126, 127
    Whooping, 3, 79, 80, 101, 112, 126, 158, 165, 210, 217
Crater Lake National Park, 147
Craters of the Moon National Monument, 70
Creeper, Brown, 39, 45, 52, 66, 74, 93, 129
Crossbill
    Red, 147, 199, 209, 212

White-winged, 88, 128, 147, 149, 199, 209, 215
Crow
Common, 92, 180, 203, 219
Fish, 60, 62, 63, 123, 157, 180
Mexican, 173
Cuckoo
Mangrove, 61, 197
Yellow-billed, 26, 65, 74
Curlew, Long-billed, 70, 101, 159, 175, 178, 184
Cypress Hills Provincial Park, 218

Darling (Ding) N.W.R., 60
Death Valley National Monument, 30
Delta-Breton N.W.R., 84
Desert Botanical Garden, 17
Desert N.W.R., 115
Des Lacs N.W.R., 139, 140
De Soto N.W.R., 77
Dickcissel, 25, 54, 73, 96, 105, 146, 162
Dinosaur National Monument, 48
Dipper (Water Ouzel), 18, 29, 43, 49, 112, 178, 209, 210, 212
Dole (Joan Hamann) Memorial Sanctuary, 34
Dove
Ground, 36, 172
Inca, 13, 21
Mourning, 25, 50, 92, 110, 115, 151
Ruddy ground, 173
Western mourning, 23
White-fronted, 166
White-winged, 19, 20, 23, 173
Dovekie, 94, 199, 200, 206
Dowitcher, 56, 145, 184
Duck
Black, 72, 92, 94, 101, 144, 156, 199, 207
Black-bellied tree, 173
Fulvous tree, 35, 43, 84
Harlequin, 11, 46, 86, 93, 185, 200, 206, 209, 211, 212, 213
Mexican, 52, 126
Mottled, 59, 60, 63, 64, 84, 85
Ruddy, 31, 33, 38, 103, 131, 170, 177, 182, 184
Wood, 130, 143, 157
Dunlin, 135, 203

Eagle
Bald, 59, 61, 62, 64, 73, 99, 100, 110, 150, 162, 165, 177, 178, 186, 187, 193, 203, 205, 210
Golden, 127, 147, 175, 178
Effigy Mounds National Monument, 77
Egret
Cattle, 61, 106, 156
Common (American), 29, 46, 82, 144, 162
Reddish, 62, 171
Snowy, 51, 181
Eider
Common, 93, 198, 199, 200, 206
King, 8, 86, 93
Steller's, 9
El Dorado Nature Center, 31
Elepaio, 68
Erie N.W.R., 149
Everglades National Park, 61

Falcon
Peregrine, 165, 206
Prairie, 32, 36, 70, 158, 175
Finch
Black rosy, 48, 49, 175
Cassin's, 18, 21, 47, 115
Gray-crowned rosy, 47, 185, 186, 209
House, 38, 68, 166
Laysan, 69
Nihoa, 69
Rosy, 49
Fish Springs N.W.R., 176
Flaming Gorge National Recreation Area, 177
Flanders Nature Center, 55
Flicker
Common, 31, 123, 171, 199, 200
Gilded, 13, 15, 17, 23
Red-shafted, 42, 45, 52, 80, 166, 218
Yellow-shafted, 63, 78, 80, 130, 152, 168, 218
Florida Keys N.W.R., 62
Flycatcher
Acadian, 143
Ash-throated, 23, 166
Beardless, 23, 48
Coues', 15
Dusky, 18

Flycatcher (*cont'd*)
  Great crested, 63, 77
  Hammond's, 33, 47
  Kiskadee, 166, 173
  Olivaceous, 15
  Olive-sided, 33, 211
  Scissor-tailed, 25, 146
  Traill's, 77, 204
  Vermilion, 17, 20, 21, 33
  Western, 32, 38, 45, 213
  Wied's crested, 13
Ford Nature Education Center, 143
Forest Glen Preserve, 73
Forillon National Park, 206
For-Mar Nature Preserve and Arboretum, 96
Fort Totten Sioux Indian Reservation, 141
Fundy National Park, 198
Frigate-bird, Magnificent, 59, 63, 84, 171, 197
Fulmar, 8, 86

Gadwall, 31, 38, 116, 138, 160, 177
Gallinule
  Common, 162, 191
  Purple, 127, 162, 171
Gannet, 123
Gateway National Recreation Area
  Sandy Hook Unit, 123
  Jamaica Bay Unit, 130
Georgian Bay Islands National Park, 201
Glacier Bay National Monument, 8
Glacier National Park, 112
Glacier National Park (Canada), 212
Glen Canyon National Recreation Area, 17
Gnatcatcher
  Black-tailed, 13, 15, 38, 166
  Blue-grey, 106, 109
Godwit
  Hudsonian, 51, 94, 121, 133, 139, 141, 171
  Marbled, 8, 33
Goldeneye
  Barrows, 10, 195, 198, 200, 206, 210, 215
  Common, 103, 133, 158, 198, 206, 219
Goldfinch
  American, 47, 88, 92, 205

Lawrence's, 15, 41, 127, 170
  Lesser, 30, 34
Goose
  Blue (Snow), 110, 121, 140, 141, 159
  Cackling, 42, 55
  Aleutian Canada, 8, 187
  Canada (notable concentrations), 64, 133, 150, 156, 182, 192
  Giant Canada, 97, 100, 138, 139, 140
  Taverner's Canada, 9
  Emperor, 8, 11
  Snow, 43, 73, 84, 99, 131, 141, 180
  Greater Snow, 181
  Ross', 32, 38, 148, 184
  White-fronted, 35, 42, 43, 79
Goshawk, 21, 50, 73, 78, 100, 134, 151, 193
Grackle
  Boat-tailed, 62, 168, 171
  Common, 92
Grand Canyon National Park, 18
Grand Mesa-Uncompahgre-Gunnison National Forest, 49
Grand Teton National Park, 193
Grays Lake N.W.R., 126
Great Meadows N.W.R., 91, 93
Great Sand Dunes National Monument, 50
Great Smoky Mountains National Park, 3, 16
Great Swamp N.W.R., 121
Great White Heron Refuge, 62
Grebe
  Eared, 38, 80, 115, 126
  Horned, 80, 150, 202
  Least, 166, 171, 173
  Pied-billed, 66, 109, 126, 182
  Red-necked (Holboell's), 35, 100, 133, 186
  Western, 71, 115, 138, 141, 160
Green Bay Wildlife Sanctuary, 191
Griffith Park, 32
Grosbeak
  Black-headed, 15, 44, 114, 176
  Blue, 7, 105, 109, 146
  Evening, 36, 134, 178, 207, 209, 211, 213
  Pine, 47, 128, 134, 199, 207
  Rose-breasted, 89, 109, 131, 203

Grouse
Blue, 18, 43, 47, 50, 70, 193
Ruffed, 93, 101, 123, 161, 188, 192, 200, 206
Sage, 70, 71, 111, 116, 248
Sharp-tailed, 96, 101, 139, 158, 215
Spruce, 10, 98, 195, 203
Guillemot, Pigeon, 186
Gull
Bonaparte's, 59
California, 33, 71, 112, 147, 195
Franklin's, 52, 80, 141, 159
Glaucous, 77, 123, 131, 198, 200, 204
Glaucous Winged, 8, 186, 213
Great black-backed, 93, 199, 206
Herring, 91, 92, 93, 94, 191, 206
Iceland, 95, 131, 198, 199, 200, 204
Ivory, 94
Laughing, 63, 181
Mew, 8, 210
Ring-billed, 13, 82, 112, 133, 141, 202, 203, 216
Ross's, 94
Sabine's, 8
Thayer's, 8
Western, 30
Goshawk, 8
Gyrfalcon, 9, 10, 48, 51

Hagerman N.W.R., 168
Harpers Ferry National Historic Park, 188
Harris Neck, 157
Hart Mountain Antelope Refuge, 148
Havasu N.W.R., 3, 32
Hawaii Volcanoes National Park, 68
Hawaiian Islands N.W.R., 68
Hawk
Black, 166
Broad-winged, 93, 100, 119, 150, 152, 172
Cooper's, 31, 36, 45, 51, 74, 95, 127, 149, 171, 191, 201
Ferruginous, 21, 115, 146, 169, 170, 184, 218
Gray, 166
Harlan's, 51, 107, 110, 139, 141
Harris', 170
Marsh, 12, 50, 51, 85, 111

Pigeon (Merlin), 38, 86, 92, 94, 102, 168, 170, 177, 179, 200, 218
Rough-legged, 52, 206
Red-shouldered, 38, 45, 64, 163, 188
Red-tailed, 18, 19, 39, 45, 50, 82, 130, 168, 180, 216
Sharp-shinned, 29, 38, 46, 107, 150, 158
Sparrow (American Kestrel), 18, 30, 38, 50, 125, 152, 170, 180, 204, 215
Swainson's, 18, 71, 80, 111, 169
Zone-tailed, 15, 127
Hawk Mountain Sanctuary, 150
Hayes Regional Arboretum, 75
Heard Natural Science Museum and Wildlife Sanctuary, 168
Hendrie Valley Sanctuary, 203
Heron
Black-crowned night, 38, 46, 51, 144, 158, 202
Great blue, 29, 49, 74, 86, 101, 102, 116, 187, 202, 205
Great white, 63
Green, 19, 46, 74, 96, 109, 152, 204
Little blue, 82, 168
Louisiana, 61
Yellow-crowned, 63, 109, 121, 123
Hershey Rose Gardens and Arboretum, 151
High Rock Park, 129
Holla Bend N.W.R., 25
Hoffman Wildlife Sanctuary, 124
Horicon N.W.R., 191
Hot Springs National Park, 26
Hueston Woods State Park, 143
Hummer, Antillean crested, 197
Hummingbird
Allen's, 31, 34, 45
Anna's, 31, 32, 34, 44, 45, 46
Black-chinned, 15, 31, 32, 36, 49
Blue-throated, 166
Broad-tailed, 18, 49, 50
Buff-bellied, 166, 172
Calliope, 21, 33, 42, 47, 210
Costa's, 20, 30, 31, 32, 34
Green violet-eared, 173
Lucifer, 166
Ruby-throated, 54, 86, 152

Hummingbird (cont'd)
 Rufous, 31, 32, 34, 49, 213
 White-eared, 166
Huron N.W.R., 98

Ibis
 Glossy, 3, 66, 91, 121, 123, 131, 135, 156, 180
 White, 59, 60, 84, 156, 157
 White-faced, 21, 42, 51, 52, 71, 84, 85, 110, 115, 126, 168, 170, 177
 Wood (Wood Stork), 7, 60, 62, 64, 66
Imperial N.W.R., 19
Inyo National Forest, 33
Ipswich River Wildlife Sanctuary, 92
Iroquois N.W.R., 130
Isle Royale National Park, 96
Itasca State Park, 100
Izembek N.W.R., 9

Jacana, 166, 172
Jaeger, Parasitic, 216
Jaeger, Pomerine, 8
Jaggar (Thomas A.) Memorial Museum, 68
Jamaica Bay Wildlife Refuge, 3, 130
Jasper National Park, 209
Jay
 Blue, 92, 156, 168, 172
 Canada (Gray), 52, 96, 147, 199, 203, 209, 219
 Green, 166, 173
 Mexican, 21, 166
 Pinyon, 18, 21, 49, 50, 115
 Scrub, 39, 44, 45, 46, 49, 64, 125, 178
 Steller's, 18, 36, 39, 46, 50, 125, 147
Joshua Tree National Monument, 34
Junco
 Oregon, 49, 147, 218
 Dark-eyed (Slate-colored), 186, 199, 205, 206

Kalamazoo Nature Center, 97
Katmai National Monument, 9
Kejimkujik National Park, 200
Kenai National Moose Range, 10
Kern-Pixley N.W.R., 35
Key West N.W.R., 62

Killdeer, 26, 35, 50, 51, 139, 150, 184
Kingbird
 Cassin's, 18, 21, 32, 35
 Eastern, 76, 80, 178, 212
 Gray, 61
 Tropical, 166, 171, 173
 Western, 17, 18, 33, 38, 49, 80, 170, 178
Kingfisher
 Belted, 11, 18, 26, 46, 81, 130, 143, 188, 199, 216
 Green, 173
 Ringed, 166, 173
Kinglet
 Golden-crowned, 150, 151, 209
 Ruby-crowned, 23, 52, 199
Kingman County Game Management Area, 79
Kings Canyon National Park, 43
Kirwin N.W.R., 79
Kite
 Everglade, 63
 Mississippi, 64, 79, 106, 145, 156, 166, 168, 171
 Swallow-tailed, 61, 63, 66
 White-tailed, 34, 39, 42, 46, 166, 171
Kittiwake, Black-legged, 206
Klamath Basin N.W.R., 35
Kodiak N.W.R., 11
Kootenay National Park, 211

Lacreek N.W.R., 158
Laguna Atascosa N.W.R., 173
Lake Isom N.W.R., 162
Lake Mead National Recreation Area, 115
Lake Meredith Recreation Area, 169
Lake Woodruff N.W.R., 63
La Mauricie National Park, 207
Land Between the Lakes, 82
Lark, Horned, 35, 50, 52, 97, 107, 111, 158, 205
Lassen Volcano National Park, 36
Laughing Brook Nature Center, 93
Laurentides Provincial Park, 207
Limpkin, 59, 63, 65, 66
Living Desert Reserve, 36
Long Lake N.W.R., 138
Longspur
 Lapland, 11, 131, 139

McCown's, 51, 111, 112, 142, 177, 218
Longwood Gardens, 151
Loon
  Arctic, 10, 210
  Common, 102, 207, 212, 213, 219
  Yellow-billed, 213
Los Angeles State and County Arboretum, 38
Lostwood N.W.R., 139, 140
Loxahatchee N.W.R., 63

Mackay Island N.W.R., 181
Mackenzie Environmental Center, 192
Magpie, Black-billed, 49, 50, 101, 160, 178, 184, 195, 210
Mallard (nests or is abundant), 80, 88, 92, 98, 116, 137, 138, 160
Mammoth Cave National Park, 82
Mammoth Lakes, 33
Manning Provincial Park, 212
Mark Twain N.W.R., 73
Martin, Purple, 74, 83, 102, 105, 180, 202
Mattamuskeet N.W.R., 135
McAshan Arboretum and Botanical Garden, 169
McCormick's Creek State Park, 75
McNary N.W.R., 184
Meadowlark
  Eastern, 25, 128, 130, 163, 168
  Western, 30, 35, 78, 138, 158, 172
Medicine Lake N.W.R., 112
Merganser
  Common (American), 60, 82, 158, 198, 203, 207, 210
  Hooded (nests), 92, 130, 149, 210
  Red-breasted, 93, 199, 202
Merlin. See Hawk, Pigeon
Merritt Island N.W.R., 64
Mesa Verde National Park, 50
Meyer Arboretum, 134
Mill Creek Park, 143
Mille Lacs N.W.R., 102
Millerbird, Nihoa, 69
Mingo N.W.R., 97
Minidoka N.W.R., 71
Missisquoi N.W.R., 179
Mississippi Palisades State Park, 74
Missouri Botanical Gardens, Arboretum and Nature Reserve, 107

Mockingbird, 26, 38, 82, 107, 166
Modoc N.W.R., 38
Monahans Sandhills State Park, 170
Monomoy N.W.R., 91, 93
Monongahela National Forest, 188
Monte Vista N.W.R., 51
Montezuma Castle National Monument, 19
Montezuma N.W.R., 131
Moosehorn N.W.R., 3, 87
Morton Arboretum, 74
Morton N.W.R., 133
Mount McKinley National Park, 3, 11
Mount Rainier National Park, 185
Mount Revelstoke and Glacier National Parks, 212
Mount Tamalpais State Park, 39
Mud Lake N.W.R., 100
Muir Woods National Monument, 39
Muleshoe and Grulla National Wildlife Refuges, 170
Murrelet
  Ancient, 9, 213
  Marbled, 9, 29, 213

Natchez Trace Parkway, 105
National Elk Refuge, 193
National Key Deer Refuge, 62
Necedah N.W.R., 192
Nighthawk
  Common, 33, 49, 74, 88, 125, 160, 200, 216
  Lesser, 20, 166
Ninigret N.W.R., 153
Nipawin Provincial Park, 219
Noxubee N.W.R., 105
Nutcracker, Clark's, 36, 43, 47, 50, 52, 112, 212
Nuthatch
  Brown-headed, 67, 88, 105
  Pygmy, 29, 41, 45, 125, 186
  Red-breasted, 147, 206, 209, 211, 212
  White-breasted, 92, 152

Oak Orchard N.W.R., 130
Ocmulgee National Monument, 66
Odessa Meteor Craters, 170
Okefenokee N.W.R., 66
Oldsquaw, 11
Olympic National Park, 185

Oregon Caves National Monument, 147

Organ Pipe Cactus National Monument, 20

Oriole
Black-headed, 166, 173
Hooded, 13, 17, 23, 34
Lichtenstein's, 166, 173
Northern (Baltimore and Bullock's), 23, 30, 34, 73, 76, 151, 170, 202, 204
Orchard, 65, 73, 105, 168
Scott's, 13, 34

Osprey, 62, 63, 121, 123, 133, 150, 180, 182, 186, 188, 203, 210

Ottawa National Forest, 97

Ouray N.W.R., 178

Ouzel, Water. *See* Dipper

Ovenbird, 54, 74, 100, 130, 143, 151, 203

Owl
Barn, 38, 68, 88, 117
Barred, 66, 73, 105, 109, 143, 168, 180, 200
Boreal, 142, 205
Burrowing, 17, 35, 79, 111, 112, 116, 117, 138, 158, 159, 170, 175
Elf, 15, 34
Ferruginous, 15
Flammulated, 21, 50, 115, 125, 175, 178
Great gray, 35, 203
Great horned, 10, 19, 34, 67, 109, 123, 170, 180, 210, 216
Hawk, 10, 179, 201, 206, 211, 219
Long-eared, 18, 74
Pygmy, 39, 47, 185
Saw-whet, 70, 74, 207, 215
Screech, 15, 26, 64, 74, 129, 130, 152, 180, 204
Short-eared, 12, 51, 175
Snowy, 199, 207
Spotted, 50

Oystercatcher, 65, 121, 135, 155

Ozark National Scenic Riverways, 109

Pacific Rim National Park, 213

Pack Monadnock Mountain, 118

Padre Island National Seashore, 171

Palo Duro Canyon State Park, 171

Parc des Laurentides, 207

Parker River N.W.R., 94, 118

Partridge, Grey, 103, 216

Pauraque, 173

Pawnee National Grassland, 51

Pea Island N.W.R., 135

Pelican
Brown, 30, 43, 59, 62, 64, 84, 135, 155, 157, 165, 187
White, 13, 35, 43, 60, 64, 110, 111, 112, 117, 137, 138, 141, 158, 217

Petrel
Bonin Island, 69
Leach's, 9

Petrified Forest National Park, 21

Pewee
Eastern wood, 88, 128, 152, 202
Western wood, 32

Phainopepla, 17, 34, 36, 42, 127

Phalarope
Northern, 33, 117, 203
Wilson's, 33, 49, 159, 184, 210

Pheasant, Ring-necked, 38, 99, 101, 111, 151, 159, 184, 191, 202

Phoebe
Black, 20, 127
Eastern, 80, 86, 93, 130, 152
Say's, 15, 23, 34, 49, 50, 158, 166

Piedmont N.W.R., 67

Pigeon
Band-tailed, 31, 47
Red-billed, 166
White-crowned, 63

Pinnacles National Monument, 41

Pintail, 38, 70, 137, 138, 159

Pipestone National Monument, 101

Pipit
Sprague's, 27, 112, 126, 141, 142, 166, 171, 218
Water, 10, 115, 182

Platt National Park, 145

Plover
Black-bellied, 135
Mountain, 111, 170
Semi-palmated, 91
Snowy, 80, 117, 126, 145, 170, 175
Upland, 25, 57, 77, 106, 107, 146, 159, 183
Wilson's, 133, 155

Point Pelee National Park, 202

Point Reyes Bird Observatory, 41
Pokagon State Park, 76
Portola State Park, 29
Prairie Chicken
    Attwater's, 165
    Greater, 100, 137, 138, 139, 141,
        160
    Lesser, 170
Prescott National Forest, 21
Presquile N.W.R., 182
Prince Albert National Park, 219
Prince Edward Island National Park,
    205
Ptarmigan
    White-tailed, 52, 112, 185, 210,
        215
    Willow, 199, 210
Puffin
    Horned, 8
    Tufted, 11, 213
Pyrrhuloxia, 13, 17, 127, 166, 170

Quail
    California, 38, 44, 45, 46, 184, 186
    Gambel's, 13, 17, 18, 20, 23, 36,
        43, 115, 116
    Harlequin, 127
    Mountain, 43
    Scaled, 126, 166, 169, 170, 171
    Valley, 32
Quetico Provincial Park, 203
Quivira N.W.R., 80

Raccoon Creek State Park, 151
Rail
    Black, 27, 41, 56, 59, 123, 146,
        162, 168, 180, 181
    Clapper, 56, 85, 121, 123, 135,
        157
    King, 63, 80, 88, 157, 162
    Sora, 72, 76, 80, 121, 126, 130,
        187, 204, 216
    Virginia, 78, 80, 86, 88, 101, 121,
        126, 130, 204
    Yellow, 27, 85
    Yuma clapper, 19, 32
Rainbow Bridge National Monument,
    18
Rancho Santa Ana Botanic Garden,
    42

Raven
    Common (Northern), 44, 70, 147,
        148, 219
    White-necked, 15, 127, 170
Razorbill, 206
Reading Nature Center, 152
Redhead, 35, 116, 133, 137, 144, 159
Redpoll, Hoary, 191, 217
Redstart
    American, 59, 77, 200, 205, 213
    Painted, 15
Reelfoot N.W.R., 162
Rice Lake N.W.R., 101, 102
Riding Mountain National Park, 216
Rio Grande National Forest, 52
Roadrunner, 13, 21, 30, 43, 126, 170
Roan Mountain State Resort Park,
    162
Robin
    Clay-colored, 123
    Rufous-backed, 173
    Western, 49, 92, 107, 123, 150,
        172, 188, 199, 203, 219
Rock Creek Nature Center, 57
Rocky Mountain National Park, 52
Roosevelt (Theodore) National Me-
    morial Park, 141
Royal Botanical Gardens, 203
Ruby Lake N.W.R., 116
Russell (Charles M.) N.W.R., 111

Sabine N.W.R., 85
Sabino Canyon Visitor Center, 21
Sacramento N.W.R., 42
Saguaro National Monument, 23
St. Lawrence Islands National Park,
    204
St. Marks N.W.R., 64
Salt Plains N.W.R., 145
Salton Sea N.W.R., 42
Salyer (J. Clark) N.W.R., 139, 140
San Andres Refuge, 127
Sanderling, 133, 199
Sandpiper
    Baird's, 95, 103, 138, 166, 167,
        171, 218, 219
    Buff-breasted, 139, 158, 159, 171
    Curlew, 56, 121
    Least, 18, 95
    Pectoral, 43, 70, 184, 186
    Rock, 9
    Semipalmated, 94, 95, 180

Sandpiper (*cont'd*)
 Spotted, 18, 152, 166, 206
 Western, 18, 148, 168
 White-rumped, 110, 121, 131, 167, 200
Sandy Hook, Unit, Gateway National Recreation Area, 123
San Jacinto State Park, 172
Sand Lake N.W.R., 159
Santa Ana N.W.R., 172
Santee N.W.R., 156
Sapsucker
 Williamson's, 15, 36, 49, 53, 125, 171
 Yellow-bellied, 59, 129, 152, 188, 199, 206
Savannah N.W.R., 156
Scaup
 Greater, 92, 131, 133, 202
 Lesser, 133
Scherman Wildlife Sanctuary, 124
Scoter
 Common (Black), 95, 103, 133, 180, 198, 210, 216
 Surf, 8, 103, 215
 White-winged, 93
Seedeater, White-collared, 173
Seneca Unit, Erie N.W.R., 150
Seney N.W.R., 98
Sequoia and Kings Canyon National Parks, 43
Shearwater
 Audubon's, 171
 Sooty, 30, 86, 95, 180, 186
Sheldon, Hart Mountain Antelope Refuges, 148
Shenandoah National Park, 182
Shiawassee N.W.R., 98
Shoveler, 31, 60, 137
Shrike
 Loggerhead, 23, 34, 92, 94, 148, 157, 166, 168
 Northern, 92, 94, 130, 134, 192, 213, 219
Silverwood Wildlife Sanctuary, 44
Siskin, Pine, 39, 42, 45, 52, 83, 134, 147, 211
Skimmer, Black, 3, 61, 64, 135, 155
Slade N.W.R., 135
Smew, 8
Snipe, Common (Wilson's), 10, 101, 157, 206, 216

Solitaire, Townsend's, 11, 34, 36, 116, 145, 147, 169, 184
Sora. *See* Rail, Sora
Souris Loop National Wildlife Refuges, 139
Sparrow
 Bachman's, 60, 63, 67, 73, 81, 105
 Baird's, 51, 101, 111, 112, 142, 166, 171
 Black-chinned, 30
 Black-throated, 15, 116, 166
 Brewer's, 15, 209, 210, 215
 Cape Sable, 62
 Cassin's, 126
 Chipping, 170
 Clay-colored, 97, 203
 Dusky seaside, 64
 Field, 26, 76
 Fox, 29, 70, 199
 Golden-crowned, 11, 215
 Grasshopper, 96
 Henslow's, 57, 81, 92, 97, 119, 192
 Ipswich, 94, 180
 Lark, 49, 109, 158
 LeConte's, 78, 98, 110, 112, 139, 162
 Lincoln's, 47
 Olive, 173
 Rufous-winged, 23, 146, 166
 Sage, 20, 30
 Savannah, 215
 Song, 91, 92, 93, 107, 128, 152, 204, 205
 Swamp, 92, 98, 202, 205
 Tree, 83, 109, 118
 Vesper, 184, 195
 White-crowned, 38, 39, 47, 131, 166, 218
 White-throated, 25, 86, 94, 118, 199
Spoonbill, Roseate, 43, 60, 61, 62, 84, 85, 171
Squaw Creek N.W.R., 110
Starling, 38, 92, 162
Stillwater Wildlife Management Area, 117
Stilt, Black-necked, 33, 63, 85
Stork, Wood. *See* Ibis, Wood
Strybing Arboretum and Botanical Garden, 45
Sullys Hill National Game Preserve, 140

Superior National Forest, 102
Surfbird, 213
Suwanee Canal Recreation Area, 66
Swallow
  Bank, 77, 182, 205, 207
  Barn, 49, 123, 180, 182, 207, 219
  Cliff, 18, 49, 86, 111, 158, 160,
    172, 195, 207
  Rough-winged, 30, 218
  Tree, 34, 92, 95, 110, 182, 186,
    205, 219
  Violet-green, 18, 33, 34, 49, 185,
    186, 193
Swan Lake N.W.R., 110
Swanquarter N.W.R., 136
Swan
  Trumpeter, 10, 38, 116, 158, 186,
    193, 195, 213, 218
  Whistling, 9, 70, 99, 117, 135, 140,
    150, 175, 178, 180, 184, 215
  Whooper, 8
Swift
  Black, 148, 171
  Chimney, 168
  Vaux's, 8, 185
  White-throated, 15, 21, 23, 36,
    125, 177

Tamarac N.W.R., 103
Tanager
  Hepatic, 21, 23, 127, 166
  Scarlet, 73, 76, 86, 88, 89, 93, 143,
    151, 203, 204
  Summer, 17, 65, 73, 131
  Western, 18, 33, 42, 186, 210
Tattler, Wandering, 9, 210
Teal
  Blue-winged, 25, 98, 138, 160, 202
  Cinnamon, 30, 35, 115, 177
  Greenwinged, 35, 52, 86, 145, 168,
    184
  Laysan, 69
Teatown Lake Reservation, 134
Tennessee N.W.R., 163
Tern
  Arctic, 8, 87, 91, 93, 95, 199, 200
  Black, 33, 51, 102, 149, 186, 219
  Caspian, 101, 204
  Common, 93, 138, 179, 199
  Forster's, 33, 84
  Gull-billed, 56, 63
  Least, 77, 126

Noddy, 62
  Roseate, 91, 121, 123, 131, 135
  Royal, 64, 171
  Sandwich, 59, 84, 171
  Sooty, 69
Terra-Nova National Park, 199
Tewaukon N.W.R., 141
Thrasher
  Bendire's, 13, 21
  Brown, 66, 92, 117, 123, 166, 173
  California, 42, 43, 44, 46
  Crissal, 19, 20, 115, 116, 127
  Curve-billed, 23, 127
  LeConte's, 30
  Long-billed, 166, 173
  Sage, 21, 30
Thrush
  Gray-cheeked, 89, 97, 206
  Hermit, 31, 39, 89, 129, 131, 199,
    206
  Olive-backed, 211
  Swainson's, 39, 74, 89, 96, 161,
    199
  Varied, 9, 212
  Wood, 55, 76, 83, 89, 143
Tishomingo N.W.R., 146
Titmouse
  Black-crested, 166, 172
  Bridled, 15, 20, 21
  Plain, 44
  Tufted, 26, 57, 74, 82, 93, 128,
    168
Towhee
  Abert's, 17, 19, 20, 23
  Brown, 42, 44, 45, 46, 47, 166
  Green-tailed, 36, 148
  Rufous-sided, 39, 42, 44, 45, 82,
    95, 128, 202
Tropic Bird
  Red-tailed, 69
  White-tailed, 197
Tucker Wildlife Sanctuary, 45
Turkey, 15, 67, 103, 123, 155, 163,
  182, 204
Turnbull N.W.R., 186
Turnstone, Ruddy, 61, 121, 181
Turtle Mountain Provincial Park, 216

Union Slough N.W.R., 78
University of California Botanical
  Garden, 46

Upper Mississippi N.W.R., 103
Upper Souris N.W.R., 133

Van Vleck Farm Sanctuary, 55
Veery, 55, 92, 123, 162, 215
Verdin, 13, 15, 19, 20, 23, 38, 43
Vireo
  Bell's, 20, 23, 26, 72, 73
  Black-whiskered, 62
  Gray, 115, 176
  Hutton's, 41, 46
  Philadelphia, 26, 92, 95, 128, 166,
    179, 203
  Red-eyed, 55, 82, 100, 145, 202
  Solitary, 47, 163
  Warbling, 96, 130
  White-eyed, 63, 123
  Yellow-green, 44, 166, 173
  Yellow-throated, 25, 103, 107, 143,
    163, 180, 191
Virgin Islands National Park, 197
Vulture
  Black, 61, 83, 163, 182
  Turkey, 57, 116, 135, 171

Wapack N.W.R., 118
Waponocca N.W.R., 26
Warbler
  Black and white, 54, 59, 121
  Blackburnian, 203, 204
  Blackpoll, 86
  Black-throated gray, 18, 32
  Black-throated green, 199, 203
  Blue-winged, 54, 75, 95, 128, 188
  Brewster's, 173
  Canada, 129
  Cape May, 89, 95, 100, 131, 137,
    152, 200, 202, 203, 219
  Chestnut-sided, 119, 205
  Colima, 166
  Connecticut, 59, 75, 97, 150, 216,
    219
  Golden-winged, 59, 60, 64, 75,
    128, 130, 171, 188
  Grace's, 21, 125
  Hermit, 36, 46
  Kirtland's, 144
  Lucy's, 13, 23
  Macgillivray's, 32, 213, 218
  Magnolia, 118, 203
  Mourning, 75, 97, 168, 188, 203
  Nashville, 47, 203
  Olive-backed, 166, 173
  Orange-crowned, 9, 45, 59, 169
  Palm, 96, 199, 200
  Pine, 63, 121, 157
  Prairie, 61, 63, 66, 73, 155, 162
  Prothonotary, 65, 83, 119, 150,
    162
  Tennessee, 216
  Wilson's, 23, 30, 38, 213
  Worm-eating, 25, 75, 128, 166
  Yellow, 30, 49, 77, 121, 203, 205,
    212
  Yellow-rumped (Audubon's, Myr-
    tle), 23, 38, 45, 94, 95, 166,
    180, 205, 211, 212, 218
Ward Pound Ridge Reservation, 134
Wassaw Island N.W.R., 157
Waterthrush
  Louisiana, 73, 114, 161
  Northern, 129
Waterton Lakes National Park, 112,
  210
Waxwing, Cedar, 54, 128, 202, 212
Wellfleet Bay Wildlife Sanctuary, 91,
  94
Wells Gray Provincial Park, 213
West Sister Island N.W.R., 144
Wharton State Forest, 119
Wheeler National Monument, 52
Wheeler N.W.R., 7
Whimbrel, 95
Whippoorwill, 109, 123, 188
White River N.W.R., 27
Whittemore Sanctuary, 55
Whittier Narrows Nature Center, 46
Wichita Mountains Wildlife Refuge,
  146
Widgeon
  American (Baldpate), 31, 60, 137
    156, 168, 180, 184
  European, 131, 133, 139
Willapa N.W.R., 186
Willet, 33, 65, 71, 157, 160
Wind Cave National Park, 160
Wood Buffalo National Park, 3, 217
Woodcock, American, 3, 55, 87, 109,
  130, 199, 202
Woodpecker
  Acorn, 21 45
  Arizona, 15
  Black-backed three-toed, 10, 96,
    185, 200, 209

Downy, 54, 151, 191, 201, 202
Gila, 13, 17, 19, 20, 23
Golden-fronted, 172
Hairy, 54, 66, 145, 168, 191
Ladder-backed, 15, 19, 20, 34, 169, 172
Nuttall's, 44, 45
Pileated, 41, 59, 67, 96, 128, 161, 200, 205, 209, 216
Red-bellied, 82, 96, 109, 152, 168, 169
Red-cockaded, 64, 66, 67, 81, 105, 135, 155
Red-headed, 66, 75, 101, 109, 172, 191, 192
Wren
  Bewick's, 25, 44, 47, 83, 84, 107, 109, 162
  Cactus, 23, 43, 166, 170
  Canyon, 15, 20, 44, 172, 176

Carolina, 7, 55, 66, 128, 163, 168, 169
House, 49, 74
Long-billed marsh, 35, 123, 158, 202
Rock, 15, 18, 20, 21, 70, 126, 158, 172
Winter, 39, 118, 147, 152, 162
Wrentit, 44, 45, 47
Wye Marsh Wildlife Centre, 205

Yazoo N.W.R., 106
Yellowstone National Park, 195
Yellowthroat, 38, 46, 55, 82, 92, 150, 180, 205
Yoho National Park, 211, 215
Yosemite National Park, 40

Zion National Park, 178

ABOUT THE AUTHOR

Jessie Kitching was born in Boston, Massachusetts, and presently lives in Forest Hills, New York. She graduated from Vassar College and subsequently spent most of her working years as a book reviewer and bibliographer. In the 1960's, after editing an East Coast Sierra Club newsletter and attending two National Audubon Society camps, she decided to try to work full time in conservation and natural history. She received a master's degree in natural history education at Cornell University, which led to freelance writing and editing and to the publication of her own newsletter, *Books about Birds*.

Ms. Kitching has walked almost the entire length of the John Muir Trail in California's Sierra Nevada; explored Glacier National Park; floated down the Snake River in the Grand Tetons; hiked down the Havasupai Indian Reservation in the Grand Canyon; rafted down the Green River in Utah; canoed in mangrove swamps on Sanibel Island; and sailed New York's Great South Bay in the Fall when boat traffic slackens and egrets are everywhere.